A Kaleidoscope of Pieces

A Kaleidoscope of Pieces: Anglican Essays on Sexuality, Ecclesiology and Theology

Edited by Alan H Cadwallader

With a foreword by Bishop Kay Goldsworthy

ATF Theology
Adelaide
2016

Text copyright © 2016 remains with the individual authors and with ATF Press for the collection.

All rights reserved. Except for any fair dealing permitted under the Copyright Act, no part of this book may be reproduced by any means without prior permission. Inquiries should be made to the publisher.

Title: Kaleidoscope of pieces : Anglican essays on sexuality, ecclesiology and theology / Alan H Cadwallader, editor.

ISBN: 9781925232752 (paperback)
9781925232769 (hardback)
9781925232766 (ebook : epub)
9781925232783 (ebook : kindle)
9781925232790 (ebook : pdf)

Notes: Includes index.

Subjects: Church of England--Doctrines.
Same-sex marriage--Religious aspects.
Homosexuality--Religious aspects .
Christian sociology.

Other Creators/Contributors: Cadwallader, Alan, editor.

Dewey Number: 261.835848

Cover design and Layout/Artwork by Astrid Sengkey

Text Minion Pro Size 10 &11

Published by:

An imprint of the ATF Ltd.
PO Box 504
Hindmarsh, SA 5007
ABN 90 116 359 963
www.atfpress.com
Making a lasting impact

In memory of the Rev'd Dr Ron Dowling
friend, pastor, scholar and priest

Table of Contents

Preface		*Alan H Cadwallader*	ix
Foreword		*Bishop Kay Goldsworthy*	xiii
Chapter 1	How Wide is the Horizon: History, Hermeneutics and Listening to What the Spirit is Saying to the Church *Alan H Cadwallader*		1
Chapter 2	Religious Diversities and Sexual Diversities: a Conflict of Freedoms *Gary D Bouma*		29
Chapter 3	Marriage and the Sacred: Fragments Straight and Gay *Sarah Bachelard*		43
Chapter 4	Friends and Lovers, Friends and Others *Duncan Reid*		59
Chapter 5	Making Decisions *Peter Sherlock*		75
Chapter 6	It Seemed Good to Us *Phillip Tolliday*		93

Chapter 7	Situating Lambeth 1.10 as Discourse in the Life of the Anglican Church *Cathy Thomson*	111
Chapter 8	Innovation, Undecidability and Human Sexual Diversity: an Anglican Ecclesial Perspective *Stephen Pickard*	135
Chapter 9	The Fear of Being Wrong *Nikolai Blaskow*	161
Chapter 10	How Do We Get It? Pray for It! Liturgical Resources for a Long Journey *Elizabeth J Smith*	183
Contributors		201
Bibliography		203
Indices		
	Index of Biblical and Other Ancient References	219
	Index of Modern Authors	223
	Index of Subjects	227

Editor's Preface

Anglicanism has always understood itself in relation to wider society both in terms of its responsibility and in terms of how it formulates its own 'society', its own way of being Church. This characteristic is grounded in an understanding of God and of God's embrace of and involvement in the world. Such an understanding is never regarded as final or complete; it does not turn the past or present (or a particular construction thereof) into an untouchable shibboleth, even though both past and present hold treasures and values that shape and resource our responses. The contingency that hangs over our decisions and understandings does not warrant fear and confusion, but rather hope and faith, which, for Christians, is geared to the future—'for who hopes for what is seen?' (Rom 8:24); faith is about 'desiring a better country', one that can be called 'heavenly' (Heb 11:16). And this too is grounded in God, for as the great, fourth-century, Cappadocian theologian, Basil of Caesarea, perceived (in his treatise on the Holy Spirit) it is precisely God's incomprehensibility that properly characterises God for us. The affirmation of incomprehensibility is in no way meant to stifle our inquiry or our courage by placing God beyond our reach, nor to negate everything we might say about God and the world. Rather, it is God's own invitation into the future, into a journey of discovery and wonder, into a world where things are always being made new. For Basil, it followed that changes *could* be made to the language of the liturgy, in order better to express the new understandings (in this case, of the Trinity) after which we had, initially, groped darkly yet into which, by hindsight, we affirm we had been lead. And for him, it sometimes required a critique of 'The petty exactitude of these men about syllables and words . . . [and] the mischief to which it tends' (ch 2.4).

God's incomprehensibility further protects us from that promethean conceit that we can be absolutely certain in our convictions, unyielding in our interpretations, inflexible in our structures and ethically unquestionable in our decisions. All such stem from the originating seduction threatening our creation: to be 'like God' (Gen 3:5). It calls for a humility that divests us of our self-protection as we wander an earth sanctified by the presence of God— 'holy ground' (Ex 3:5). This is the God whose being is safeguarded from our predictive control by an ineffable name that precludes fixity: 'I am what I am/I will be what I will be' (Ex 3:14). Both meanings are held in this sacred name—unveiling and veiling at the same time. This was the name given in the defining biblical story about a future and a hope, liberation and transformation, that is the proper 'Exodus' of our received tradition. The promise of God that comes from God's own being is not to deliver the blueprint but to lead; and this journey is away from surety into a country yet to be shown (Ex 3:8 cf Gen 12:1).

The Anglican Church of Australia finds itself in just such a sacred moment. It is poised before a future, a country we don't completely understand and yet one that calls us out, indeed, calls us home. We are located within a society that God has embraced and, by the Spirit of the incarnate Jesus, has committed to. Our responsibility lies precisely there, to be part of what God has committed to. Our future is inextricably bound up with that commitment of God (Rom 8:17–23 cf Jer 29:7). It cannot be avoided by obfuscations about a lack of readiness, by positing conspiracies of attacks on our previous positions or by a retreat into border-protected bunkers in the name of the preservation of purity and the sanctity of our 'temples'. Such resistance has a long history and remains alive in debates inside and outside the church. The incarnate one is just as likely to accuse us of having become 'a cavern [the Greek word can mean 'grave'] of terrorists' (Mk 11:17) by our failure to offer welcome and inclusion, by our fear of journeying into an (in part) unknown future, and perhaps, above all, by our resistance to the faith of others different from ourselves. Ours is a faith that calls us out, saying, 'come over here' (Acts 16:9). To hold back, to refuse to move may not only signal our own death; it may cause severe harm to those to whom and with whom we are called.

The essays in this volume have been written by those deeply concerned about the future of the Anglican Church of Australia, a future which in many ways is being defined pastorally, theologically and ecclesiologically by its attitudes to those identifying as 'LGBTQIA', that is by sexual identities other than the normalised 'heterosexual' identity asserted as held by the majority. I am profoundly grateful for their courage and willingness to venture where others have, at times, timidly held back. They are keenly sensitised to those people of faith who, in various ways, do not and have not been permitted to sit in a church where they are welcomed, included and affirmed as people of the God of welcome, inclusion and affirmation. They recognise that, even as members of a church in a position of less security and influence in Australian society, their responsibility remains to be the church in and for the world. That responsibility has never been more weighty. Those who have written do not hold identical views; they do not write with absolute surety about how the church should respond, even in the variety of matters that they address. In this sense, the collection is a 'kaleidoscope of pieces'. They do offer reflections, insights and perspectives on how the church might move into a future where God is calling, beckoning, bidding us welcome. And they understand that the 'us' who are welcomed are, ourselves, a kaleidoscope of pieces, intricately, wonderfully and mysteriously made, not defined or prescribed by our sexual identities but rather by the image of that God who will be what God will be. Yes, we do not yet know what will be the outcome. As Paul of Tarsus acknowledged, 'now we see in a mirror dimly' (1 Cor 13:12) but, bidden by the One who is love, we may yet not only come to apprehend that love but, ourselves, *be* the image of that love. Love bids us welcome; may we not draw back.

Alan Cadwallader

Foreword

Rt Rev'd Kay Goldsworthy
Bishop of Gippsland

The early twentieth-century poet Rainer Maria Rilke's *Book of Hours: Love Poems to God* includes a poem written in 1905, 'I am too alone in the world'. It includes these lines: 'I want to unfold. I don't want to stay folded anywhere, because where I am folded, there I am a lie.'

Over recent decades there has been an incredible unfolding taking place regarding the place of gay and lesbian people in society not only in Australia but in many parts of the world. Conversations with gay friends in the 1970s, in which they dared to voice hopes and dreams for life-long partnerships, simply did not include the word *marriage*. Come to think of it, neither did they include the term *civil union*. Such conversations with Christians revealed a yearning for the same things most people simply took for granted: someone to love, someone to love them, the intimacy and friendship of a life shared in a faithful monogamous relationship, the anticipation of building a life, and growing old together—'the mutual society, help and comfort that one ought to have of the other, both in prosperity and adversity.'

When Thomas Cranmer wrote these words and inserted them into the marriage service in *The Book of Common Prayer*, he knew what he was talking about. As the first married Archbishop of Canterbury he had been scrutinising a rite devised by generations of medieval celibate clergy. 'At first sight, the result is a conservative rendering into English of the Sarum rite, but throughout there are small changes and expansions to bring a new warmth and humanity into the service', as Diarmaid MacCulloch, Cranmer's most recent biographer points out. 'Few medieval theologians would have extended the reasons for marriage beyond the avoidance for sin and the begetting of children; the classical list of Thomas Aquinas was *fides, proles, sacramentum*, and no mention of enjoyment. However, the Archbishop had at least sixteen years' experience of Margaret Cranmer's society, help and comfort in prosperity and adversity when he and his drafting team finalized these words.[1]

Other yearnings also came to the surface in conversations with friends: a yearning for building a family, for instance, and the dreadful grief of knowing that this would never be the case, and, of course, a yearning for there to be, within the community of the baptised, both the recognition and welcome promised in Christ crucified and risen.

Life does move on. We grow into the future, and debates, deliberations and actions continue both beyond and within the Christian community about same sex attracted people sharing the same dignity as all other followers of Christ. Far from subsiding, or fading away, this conversation has become fixed in the public square not around who may be ordained, but around who may be married. A cursory online investigation regarding the places in which same-sex marriage is allowed reveals no fewer than twenty very different countries and cultures where marriage equality is already enshrined in law. Alongside this, has come Ireland's recent referendum in support, laws allowing same-sex marriage will be in effect in 2016 in Finland and Greenland, and the Supreme Court extending marriage equality across the United States of America, all of which indicate an incredible momentum impossible to withstand. As philosophers and commentators have noted, indeed, as conveyed by the seasons of Advent and Lent, 'History only moves forward.'[2]

Kaleidoscope of Pieces follows two previous collections of essays, *Five Uneasy Pieces*, focussing on scriptural texts used to argue against the legitimacy of homosexual expression within Christian life, and *Pieces of Ease and Grace*, opening up fresh insights into readings offering pastoral and transformative support to those whose self-identification is not heterosexual.

---

1. D MacCulloch, *Thomas Cranmer: A Life* (New Haven/London: Yale University Press, 1998), 421.
2. N Berdyaev, *Christian Existentialism: A Berdyaev Anthology*, edited by DA Lowrie (London: George Unwin & Allen, 1965), 281; BC Crafton, *Let Us Bless the Lord, Year One: Advent through Holy Week* (Harrisburg, PA: Morehouse, 2004), 168; A Cooper, 'I think Visibility is Important' available at <http://www.huffingtonpost.com/2012/09/10/anderson-cooper-coming-out-talk-show_n_1871048.html>

This collection of essays has been written in response to issues raised in the previous volumes and ongoing debates in the life of the Church which call for a wider theological analysis, and theological reflection on recognising the dignity of gay and lesbian people of faith. Cathy Thomson locates the issues and pressures which led to the resolution of the 1998 Lambeth Conference, now known colloquially throughout the Anglican Communion as 'Lambeth 1.10'. Her essay provides a context for the unfolding story of this resolution in the wider life of the Church, and its impact on the theology and developing ecclesiology of the Communion.

These essays do what good theological investigation requires. They both confront and challenge through scholarly investigation. Sarah Bachelard asks what it means for marriage itself to become an idol. What impact does this have on those outside marriage, allowing them to be excluded and devalued? Questions of sacrifice, sanctification and what she frames as 'the vowed life' are explored in relation to unquestioning acceptance of things declared sacred or profane, and the need for such claims to be tested in the light of God's holiness in Jesus Christ.

Peter Sherlock asks readers to consider how it is that Anglicans make decisions in practice, our synodical and other governance structures for decision-making. Of sexuality, he says, 'the category of sexuality is one on which all Anglicans must take a stance. There is no neutral position'. By drawing attention to the ways in which decisions have been arrived at in relation to the ordination of women as priests and bishops, as well as recent decisions in two Australian dioceses, he invites us to reflect on the theological task which allows grace to unfold, inviting same-sex attracted people to be at the centre of our wrestling with these questions before the Church.

Alan Cadwallader asks readers to look back to the theological inquiry of two of Anglicanism's great biblical scholars, Westcott and Lightfoot, in order to look forward. Stephen Pickard focuses on Acts 15:28 to investigate how it is that movement takes place from something which seems good only to us, to what can by affirmed as good also to the Holy Spirit.

Each essay does help open a window, or perhaps to bring more nuanced colour and texture, a different view, like looking though a kaleidoscope, to highlight more of the theological, spiritual and ecclesiological depths in relation to human sexuality, and to homosexuality in particular. If it is true as Rilke said a hundred years ago that 'where I am folded, there I am a lie', then surely this is the case not only for individuals but also for the Church as a whole, called in Christ to unfold completely as we live into the life to which we have been called.

+ Kay

Chapter One
How Wide is the Horizon:
History, Hermeneutics and Listening to What the Spirit is Saying to the Church

Alan H Cadwallader

> *You may write me down in history*
> *With your bitter, twisted lies*
> *You may trod me in the very dirt*
> *But still, like dust, I'll rise*
> 　　　　　'Still I Rise' Maya Angelou

A Victorian rendition of the interpretation of the Bible

In 1895, the Bishop of Durham prepared a series of notes for a committee of English Bishops that was focused on the 'Organisation of the Anglican Communion'. The preparations for the Lambeth Conference of 1897 were in full swing. The printed notes were emblazoned with a superscript 'Strictly Confidential'.[1] It was not the first time that the thoughts of Brooke Foss Westcott, formerly Regius Professor of Divinity at Cambridge University, had been shielded from public gaze by his friends.[2] Westcott was a biblical scholar, one

---

1. Lambeth Palace Library (Papers of the Bishop of Salisbury [John Wordsworth], 1896–1911; hereafter *LPL*), Volume 1401, folios 5–6. Quotations hereinafter that are not footnoted come from this document. Wordsworth had served on the New Testament Committee for the Revision of the Authorised Version, though his conservative predilections at one stage had him teetering on resignation (Lightfoot to Westcott 24/6/1874; Auckland Castle Episcopal Records [Durham University Library, Palace Green] 3.13.9/21; hereafter *ACER*).
2. Edward White Benson (Bishop of Truro, Archbishop of Canterbury) Diary May 17, 1893, Cornwall Record Office (TCM 150): 'Bp of Durham addressed us very powerfully but it would be rather perilous to publish some of the things he said just now.' Thirty years or more earlier, another of Westcott's Birmingham friends, Joseph Barber Lightfoot, had advised Westcott against the publication of his

who, along with his friends Joseph Barber Lightfoot and Fenton JA Hort—dubbed 'the Cambridge Triumvirate'—had dragged English scriptural scholarship kicking and screaming into the modern age. Westcott's commentaries on the Gospel of John and the Epistle to the Hebrews, in particular, continue to be reference points for contemporary interpreters, and his work with Hort on establishing the text of the New Testament on sound genealogical principles has provided the foundation for almost all subsequent critical editions.[3] Six of his seven sons were ordained and grandsons would follow. He served on a number of Government bodies, including the Ecclesiastical Courts Commission in the 1880s. His credentials are impeccable. Why then the veil of secrecy from his fellow bishops?

The paper was titled 'Notes on the Critical Study of Holy Scripture'. Westcott's address to his fellow bishops laid out a distillation of his thoughts on the Bible and its interpretation. This same topic is the lode-stone of debate, even conflict, in the contemporary church as it variously addresses and avoids the subject of homosexuality—just as the church exhibits the same equivocating reaction towards those who, in the rainbow of human sexual sensibilities, identify as lesbian, gay, bisexual, transgender, intersexual, queer or asexual or those who resist any such label (including 'straight'). Westcott, ever the optimist

---

essay on the then-recent Marian manifestations at La Salette in France, for fear of confusion and thereby damage to his reputation: Lightfoot to Westcott 3/11/[1865] (*ACER* 3.13.3/2). It was conjectured that Westcott was denied an earlier place at Cambridge (prior to gaining the professorship in 1870) because of his supposed 'German' sympathies in biblical scholarship. See Lightfoot to Westcott 15/8/1861 (*ACER* 3.13.4/11). The *Edinburgh Review* paired '. . . Romanising Tractarianism or German neology' as the twin dangers for the Church of England (vol 96 (1852): 274). On both counts, Westcott, in his fledgling career, was viewed with suspicion by the Establishment in institution and church.

3. Eberhard Nestle, wrote to Westcott with a gift of his own critical edition of the Greek New Testament in 1900 (the progenitor of the most recent critical Greek edition), stating, 'I testify once more with the greatest pleasure, I never handled a book made up with so much care and thoughtfulness in the smallest details as your edition.' (Letter, March 1898, affixed to *Novum Testamentum Graece*, [Stuttgart: Privilegierte Württembergusche Bibelanstalt, 1898] edited by E Nestle; Westcott House Archives Books §2; hereafter *WHA*). See also JH Petzer, 'The History of the New Testament—Its Reconstruction, Signfiicance and Use in New Testament Textual Criticism', in *New Testament Textual Criticism, Exegesis and History*, edited by B Aland and J Delobel (Kampen: Kok Pharos, 1994), 15–16.

and fearless appropriator of new developments in society and philosophy, began with the observation that just as 'former periods of spiritual revival have been marked by fresh interest in the study of the Bible' so, correspondingly, 'the character of the study in each age has corresponded with the character of the age'. For Westcott, one of the chief characteristics of his age was 'the scientific study of history'. This was far from confined to the Bible. Indeed, one of Westcott's colleagues,[4] Henry Gwatkin, recognised that the taxonomy of the genealogical arrangement of New Testament manuscripts for textual criticism owed much of its impulse to the stemma arrangement in botany.[5] Westcott was certainly familiar with Charles Darwin's work,[6] even as he had imbibed his own father's promotion of botanical inquiry in the Westcott home city of Birmingham.[7] The intellectual trends of the age were not quarantined to any one discipline, even

---

4. In fact, the Westcott family for a time lived next door to the Gwatkins in Scrope Terrace, Cambridge.
5. HM Gwatkin, *Studies of Arianism* (Cambridge: Deighton, Bell & Co, 1882), preface. See also SC Carpenter, *Church and People, 1789-1889: A History of the Church of England from William Wilberforce to 'Lux Mundi'* (London: SPCK, 1933), 513-15.
6. A Westcott, *Life and Letters of Brooke Foss Westcott* (London: Macmillan, 2 vols, 1903), 1.335. The wrestling with the issues of evolution in fact goes back earlier, in part because Lyle, a forerunner to Darwin, had influenced a generation of Cambridge students into collecting rocks and ferns: Westcott to Lightfoot 7/12/1852 (Durham Dean and Chapter Library, Lightfoot Papers; hereafter *DDCL*). Hort regarded Darwin's Origin of Species as unanswerable and 'a treat to read' (Hort to Westcott 10/3/1860), proposing even to write on it: AF Hort, *Life and Letters of Fenton John Anthony Hort* (London: Macmillan, 2 vols, 1896), 1.414-5, 432-3. When Westcott was a master at the Harrow School, his colleague FW Farrar (later Dean of Canterbury) had written a book called *Chapters on Language* (London: Longmans, Green & Co, 1865) which led to supportive correspondence with Charles Darwin on the parallels between the evolution of language and the evolution of life: Farrar to Lightfoot 7/11/1865 (*DDCL*, Lightfoot Papers). On the key role of English clergy in the mustering of evidence, especially of geology and botany, see PW Armstrong *The English Parson Naturalist A Companionship between Science and Religion* (Herefordshire: Gracewing, 2000). I am grateful to Patrick Armstrong (Emeritus Professor at the University of Western Australia) for filling in some of the details of the Darwin correspondence.
7. See GB Knowles and F Westcott, *The Floral Cabinet and Magazine of Exotic Botany* (London: William Smith, 3 Vols, 1837-40).

though each advance or movement in those trends did not occur without contestation or the postulation of alternatives.

Westcott laid out how wide-ranging the 'change in attitude towards the Bible' was. It repudiated three main assumptions that had governed various Christian approaches to the Bible at the advent of the Victorian age:

> I that 'the authority of the several books' (including the Apocrypha) could be 'placed beyond the range of historical enquiry';
> II that 'the current text was free from corruption to which other ancient texts are liable';
> III that 'the interpretation of the Bible was guarded by an authoritative tradition'.

The Cambridge Triumvirate in their various publications clearly revealed their willingness to engage the full sweep of historical data that was available at that time. Lightfoot's commentary on Colossians, for example, incorporated recently published inscriptions and coins to elucidate the background to the history of Colossae.[8] Indeed, both Lightfoot and Hort (amongst a number) were enlisted by the English archaeologist, John Wood, who had returned from his long foray in the ruins of Ephesus laden with an array of inscriptions that needed deciphering.[9] Westcott himself maintained a keen interest in ancient coins and what insights they could yield into ancient times.[10] As he insisted repeatedly, 'the data must be ascertained with the utmost possible exactness, and then interpreted'. This evidence therefore challenged the sense that the Bible was somehow preserved from the issues of transmission that beset every other ancient book, even

---

8. See AH Cadwallader, 'Refuting an Axiom of Scholarship on Colossae; fresh insights from new and old inscriptions', in *Colossae in Space and Time: Linking to an Ancient City*, edited by AH Cadwallader and M Trainor (Göttingen: Vandenhoeck & Ruprecht, 2011), 153–156.
9. The inscriptions were included as an eight part appendix in his *Discoveries at Ephesus* (London: Longmans, Green & Co, 1877).
10. He wanted the library in the newly established Cambridge Divinity School (later Westcott House) to have a display of coins or casts thereof: Westcott to JW Clark 22/1/1883 (Cambridge University Library Add 8953/100-1; hereafter *CUL*). See also Westcott to CW King 5/6/1879 (Trinity College Ms O.10A.13.59), Arthur Westcott to his mother 21/12/1893 (*CUL* Ms 8316.3 No 161).

though, for some, such as John Burgon, Dean of Chichester Cathedral, this mortally offended the dogma of divine providence.[11] Westcott was clear that 'we have no right to determine by presuppositions what must be the character of the pages of revelation'. Accordingly, traditions of interpretation, dogmatic commitments, perhaps even the very Articles of Religion of the Church of England that he loved, were not to pre-determine the scope and direction of research. Indeed, all too often these yielded interpretations that rested 'on unsubstantial foundations'.[12] In a public essay on the Revision of the Authorised Version of the New Testament, a revision in which he had been involved for over a decade, Westcott wrote, 'There is no doubt a restless desire in man [sic] for some help which may save him from the painful necessity of reflection, comparison, judgment. But the Bible offers no such help.'[13]

The sort of inquiry Westcott was advocating to his fellow bishops, was to be sustained by 'absolute freedom'. Westcott had seen in his more than sixty years of involvement in the Church of England, too many examples of those who had suffered quite extreme damage at the hands of bishops and others who held the power (*de jure* or *de facto*) of preferment. The most flamboyant was probably the storm that erupted with the publication of *Essays and Reviews* in 1861, though one could easily explore the careers of Herbert Marsh, JW Donaldson, FD Maurice and Bishop Colenso to harvest poignant illustrations of the point. Heresy charges, court proceedings, damage to reputations and preferment were flung at the seven authors with such vehemence that one of them (the Reverend Benjamin Jowett)

---

11. Accordingly, Burgon vehemently defended the received ending of Mark's Gospel: JW Burgon *The Last Twelve Verses of the Gospel according to S Mark vindicated against recent critical objectors* . . . (Oxford/London: J Parker, 1871). Burgon declaimed that 'Profane literature has never known anything approaching to it [the preservation of the text] . . . because—the good Providence of God so willed it.' (*The Revision Revised* [London: John Murray, 1883], 334). It was not that Westcott did not hold to the providence of God (Westcott to Lightfoot 28/4/1860 [*DDCL* Lightfoot Papers]). It was rather that his understanding of providence was more subtle and far less mechanistic and hermetically sealed than Burgon's.
12. Here, Westcott was clearly marking out a distinction in the approach to the Bible from that favoured by John Henry Newman. See AH Cadwallader, 'Star-cross'd lovers: John Henry Newman and the Revision of the Bible', in *Australian eJournal of Theology* 19.3 (2012): 229–43.
13. *Lessons from Work* (London: Macmillan, 1901), 149.

never wrote on biblical matters again, confining himself to ancient Greek philosophical texts.[14] Westcott was appalled at 'the extreme violence of the language used against' the book and its authors, who were labeled 'infidels and the like'.[15] Lightfoot shared his consternation at the vilifying dismissal of the writers and their ideas: 'It is grievous to have to complain of the whole bench of bishops: but that the Essayists should be condemned indiscriminately and then be told that they have no business in the Church, is surely monstrously unjust.'[16] Lightfoot lamented that 'one of the evil effects of the publication of Essays and Reviews [was] that people in authority here have become more timid than ever.'[17]

The irony was that in the thirty years' interval from its publication to Westcott's address to the Lambeth gathering, another of the contributors to *Essays and Reviews*, Frederick Temple, had become a member of the episcopal bench; shortly (in 1896) he would be the new Archbishop of Canterbury![18] It was a clear indication that the issues that caused so much contumacious conflict at the outset had, in a relatively short period, become an accepted part of dialogic conversation, not unlike the change to the doxology introduced by Basil of Caesarea in the fourth century[19] through to the ordination of woman at the end of the twentieth century.[20] Nevertheless, enough

---

14. Westcott had early expressed his appreciation of Jowett's work, even if he disagreed with him about the 'uncertainty' of Scriptural language (Westcott to Lightfoot 1/9/1855 *DDCL* Lightfoot Papers).
15. Westcott to Lightfoot 30/1/1861 (*DDCL* Lightfoot Papers).
16. Lightfoot to Westcott 18/2/1861 (*ACER* 3.13.4/9).
17. Lightfoot to Westcott 5/10/1861 (*ACER* 3.13.4/13).
18. Temple, then Headmaster of the Rugby School, was made Bishop of Exeter in 1869, on condition that he withdraw his essay from any subsequent editions of *Essays and Reviews*. It seems that the inducement of promotion outweighed the commitment to the dissemination of his ideas. He was promoted further, to the bishopric of London, in 1885. Compliance had its rewards, though initially it was severely troubled: see V Shea and W Whitla (editors), *Essays and Reviews: The 1860 Text and its Reading* (USA: University of Virginia Press, 2000), 858–75.
19. Basil of Caesarea, 'On the Holy Spirit' 1.3. Basil had been severely criticised for changing the doxology to 'Glory to the Father with the Son together with the Holy Spirit' to more exactly indicate the Trinitarian equality of the persons. For the significance of this ancient argument for contemporary issues, see K Giles, *The Trinity and Subordinationism: The Doctrine of God and the Contemporary Gender Debate* (Downers Grove, IL: IVP, 2002). See further below.
20. See generally E Lindsay and J Scarfe (editors), *Preachers, Prophets and Heretics:*

heat remained in the debates over scriptural authority for Westcott's address to be x-rated as 'Highly Confidential'. Perhaps the bishops were protecting Westcott himself—he had barely scraped into selection for Durham because a number of candidates that the then Prime Minister, Lord Salisbury, had proffered in his recommendation to Queen Victoria, had declined.[21] Westcott's presidency of the Christian Social Union, from which he articulated a Christian Socialist position on biblical and theological grounds,[22] was regarded by Salisbury as too controversial for the unity, solidarity and compliance required of a bishop. Even after Westcott had won a resolution of the miners' strike/mine-owners' lock-out in 1892, he was still regarded in some quarters with suspicion, though lauded as 'the miners' bishop' in the north,[23] and as the Anglican trumping of the Catholic Cardinal Manning's conciliation in 1890 of the London dock strike.[24] Westcott's express mention of 'academic freedom' indicated that oft-caricatured 'heady' debates over history and hermeneutics were embroiled in and deeply affected by political and activist involvements—from all sides.

Anglican Women's Ministry (Sydney: UNSW Press, 2012).
21. Lord Salisbury fished for various reasons to reject Westcott, but it is clear that he thought Westcott too disruptive: Lady G Cecil, *Life of Robert, Marquis of Salisbury* (London: Hodder & Stoughton, 4 vols, 1932), 4.209–11. Salisbury had offered Durham, through the Queen, to Bishop Francis Jayne of Chester, to Bishop William How of Wakefield (both recent appointments) and even sounded out a former Harrow student of Westcott, Randall Davidson (then Dean of Windsor). Westcott's speech at the Hull meeting of the Christian Social Union in 1891 caused a furore in Conservative political circles (J Clayton, *Bishop Westcott* [London: AR Mowbray, 1906], 164). Salisbury refused to countenance Westcott as Archbishop of York (following William McGee's death in 1891) because of 'the socialist tendencies of the speeches he has made since he became a bishop' (quoted in B Palmer, *High and Mitred: Prime Ministers as Bishop Makers 1837–1977* [London: SPCK, 1992], 121).
22. BF Westcott, *Christian Social Union Addresses* (London: Macmillan, 1903).
23. See G Patrick, *The Miner's Bishop: Brooke Foss Westcott* (Peterborough: Epworth, 2nd Ed, 2004).
24. On the significance of Manning's intervention, see J Atherton, *Christianity and the Market: Christian Social Thought for our Times* (London: SPCK, 1992), 178; T McCarthy, *The Great Dock Strike 1889* (London: Weidenfeld and Nicolson, 1988), 148. The confessional snootiness of some Anglican devotees (especially given that Manning was a convert from Anglicanism) was recognised as playing a part in the exaltation of Westcott's achievement: G Best, *Bishop Westcott and the Miners* (Cambridge: Cambridge University Press, 1966), 21.

Some of these interventions that impacted the formal intellectual arguments were public; others prowled behind the scenes.

The historical study of the Bible revealed, for Westcott, the enormous diversity contained within its pages, as, for example, in the different understandings of the Messiah. Moreover, for Westcott, the Bible had set in train an unfolding of revelation, a method of divine interaction with the world that remained on-going. Whilst the Bible provides the consummate expression of that revelation, all human religious and scientific endeavour make their contribution to that revelation: 'we also are placed in an age of revelation,' he said. Most significantly, this revelation means that ultimately the Bible belongs not in the schools but 'into life', just as life makes its own contribution to the understanding of the expansiveness of revelation in which the Bible participates, bringing all not to itself but 'to Christ himself'. Moreover, as Westcott reflected on his time in the decade-long work of the Revised Version of the New Testament, the 'most free inquiry into the meaning of the sacred writings brought together in spiritual fellowship men widely separated by confessional differences'.

What can be deduced from this doyen of Anglican commentators provides a means of negotiating some of the claims, counterclaims and power dynamics in the recent debate over (homo)sexuality and the place of those identifying as of different sexual expression. The two recent Australasian volumes, *Five Uneasy Pieces* and *Pieces of Ease and Grace*, pointedly directed attention again to the Bible and how it might be used to aid contemporary reflection, perception and even decision-making about the variety of sexual identities within and beyond the church. Whilst none of those who contributed to these volumes regarded the Bible as the only source of knowledge for such work—as in Westcott's expansive understanding of revelation— nonetheless two factors privileged the initial focus on the Scriptures. The first was simply that each of the contributors had a love, respect and debt to the Bible, 'the book' said Westcott, 'unlike any other book'.[25] The second was that the Australian context (less so for New

---

25. This was a favorite slogan of Westcott, built on Jowett's call in *Essays and Reviews* to treat the Bible as literature like any other. Westcott admitted the methodology but declaimed that the emergent result was the singular standing of the Bible. See his Introduction to the Study of the Gospels (London: Macmillan, 1860), 389, and his essay in *The Expositor* III.5 (1887): 84.

Zealand) has been heavily constrained to what is loosely called biblical perspectives on sexuality, and to a particular approach to the Bible that dominates church pronouncements in the media and therefore, perceptions of what the church appears to hold.[26] In this sense, control of the debate has been housed in one particular party and this control enabled the setting of the agenda for debate.[27] The collections of essays were a sincere effort to demonstrate not only that the Bible may not speak as unequivocally in one direction as might appear but, indeed, the Bible could be read with integrity as offering embrace, love, inclusion and authenticity for those whose sexual identities do not conform to what is espoused as the normative and majority heterosexual, marital position.[28]

Inevitably, such readings prompted a number of responses, some laudatory, some less exemplary. In many ways, they reiterate the various dimensions of the critical study of the Bible identified by Westcott. These are:

1. Approaches to the Bible are determined by the characteristic commitments of the age in which those approaches manifest.
2. The interpretation of the Bible requires substantial human effort in critical methodologies.
3. The interpretation of the Bible frequently is designed to reinforce entrenched positions.
4. Interpretation of the Bible does not occur in an intellectual vacuum but has real and immediate implications for human beings, frequently at the price of intellectual freedom.

---

26. See W Lawton, *The Better Time to Be: Utopian Attitudes to Society Among Sydney Anglicans, 1885 to 1914* (Kensington, NSW: UNSW Press, 1990); T Frame, *Anglicans in Australia* (Kensington, NSW: UNSW Press, 2007); M Jensen, *Sydney Anglicanism: An Apology* (Eugene, OR: Wipf & Stock, 2012).
27. See H Hearon, '1 Corinthians', in *The Queer Bible Commentary* (London; SCM, 2006), 608.
28. This was recognised in a substantial review of *Pieces of Ease and Grace* by Megan Daffern in the *Journal of Theological Studies* (NS) 66 (2015): 277–79.

The considerations of the age

The nineteenth century saw the development of two anchors for intellectual inquiry: science and history. Westcott was confident that the two could be held together without irresolvable tension for the articulation and demonstration of the absolute truth of Christianity: '...the attempts, however imperfect, to bring our Faith into actual contact with the most varied facts of life, reveal its breadth and grandeur and vitality'.[29] He added a third anchor as part of his own foundational platform, namely, language (to which I shall return below). For him, the fostering of antagonism between these elementary principles reflected more on the limits of our own understanding than on any fundamental rupture: 'Man... introduces his own limitation into all the subjects which he tackles'.[30] Though the present day sees these elements frequently in conflict, they remain the key elements: science, history and language. The philosopher of religion, Mark Taylor has demonstrated how much of the intellectual cartography drafted in the nineteenth century continues to drive and direct debates today.[31]

It is not merely the discoveries in any of these fields that are valued as important—such as saw the American Psychiatric Association repudiate its own classification of homosexuality as a 'mental disorder' in 1973.[32] Rather more critical has been the burgeoning of methods by which these elements are to be explored. Indeed, the insight should be pressed further. It is not that a particular method is somehow privileged for exploring a pre-existing deposit of information, though, as will be seen, this *is* the argument of some. Rather, it has become a standard recognition in these various fields

---

29. 'Christianity as the Absolute Religion' in his *Essays in the History of Religious Thought in the West* (London: Macmillan, 1891), 342-61 (at p 359).
30. Westcott to Lightfoot 7/12/1852; Westcott to Lightfoot 5/5/1860 (*DDCL* Lightfoot Papers).
31. MC Taylor, *About Religion: Economies of Faith in Virtual Culture* (Chicago: University of Chicago Press, 1999).
32. It was not until 1990 that the World Health Organisation finally removed homosexuality from its list of 'disorders'. The 1975 resolution of the American Psychological Council was particularly telling: 'Homosexuality per se implies no impairment in judgment, stability, reliability, or general social and *vocational* capabilities ...' (My emphasis). See JJ Congar, 'Proceedings of the American Psychological Association', in *American Psychologist* 30 (1975): 620-51.

that they exist as fields of inquiry precisely because of the methods used to exposit them. In this sense, the limits of discernible results and of the understanding attached to them, are pre-determined by the methods used. As Chris de Wet notes, 'Different methods not only highlight different dimensions of texts, but they also have the ability to address the contemporary context of the historian in different ways.'[33] History, frequently seen as the paramount concern for Christianity, therefore becomes complicated precisely by, firstly, the range of material harnessed, secondly, the method(s) used for their analysis and, thirdly, the assumptions governing the choice of method. It is difficult to separate these because each affects the other.

Christianity has, in the modern era, been dominated by reference to the past, whether it be tracking an authentic episcopal succession for Anglican bishops[34] or, pressing further back, espousing a creation pattern (if not edict) for heterosexual (marital) normativity.[35] The difficulty is that access to this history has been via documents intended for transmission—like the Bible and the array of literary artefacts associated with it. Because such literature has been privileged as the means of access to the past, history has been read out of such documents (whether gospels, epistles, law-books), even if that is acknowledged as not the primary intent of the genre.[36] Whilst the yield of historical data has varied enormously in the estimation of scholars over the last two hundred years, this literature has held

---

33. C de Wet, 'On Method in the Study of Early Christian History: Problems, Limits and Challenges', in *Journal of Early Christian History* 3.2 (2013): 1.
34. This came to a head in Westcott's time with the so-called 'Bishop of Lincoln' case, where his close friend Edward White Benson (d 1896), Archbishop of Canterbury, set himself to lay out plainly 'the historical position of the English Church'. See Westcott's 'Memoir of Benson' 2/3/1898 *CUL* Add 7683. For the details of the court case, including the historical schema employed, see ES Roscoe, *The Bishop of Lincoln's Case* (London: William Clowes, 1889).
35. It is crucial to recognise that the so-called 'creation hermeneutic' used to determine responses to the homosexuality debate (so Giles, *infra*) itself involves a choice over the meaning of the key text: Gen 2:24. See M Warner, '"Set in Tradition and History": Genesis 2:24 and the Marriage Debate', in *Pieces of Ease and Grace: Biblical Essays on Sexuality and Welcome* (Adelaide: ATF Press, 2013), 1–15.
36. Lightfoot to Westcott 1/7/1863 (*ACER* 3.13.4/32). On the subtleties of Lightfoot's understanding of history, see G Treloar, *Lightfoot the Historian: The Nature and Role of History in the Life and Thought of J.B. Lightfoot (1828–1889) as Churchman and Scholar* (Tübingen: Mohr Siebeck, 1998).

the unconscious privileged position, not least, in this case, because of the sacredness attached to the Bible, and, almost by extension, to apocryphal and classical texts. That yield is then given a status of objective reality that obfuscates the role of the interpreter and the method used.[37]

It is not coincidental that the historical-critical method, so-called, arose within the ambit of European imperial powers (and their colonial imitators) who were concerned to justify their rising position by reference to an authorised inheritance of the past for which they were the self-appointed guardians and successors. The method has become naturalised as the authentic approach to the interpretation of ancient texts,[38] with other methods more or less dismissed as serving the interests of 'identity politics'.[39] At one level, practitioners of the historical-critical method are themselves engaged in a form of identity politics on behalf of (an) empire—'a form of intellectual ethnocentrism', as Pierre Bourdieu dubs it[40]—albeit concealed under the guise of normativity and consensual allegiance in the academy. Inevitably then, the glittering testamentary inheritance was privileged, albeit subject to contest not only between the imperial powers but also amongst various groups in each empire looking to be the predominant articulators for, or at least within, that empire. History was being courted for ideological purposes, even if it could also be used to expose such expropriation.[41]

In our own day, the same drive for comprehension of the treasures of the past—what Lightfoot deemed 'completeness' without

---

37. See W Wink, *Manifesto for Biblical Studies* revised and re-published as *The Bible in Human Transformation* (Philadelphia: Fortress Press, 1973).
38. Sometimes it is distinguished from a philological or grammatico-linguistic approach; sometimes it is blended as in the phrase 'grammatico-historical' used, for example, by the nineteenth century Catholic biblical scholar, Cardinal Nicholas Wiseman. See N Wiseman, *The Real Presence of the Body and Blood of Our Lord Jesus Christ in the Blessed Eucharist, Proved from Scripture* (Dublin: James Duffy, 1836), 37.
39. See FJ King, 'Review of Five Uneasy Pieces', in *Colloquium* 46.1 (2014): 134.
40. P Bourdieu, 'Thinking about Limits', in *Theory, Culture, Society* 9.1 (1992): 37–49, at p 39.
41. Note the caution about this possibility in the Inter-Anglican Theology and Doctrine Commission, 'Summary Argument for the IATDC's "Communion Study"' (2006) §5, sourced from <http://www.anglicancommunion.org/ministry/theological/iatdc/docs/2006study.cfm> last accessed August 2014.

prolixity[42]—predominates. It is an inheritance of the scientific method begun in the seventeenth century but reaching general acceptance and practice in the nineteenth century.[43] The work of Robert Gagnon and Bill Loader reflects this concern.[44] Indeed, John J Collins confers the epithet 'the Kinsey of biblical sexuality' on Loader.[45] Academicians certainly privilege comprehensive treatments—from these, solid comparative results and predominating tendencies can be delineated. It was what drove the twenty-five years of gathering and evaluation of ancient manuscripts by Westcott and Hort for their edition of the New Testament.[46] To be accused of missing out some author or some evidence becomes then not merely a demerit point for an author but a betrayal of the global reach of the method,[47] even though Loader,

---

42. Lightfoot to Westcott 4/12/1859 (*ACER* 3.13.4/3); cf 'comprehensive' in Westcott, Lessons from Work, 120. Nonetheless, Lightfoot also held that completeness was not for this world! Lightfoot to Westcott 18/5/1869 (*ACER* 3.13.8/7). Part of Westcott's commitment to the translation/revision of the Apocrypha for the Revised Version was precisely because of the two-century, historical gap between the (Protestant) Old Testament and New Testament. The resultant addition to the Revised Version was published in 1895.
43. See R Yeo, *Notebooks, English Virtuosi and Early Modern Science* (Chicago: University of Chicago, 2014).
44. RJA Gagnon, *The Bible and Homosexual Practice: Texts and Hermeneutics* (Nashville: Abingdon, 2002). The five main books in the series by William Loader called *Attitudes towards Sexuality in Judaism and Christianity in the Hellenistic Greco-Roman Era*, are *Enoch, Levi, and Jubilees on Sexuality*; *The Dead Sea Scrolls on Sexuality*; *The Pseudepigrapha on Sexuality*; *Philo, Josephus and the Testaments on Sexuality* and *The New Testament on Sexuality*, all published by Eerdmans, 2007–2012. Additional books aimed at different readerships have also been published.
45. Back matter to W Loader *Making Sense of Sex: Attitudes towards Sexuality in Early Jewish and Christian Literature* (Grand Rapids: Eerdmans, 2013).
46. Kurt Aland's perfunctory dismissal of his English forebears, 'that neither Westcott nor Hort ever actually collated a single manuscript but worked completely from published material', is simply wrong: K and B Aland, *The Text of the New Testament* (Grand Rapids: Eerdmans, 1987), 18. See AH Cadwallader, *The Politics of the Revised Version* (Sheffield Phoenix forthcoming).
47. This is one of the refrains of King's critique in his review of *Five Uneasy Pieces*, albeit recognising that the book is 'aimed at a popular market' (p 133). Moreover, the suggestion that my essay in that collection rules out 'all possible engagement with OT texts' is simply wrong, as the argument about 'sleeping with the father by robbing him of his wife' is grounded in a reading of the incest prohibitions in Leviticus (Lev 18:7–8 in particular; Lev 20 in general) that marginalise the integrity of the woman/wife by accenting the honour, if not the ownership, of

in spite of the magisterial sweep of his research and his rejection of selective reading,[48] acknowledges the possibility of both omissions in the collection of data and the distortion in analysis caused by a scholar's situational perspective.[49] Nevertheless, Westcott's recognition of human limitations does not, it seems, extend to the method itself.

In a sometimes-conflicted mixture of the desire to harness all the material with yet a privileging of literary texts,[50] sexuality in the ancient world is explored largely through writings that predominantly, though not exclusively, seek to be prescriptive,[51] even though Loader

---

the man/husband. See 'Keeping Lists or Embracing Freedom', in *Five Uneasy Pieces*, 58–60. This has been recognised by other readers: see KR Lings, *Love Lost in Translation: Homosexuality and the Bible* (USA: Trafford Publishing, 2013), 232–34. There have been a number of repeated efforts to argue for an etymology for the word *arsenokoitēs* that aligns it with homosexual rather than incestual practice, that is, baldly, 'man-bedder'. See for example, Gagnon, *Bible and Homosexual Practice*, 312; KR Giles, 'Paul's Condemnation of Porneia: Sexual Immorality in 1 Corinthians 6:9–10', in *Ethos: Centre for Christianity and Society* blog, at <www.ethos.org.au/Online-Articles/Blog> last accessed August 2014; D Cooper-Clarke, 'An Evangelical Perspective on the Morality of Homosexual Behaviour', 11, sourced from <www.bioethicscolloquium.com.au> last accessed August 2014. Given that my suggestion serves an alternate etymological genealogy (from that largely derived from Gagnon's work), it demonstrates that etymological arguments do not give certainty; greater confidence in meaning is therefore found by referring to the overall context in which the term is deployed, that is, as deriving from the situation briefly described in 1 Cor 5:1ff. That this would resonate in a Greco-Roman and not simply a Jewish context is indicated by (Ps-) Quintilian *Minor Declamations* §335.

48. Loader, *Making Sense of Sex*, 3.
49. Loader, *Making Sense of Sex*, 141.
50. Here, the old artificial distinction between *Kleinliteratur* and *Hochliteratur* that saw New Testament writings classified with papyri under the former as 'popular' to distinguish it from the high literature of classical and elite Hellenistic writings, is misleading. The New Testament texts were not private—even Philemon is addressed to the church (v 2)—and were intended (by author and/or recipients) to gain the sort of hearing and remembrance that required a measure of preservation and transmission (for example Jn 20:30–31, 1 Cor 5:9, 16:1, 1 Thess 5:27, 2 Thess 2:15, Col 4:16, 2 Pet 3:15–16, Rev 2:7, 11, 17, 29, 3:6, 13, 22, 22:18–19). In any case, the 'papyri' include everything from ephemeral shopping lists to previously unknown works obviously intended for transmission and performance.
51. A review of the Index in Loader's summative volume (2013) confirms what is found in the previous extensive treatments, namely that literary texts are the fare for analysis. Loader does recognise however that narrative tales also exist beside more legislative or juridical texts.

reframes this designation under the generic heading of 'attitudes to sexuality'. From this it is deduced that the Judeo-Christian attitude towards homosexuality is unequivocally negative and further that Jesus, as fundamentally a conservative, adopts a strict sexual ethic.[52] Gagnon and Loader part company however on the question of the hermeneutical application for today of this large, literary, textual data accumulation and description.[53] Two main criticisms adhere to this historicist approach: the privileging of literary texts and the privileging of a particular method. These are not new criticisms of the use of history. In EH Carr's colorful language, 'what the historian catches will depend, partly on chance, but mainly on what part of the ocean he chooses to fish in and what tackle he chooses to use'.[54] I shall deal with these in turn, and then add a third element.

A. The failure to look beyond literary texts

This criticism is not to provide my own accusation of incompleteness but rather to illustrate that the selective choice of the type of evidence can jaundice the results and create the false impression that the literature surviving from history *is* the history. Both Hort and Westcott longed for some insight into 'common spoken Greek' which they suspected was 'sedulously excluded from the literary language'.[55] Their encounters with inscriptions had already given weight to their suspicion of the gulf between transmitted scribal literature and the language (and hence, potentially, the attitudes) of the *hoi polloi*. But the revolutionary advent of papyri was, for them, barely visible on the horizon. Sometimes dubbed 'sub-literary', 'para-literary' or 'documentary' sources, papyri have a peculiar value. These materials provide an insight into ordinary life that frequently is either missing from more literary works or is given a particular slant for heuristic or polemical purposes in such works.[56] Sometimes, the evidence is

---

52. Loader, *Sexuality in the New Testament* (Louisville, KY: WJKP, 2010), 34.
53. Loader, *Sexuality in the New Testament*, 120–26.
54. EH Carr, *The Making of History* (Harmondsworth: Penguin, 1987), 23.
55. Hort to Westcott 5–6/9/1859 (*CUL* Add 6597 [Hort Correspondence]).
56. This is not to say that papyri chart all the ocean of ancient life. Quite apart from the limitations on survival imposed by climate—the sweep of latitude from Egypt to Jordan providing the optimum circumstances for preservation—the material

quite disruptive of the history derived from literary sources; indeed sometimes that evidence has either been sidelined from consideration or explained away.[57]

Though Loader defines 'sex' and 'sexuality' in the broadest terms so as to glean as much information as possible, that exemplary ambition does not extend to the information that comes from documentary sources. So, the 'Jewish whore Salome' flung as a mocking vilification of the lineage of a Roman emperor (Claudius) in an Egyptian source (titled by scholars, *The Acts of the Pagan Martyrs*) is a crucial example of how rhetoric can paint disreputable, generalised and sexualised pictures of a despised ethnic group.[58] One wonders if the same tendency, evident in some Christian commentary that holds to a measure of reality about the Gentile world (and Paul's attitudes) in Romans 1 or the vice-list in 1 Corinthians 6, were applied equally here, then Jews or at least Jewish women would appear very differently. As Loader acknowledges, plotting the line between rhetoric and reality, the pun and the punch, can be difficult.[59]

More significant is a letter (or strictly, two letters) in the Zenon papyri.[60] In 257 BCE, an influential Jewish businessman, Toubias, informed Apollonios (an official [a *dioiketes*] in the service of King Ptolemy Philadelphos of Egypt), that he has sent as a gift to him—a eunuch and four boy slaves—for whom he gave detailed descriptions, including that two were circumcised and two were not. It is a clear indication of the wealth, autonomy and influence of the Tobiad family and how, in a period of Ptolemaic control of Palestine and the Transjordan, they were able to maintain their privileged commercial and administrative position. That is, the provision of gifts, tailored to

---

that has survived has its own limitations. See RS Bagnall, *Everyday Writing in the Graeco-Roman East* (Berkeley, CA: University of California Press, 2012), 58–60.

57. This is the thinly veiled suggestion of JEG Whitehorne, 'Sex and Society in Greco-Roman Egypt', in *Actes du XVe congrès international de papyrology*, Pt 4, edited by J Bingen and G Nachtergael (Brussels: Fondation Égyptologique Reine Élisabeth, 1979), 240.
58. See HA Musurillo, *The Acts of the Pagan Martyrs: Acta Alexandrinorum* (Oxford: Clarendon, 1954), 24.
59. Loader, *Sexuality in the New Testament*, 12–14.
60. *PCairo Zenon* I.59076.

the interests and proclivities of Greek-Egyptian authorities,[61] was one of the means by which Tobiad interests were served.

When these documents were first gathered into a collection of Jewish papyri, the editors were coy about the ethnicity of the circumcised boys and the role of the eunuch, just as they were about the thanksgiving to the gods in Toubias' opening greeting. They proposed that circumcision was not the preserve of Jews—correct as a general observation[62]—that the possibly Hebrew names of the two were not necessarily their own but given by their owner, that the eunuch was the boys' teacher (probably in household scribal tasks)[63] and that the formulaic opening to the correspondence was written by a Greek scribe who simply imposed his own convention.[64] Moreover, Toubias himself was tarred with a Hellenistic brush, being identified as the forefather of those who 'were the champions of the Hellenistic movement among the Jews in Palestine'.[65] Such subtle efforts to isolate Toubias from more general exemplary Jewish values and practice has continued amongst commentators on this papyrus.[66]

---

61. T Rajak, *Translation and Survival: The Greek Bible of the Ancient Jewish Diaspora* (Oxford: Oxford University Press, 2009), 81.
62. See Herodotos 2.104.2–3.
63. This rests on an insecure reconstruction of the papyrus.
64. The occurrence of Jewish names amongst voluntary associations that honour various gods, should qualify such easy explanations. See W Horbury and D Noy, *Jewish Inscriptions of Graeco-Roman Egypt* (Cambridge: Cambridge University Press, 1992), §154, p 246; cf PCowley 14; 21.2; CPJ 39, 427. See also, ARR Sheppard, 'R.E.C.A.M. Notes and Studies No. 6: Jews, Christians and heretics in Acmonia and Eumeneia', in *Anatolian Studies* 29 (1979): 169–80; A Vincent, *La Religion des Judéo-Araméens d'Eléphantine* (Paris: Guethner, 1937), 92–96. The letter's detailed descriptions of the young boys indicates that Toubias was well aware of Ptolemaic conventions, beyond the mere greeting; if he is concerned that the former be included, he can reasonably be held responsible for the latter salutation. See M Popovic, *Reading the Human Body: Physiognomics and Astrology in the Dead Sea Scrolls* (Leiden: Brill, 2007), 279.
65. VA Tcherikover and A Fuks (editors), *Corpus Papyrorum Judaicarum* [*CPJ*] (Cambridge, MA: Harvard University Press, 1957), vol 1, §4, p 127. For the succession, see M Hengel, *Judaism and Hellenism*, translated by J Bowden (London: SCM, 1974), 1.59.
66. See, for example, JL White, *Light from Ancient Letters* (Philadelphia: Fortress Press, 1986), §16, p 39; I Bieżunka-Małowist, 'La traite des esclaves dans l'Égypte', in *Archaeologia Polona* 14 (1973): 150; RF Collins, 'A Significant Decade: The Trajectory of the Hellenistic Epistolary Thanksgiving', in *Paul and the Ancient Letter Form*, edited by SE Porter and SA Adams (Leiden: Brill, 2010), 160.

There has even been an attempt to argue that Toubias was not a real Jew.[67] Nevertheless, given a willingness to allow that practice did not always equate with beliefs encoded or prescribed in literature, it can reasonably be asserted that Toubias was nothing 'but a loyal Jew who was not bothered by a polytheistic greeting'.[68] Moreover, it is clear that trade in slaves between Palestine and Egypt was common at this time, with Toubias at both ends of commercial and munificent exchange.[69] The commodification of human bodies can be recognised in the ease with which Toubias writes another letter on the same day that this time accompanied delivery of gifts of animals such as dogs, intended for the same king.[70]

The most recent detailed analysis of the papyrus[71] repudiates efforts to somehow exonerate Judaism from the troubling elements in this papyrus. The Damascus Document known at Qumran (and elsewhere) may later prohibit the sale of Jews as slaves to non-Jews,[72] but this does not appear to have been a concern for Toubias or other Jews in Palestine in the mid-third century BCE. Indeed Krautbauer, Llewellyn and Wassell consider that the role of the eunuch was to be a 'personal attendant' to Apollonios and that the four, young boys, were 'not yet "fit" to go' to him, because they were not yet castrated. Their value lay in their pre-pubescent state.[73] Even though I think

---

67. L Doering, *Ancient Jewish Letters and the Beginnings of Jewish Epistolography* (Tübingen: Mohr Siebeck, 2012), 85–86.
68. LL Grabbe, *Judaic Religion in the Second Temple Period: Belief and Practice from the Exile to Yavneh* (London: Routledge, 2000), 40. Jewish reverent acknowledgment of other gods is known elsewhere: CIJ 2.1537. See KB Stern, 'Vandals or Pilgrims? Jews, Travel Culture and Devotional Practice in the Pan Temple of Egyptian El-Kanais', in *'The One who Sows Bountifully': Essays in Honor of Stanley K Stowers*, edited by CJ Hodge, SM Olyan, D Ullucci and E Wassermann (Providence, RI: Brown University Press, 2013), 177–88.
69. He received a slave girl named Sphragis, for example: *CPJ* 1. Apollonios had a Jewish slave-girl named Johanna in his Egyptian household: *CPJ* 7. Other such trafficking is mentioned; cf *CPJ* 126.
70. *CPJ* 5.
71. A Krautbauer, S Llewellyn and B Wassell, 'A Gift of One Eunuch and Four Slave Boys: P. Cair.Zen. I 59076 and Historical Reconstruction', in *Journal for the Study of Judaism*, 45.3 (2014): 305–25.
72. *CD* 12.10–11.
73. Krautbauer, 'A Gift', 323–4.

they underestimate the careful distinction between circumcised and uncircumcised as part of the present (not just future) value of the boys,[74] the general point is plain. An aristocratic Jew who courted close connections with high-priestly families,[75] felt completely at liberty to provide outlets for same-sex and pederastic desire in his powerful Ptolemaic connection. Indeed, the more likely reconstruction of the papyrus that describes the slaves as 'house-born' (*oiketika*) combined with 'well-born' (*eugenês*) may indicate that Toubias knew full-well who had taken responsibility for training if not fathering the boys.

Given recent scholarship highlighting the sexual use of slaves (whether male or female),[76] it is striking that such considerations have usually not entered the discussions of Jewish and Christian beliefs and practices, nor gained the more subtle analysis that literary references were frequently heard in class tones—a sexual offence impugned as shameful against an equal was often regarded as inconsequential when committed against a slave.[77] Also clear is that even though a variety of Jewish writings can slam the array of Gentile nations for their rampaging unnatural sexual appetites,[78]

---

74. Cf *CIL* 4.1375, 1655.
75. Toubias' son, Joseph, married one of the Oniad daughters (Josephus *Antiquities* 12.160).
76. SB Pomeroy, *Women in Hellenistic Egypt: from Alexander to Cleopatra* (Detroit, Mich: Wayne State University Press, 1990), 143; JA Marchal, 'The Usefulness of an Onesimus: The Sexual Use of Slaves and Paul's Letter to Philemon', in *Journal of Biblical Literature,* 130 (2011): 749–70.
77. Thus a certain Hierocles is most concerned to clear his name of offences against ephebes-in-training at the Alexandrian palaestra (*Papiri greci e latini* [*PSI*] 4.340). No such concern appears to attach to slaves or even in regard to those who willingly enter same-sex connections (Compare Ps-Quintilian *Minor Declamations* §298; *POxy* 1160). See generally, F Ivarsson, 'Vice Lists and Deviant Masculinity: The Rhetorical Function of 1 Corinthians 5:10–11 and 6:9–10', in *Mapping Gender in Ancient Religious Discourses,* edited by T Penner and C Vander Stichele (Leiden: Brill, 2007), 166.
78. As in the *Sibylline Oracles* 3.596–600. Loader does not deal with the rhetorical generalisations operating to reinforce and privilege (Jewish) ethnic (and hence ethical) distinctions from reprobate Gentiles: *Pseudepigrapha on Sexuality,* 61; contrast JDG Barclay, *Jews in the Mediterranean Diaspora: From Alexander to Trajan (323 BCE–117 CE)* (Edinburgh: T&T Clark, 1996), 218–25.

the same charge was also leveled against Jews.[79] Conversely, within societies, sexual behaviours can be vilified as a means of degrading an individual, without any sense that the entire race or group comes under such a judgment.[80] The purpose may or may not be absolutely to castigate a behaviour; rather, the primary intent is to denigrate an opponent (real or perceived) either for the public humiliation of that opponent or for the reinforcement of one's own group boundaries. The easy rhetorical slide is to claim that 'guilty of one fault, guilty of all' and further, the 'guilty individual implies the guilt of the group'.[81]

Overall then, the danger is that, when historical investigation is promoted, some types and registers of literature may be overlooked by a privileging of certain surviving texts, and that this distorts the resultant picture. But further, in the very act of making such a choice, an interpreter becomes a witting or unwitting re-iterator of the dominant tendencies (their own rhetoric) in those documents, either by generalising from those documents or by privileging their contents.[82] The *method* of inquiry thereby becomes as problematic as a restricted harvest of evidence. To this I turn.

---

79. 'the lecheries of circumcised Jews' writes the satirist Martial *Epigram* 7.30; see also Martial's satirical pilloring of the Jew Menophilus: *Epigram* 7.82 cf 11.94 (an anonymous Jew). Juvenal's use of verpos for 'circumcised' in *Satires* 14.104 may be designed to evoke the ithyphallic propensity of Priapus. I wonder whether the Pompeii graffito belittling the slave Martha (*CIL* 4².5244) is to be grouped here as well. Carlo Giordano and Isodoro Kahn report on the notorious activities of a certain Jonah of Pompeii: *CIL* 4.1782, 2402, 2403, 2406, though argue that these reflect 'the easy mockery to which the Jews more than others were exposed': *The Jews in Pompeii, Herculaneum, Stabiae and in the Cities of Campania Felix* (Rome: Bardi, 3rd ed, 2001), 47; there is considerable doubt however as to whether Jonas or Jonis (a Greek female name) should be read: see J Gunderson, 'Inscribing Pompeii: a Re-evaluation of the Jewish Epigraphic Data' (unpublished MA thesis, University of Kansas, 2013). None of these primary sources finds a mention in Loader's project.
80. See, for example, Seneca's condemnation of wealthy Romans 'who make sure boyhood's glow lasts into a time not its own' (*Epistle* 122.7; cf *Controversies* 10.4.17). For Seneca, this was decidedly 'un-Roman', even though committed by a Roman. Compare also, for a (later) Jewish example, D Baile, *Eros and the Jews: from Biblical Israel to Contemporary America* (NY: BasicBooks, 1992), 146–47.
81. Ivarsson, 'Vice Lists and Deviant Masculinity', 167. Ivarsson suggests that this may enlighten why Paul wants, in some cases, the separation of certain members, so that the group not be tarnished by association.
82. See E Schüssler Fiorenza, 'Challenging the Rhetorical Half-Turn: Feminist and Rhetorical Biblical Criticism', in *Rhetoric, Scripture and Theology: Essays from*

B. The failures in method

A number of responses to *Five Uneasy Pieces* has concentrated on one or other method used to interpret texts.[83] One writer, in an echo of nineteenth century episcopal branding of the *Essays and Reviews* authors as 'infidels', has declared that the methods employed in at least two of the essays were 'not compatible with Christian interpretative tradition'.[84] The irony is that the literary and historical methods so severely criticised in Victorian England are the very methods advocated by William Loader but which are, in his assessment, critically absent from the readings of Scripture in *Pieces of Ease and Grace*.[85] For all the efforts to establish a Christian method for reading the Christian Scriptures, such a qualified and qualifying method not only varies across the ages of the history of interpretation. It also owes a considerable debt in the methods for the interpretation of literature and history to prevailing norms in non-biblical interpretation. Thus, the contemporary method called 'intertextuality' that has gained a measure of scholarly status,[86] derives its theoretical base from the work of the Marxist-feminist Julia Kristeva.[87]

Long ago, Walter Wink exposed the atheistic roots of the historical critical method itself, whilst continuing to harness its advantages for biblical interpretation.[88] His insights remain valid, namely, that the

---

the 1994 Pretoria Conference, edited by SE Porter and TH Olbricht (Sheffield: Sheffield Academic Press, 1996), 45–47.
83. See for example, G Preece, 'Accommodation of gay culture not scriptural', in *The Melbourne Anglican* 6/3/2012.
84. MR Stead, 'Herman Who? The Hermeneutics of the Homosexuality Debate', 24 (see also pp 9, 10, 25); <stjamesturramurra.org.au/stead/files/HermanWho TheHermeneuticsoftheHomosexualityDebate.pdf> last accessed August 2014. For a similar argument for a 'Christian' method of interpretation, see O Bayer, 'Hermeneutical Theology', in *Philosophical Hermeneutics and Biblical Exegesis*, edited by P Pokorný and J Roskovec (Tübingen: Mohr Siebeck, 2002), 103–20.
85. Communication from Bill Loader 23/10/2013.
86. See, for one example among many, MR Stead, *The Intertextuality of Zechariah 1–8* (New York: T&T Clark, 2009).
87. Such is the accreditation in J Still and M Worton, 'Introduction' to *Intertextuality: Theories and Practices*, edited by M Worton and J Still (Manchester: Manchester University Press, 1990), 1.
88. The initial booklet, almost a tract, was called *Manifesto for Biblical Studies*. It was revised and enlarged in a more formally published volume, *The Bible in Human Transformation*, cited above.

historical critical method is not a guarantee of an objective result either of the author's intention or of a complete historical reality: 'nothing can be thought unless through instruments of thought which are socially constituted'.[89] For some, there has been a revival of the nineteenth century fear that this method would work against Christian faith.[90] Rather this method (as any) can act as a veil to obscure the values, commitments (tacit or acknowledged) and unifying drive of the interpreter, even as it parades itself as value-free and open to variegated voices. One reviewer of Loader's work for example, noting that it is hard to reconcile a supposedly conservative (Jewish) Jesus with a prioritisation of singleness or a commendation of eunuchs or a privileging of prostitutes (Lk 20:34–35 cf 1 Cor 7:7-8; Matt 19:12; 21:31-32) asks a question that reveals the intricate infusion of the interpreter's values into interpretation: 'whether, how and to what extent have heterosexist and homophobic presuppositions (majority propaganda) distorted translations, exegesis and hermeneutics (for centuries, but including contemporary interpreters)'?[91]

This should not be taken as endorsing one method over another. To label some methods as concerned with self-serving, identity politics and apologetics or as a failure in attention to the distance between the ancient texts and our own times, is to obfuscate the recognition that *all* methods are limited in their scope, and are themselves developments of persons embroiled in an unfolding historical process. Rather, the eclectic reliance upon a variety of methods can actually yield unacknowledged, even surprising treasures. Feminist criticism, treated with considerable suspicion by some who adhere to the historical-critical method,[92] has unlocked a huge return both for an understanding of the first century Jesus/ *basileia* movement and for transformative living in the present

---

89. Bourdieu, 'Thinking about Limits', 40.
90. See AH Cadwallader, 'History as Bulwark, Bridge and Bulldozer: *Dei Verbum* and Ecumenical, Biblical Endeavour', in *God's Word and the Church's Council: Vatican II and Divine Revelation*, edited by C Monaghan and M O'Brien (Adelaide: ATF Press, 2014), 207–24.
91. TD Hanks, 'Tom Hanks Paper on Loader, SBL 2013' available from Other Sheep: Multicultural Ministries with Sexual Minorities <http://www.fundotrasovejas.org.ar/ingles/resenas/Loader%20Romans%202010.pdf> last accessed August 2014. (A slight adjustment to syntax has been made, for clarity.)
92. *The Interpretation of the Bible in the Church* (1993) section E.2.

day.[93] To be sure, feminist criticism can be apologetic but this is not something from which grammatico-linguistic and historical-critical methods are themselves immune. An off-shoot of feminist and queer methods of criticism—masculinity studies—has brought similar benefits in understanding how early Christian male leaders operated in the world of their day, questions and insights about which earlier generations of commentators were deafeningly silent, even as they proclaimed certain methods and expositions as 'muscular'.[94] These contests about methods and results often present as belonging in a rarefied world of intellectual debate. One might wish that were the case, either as a relegation to an angels-on-the-head-of-a-pin irrelevance or as a denial of the ecclesial politics that frequently foster and depend upon such debates. But just as considerable German scholarship culminating in the 1930s was concerned to explore the Galilean as distinct from the Judean origins of Jesus as a sequestering of the man of Nazareth from his Jewishness,[95] the impact on people can be frighteningly, horrifically real. The setting and consequences of the sexuality 'debate' in the Anglican Church of Australia reflect on the conduct of the church and the non-intellectual pressures that shape how the debate proceeds.

C. The politics of ecclesial debate over sexuality

This subject itself warrants a more detailed analysis than can be given here.[96] But enough can be outlined to demonstrate that the debates over sexuality in the Anglican Church of Australia are embedded in real consequences for people at the academic, career and pastoral

---

93. See as but one example, W Cotter, 'Women's Authority Roles in Paul's Churches: Countercultural or Conventional', in *Novum Testamentum*, 36.4 (1994): 350–72.
94. See AH Cadwallader, 'Male Diagnosis of the Female Pen in the late Victorian Britain: Private Assessments of Supernatural Religion', in *Journal of Anglican Studies*, 5 (2007): 67–86.
95. See H Moxnes, *Jesus and the Rise of Nationalism: a New Quest for the Nineteenth Century* (London: IB Tauris, 2012).
96. For examples of the links between theology and political decision-making and impacts on the lives of people, see M Maddox, *God under Howard: The Rise of the Religious Right in Australian Politics* (Crows Nest: Allen & Unwin, 2005); R Boer, *Political Myth: On the Use and Abuse of Biblical Themes* (Durham, NC / London: Duke University Press, 2009), especially 116–43.

levels, to name some of the dimensions. In this sense, little has changed since the fiery debates of the nineteenth century that led Lightfoot to bemoan 'ecclesiastical terrorism' and 'monstrous injustice'[97] and Westcott to fear an 'internecine war'.[98]

Within six months of the release of *Five Uneasy Pieces*, a 'riposte',[99] titled *Sexegesis*,[100] was launched contemporaneously in six venues across Australia. Copies were distributed to every member of the Diocesan Synod in Brisbane. Another response appears to have been written for the Doctrine Commission in preparation for the annual meeting of Australian bishops to which Bill Loader was invited to provide his take on the biblical understanding(s) of sexuality.[101] One bishop declaimed with exuberance about *Sexegesis*, 'What's interesting is that this is not a book by the usual suspects. We in Sydney have had almost nothing to do with it.'[102] To the extent that the editors championing the work were from Melbourne and Brisbane, this was accurate. However, the collection included one piece, acknowledged with thanks as having been written at 'short notice, due to an unexpected change in content'.[103] A relatively short time later, a more detailed, measured and thoughtful engagement with the same chapter in *Five Uneasy Pieces* appeared on the Ethos Centre website.[104] In that paper, Kevin Giles gave considerable space to distinguishing

---

97. Lightfoot to Westcott 7/2/1861 (*ACER* 3.13.4/7); and see above.
98. Westcott to Lightfoot 19/2/1861 (*DDCL* Lightfoot Papers).
99. This was the language of Marshall Ballantine-Jones of Youthworks, the alternate publishing identification for the book: see *Eternity Newspaper* 14/6/2012. It was not the language of the editors.
100. M Bird and G Preece (editors), *Sexegesis: An Evangelical Response to Five Uneasy Pieces on Homosexuality* (Sydney South: Anglican Press Australia, 2012).
101. Stead, 'Herman Who?', cited above.
102. 'Sexegesis brings Australian authors together', sourced at <http://sydneyanglicans.net/news/sexegesis-brings-austraian-authors-together> last accessed August 2014.
103. New Cranmer Lobby, 'Acknowledgements', in Bird and Preece, *Sexegesis*, 4. The included chapter was P Barnett, 'God, Creation and Sexuality in First Corinthians: A Response to *Alan Cadwallader*', in *Sexegesis*, 105–16.
104. K Giles, 'Paul's Condemnation of Porneia: Sexual Immorality in 1 Corinthians 6:9-10', sourced at <http://www.ethos.org.au/Online-Articles/Blog/Paul-s-Condemnation-of-Porneia--Sexual-Immorality-in-1-Corin> last accessed August 2014. The Director of *Ethos: EA Centre for Christianity and Society* is Gordon Preece, one of the editors of Sexegesis. Giles' paper was subsequently published in *Zadok* 116 (2012): 13–18.

women's liberation from the issue of homosexuality. Giles has been a long-term and eloquent proponent of women's ordination[105] and he was concerned to isolate that issue from what he considers the cultural accommodation fostering the debate over homosexuality in relation to church institutions such as marriage and ordination. However, the acceptance of his paper into the *Sexegesis* collection was made contingent on his removal of the offending section about the emancipation of women. The pressure did not come from the editors but from 'Sydney [who] were paying for the book',[106] whether this meant under-writing or subvention. The paymaster had become the piper; but Giles refused to dance to the tune, in spite of some hard playing, and, as a result, his contribution was not included in the book.

Giles is not the only one to have felt the impact of economic-political manoeuvrings. Pastoral licenses have been revoked for those who have dared to acknowledge their homosexuality, vetoes have been threatened against preferment to particular elevated positions in the church simply on the basis of expressions of support for gays and lesbians, and, perhaps most concerning for an Anglican polity that avows 'dispersed authority',[107] one synod resolution recognising same-sex relationships has been twice vetoed by the diocesan.[108] The Anglican Synod prayer for *corporate* guidance for 'them/us' in 'wisdom and understanding'[109] seems therefore to be readily thwarted by individual decision, simply on the basis of an agreement

---

105. See his *Patterns of Ministry among the First Christians* (North Blackburn, Vic: CollinsDove, 1989); *Better Together: Equality in Christ* (Brunswick East, Vic: Acorn Press, 2010).
106. Email correspondence Giles to Cadwallader 4/8/2014, 18/8/2014.
107. B Kaye, *Conflict and the Practice of Christian Faith: The Anglican Experiment* (Cambridge: Lutterworth, 2011), 125–37. A clear instance of the operation of this authority of the people, was demonstrated in the decision by Bp David McCall, a long-time opponent of women's ordination, to follow the lead of the clergy and laity of his synod in the Diocese of Willochra and move to ordain women in 1997.
108. See *The Australian* 29/10/2013. The formal motion was in three parts, recognising diversity in understandings, widespread church support for 'civil unions' and that legal recognition of same-sex relationships can co-exist with heterosexual marriage.
109. See the Synod prayer (for use at Diocesan and General Synod meetings), *A Prayer Book for Australia* (Alexandria, NSW: Broughton Books, 1995), 213.

or protocol previously made amongst bishops. The protocols are asserted to 'express the common mind of the bishops as determined by consensus at our National Meeting ... [and] it is expected that our bishops will abide by them as an expression of the bonds of affection and unity that we share in the gospel and our collegiality in episcopal ministry.'[110] As high-sounding as this might seem, it places the bishops above the mind of the church, rather than expressing that mind and ensures that individual bishops act as agents of a group separated from the diocese that elected them in response to the leading of the Spirit.[111] Accordingly pre-determined decisions over-ride what the synod of a diocese discerns as the leading of the Spirit. Maintaining 'the unity of the Spirit in the bond of peace' can appear to belong to an elite group rather than the wider body of Christ seeking to live out its discipleship in its local community. To tune episcopal ears to the voice of the Spirit coming from outside that group (such as Archbishop Peter Carnley did in relation to the ordination of women in an Australian diocese, or Bishop John McIntyre has done in relation to the appointment of a gay member of clergy) unleashes cries of acting against the Church, by which is meant acting against the 'consensus ... of the bonds of affection and unity' amongst bishops. Hearing what the Spirit is saying to the church can therefore be a confounding discernment.[112]

One might argue that the model of distinction from the Gentiles (Mk 10:41–5) calls the church into a practice diametrically opposed to 'a world where oneness is often forced by dominance,'[113] but fine-sounding words need to find expression in action to avoid the charge

---

110. The 'Protocols from the Australian Bishops' are to be found at <http://www.anglican.org.au/governance/Pages/bishops_protocols.aspx> (last accessed September, 2014). The particular protocol related to homosexuality was Protocol 15 which was replaced by a more general Protocol 19 in April 2014, largely in response to the difficulties arising from Bp John McIntyre's concern to place issues of justice and the mind of the wider body of Christ above the terms of the previous episcopal protocol. Nevertheless, the model of discerning the Spirit is fraught.
111. Note the chapters by Phillip Tolliday, Peter Sherlock and Stephen Pickard in this collection.
112. So GM Griffin, 'Christian Attitudes to Sexuality: An Historical Romp', in *Ministry, Society and Theology* 7/2 (1993): 6.
113. J Driver, *A Polity of Persuasion: Gift and Grief of Anglicanism* (Eugene, OR: Cascade, 2014), 145–46.

of self-serving mystification. Outside of Anglican polity, the impact of such decisions ranges from bemusement to oppression. Westcott's concern of more than a hundred and fifty years ago does not seem to be allayed: 'The only result of such wild clamour must be to make people believe that the voice of authority alone, not reason' rules.[114] Clearly, such 'authority' for Westcott was authoritarian.[115]

The rhetoric in any espousal of irenic debate is difficult to match against such actions and shows that biblical interpretation is more than simply about the part of the ocean fished and the tackle used. It is about the industry with vested interests, commercial clout and regulatory reach that undergirds its involvement in fishing. As Pierre Bourdieu noted, 'Behind epistemological choices there are social forces. We all know that violence hides behind the most noble and pure *statements*.'[116]

Conclusion

When the York Convocation met in 1892, Westcott had recently joined the ranks of the episcopate. It was recognised that the fever of debates of previous decades about the way the Bible could be interpreted or translated had given way to a greater acceptance. What had once appeared contentious, now seemed almost innocuous, though other issues (such as the government's investment in the opium trade) stepped in to keep the adrenalin flowing. Even though differences of opinion remained over the Bible, they were no longer turned into reactionary or revolutionary positions, where each anathematised the other.[117] Rather, the church was again seeing itself as the richer for its diversity, even in the way the Bible was read and understood.

In the hundred and more years since Westcott and his Cambridge confreres bequeathed their work to the church, many of the debates have followed similar lines indicating that many of the questions have not been concluded. The particular issue of homosexuality in the church has re-fueled issues about the Bible and its interpretation.

---

114. Westcott to JF Wickenden 25/2/1861 (in Westcott, *Life and Letters*, 1.215).
115. See P Avis, *Authority, Leadership and Conflict in the Church* (London: Mowbray, 1992), 39, 85.
116. Bourdieu, 'Thinking about Limits', 48.
117. See Carpenter, *Church and People*, 508.

But the debates about history and hermeneutics, fired by a concern that some leading be given to the church for the future, cannot be depersonalised. Individuals and communities are involved, either delivering or receiving the impact of ideas and decisions based upon them.

I write this shortly after the untimely death of Bishop John McIntyre of Gippsland. Although John's legacy covers many fields, his lone public defence of ordained and lay gays and lesbians in the church offered hope that fine words of justice, equality and freedom—the impulse of the good news of Jesus—actually could be grounded in social and ecclesial reality. As he wrote, 'I pray the time is not too far off when we can at last celebrate appropriately the ministry of gay and lesbian people in the church, in and through whom God has been ministering to us for so long.'[118]

---

118. Personal communication 21/3/2012.

Chapter Two
Religious Diversities and Sexual Diversities: a Conflict of Freedoms

Gary D Bouma

The Marriage Equality movement has brought to the surface underlying divisions within the Anglican Church as well as other religious groups. Marriage Equality is one of the fronts along which the increased recognition and acceptance of diversities, including the normalcy of multiple genders and sexualities, is progressing. There has been a concomitant increase in the numbers and percentages of people in most Western nations—including those who identify as Christian—who accept homosexuality and support the introduction of same-sex marriage, also known as Marriage Equality.[1]

The challenge

The press for Marriage Equality challenges religious communities and leaders in two ways, as in this movement many couples are seeking recognition of both their love and their faith. This combination of two urgent requests stands in stark contrast with the stereotypes about the 'gay lifestyle'—used by those opposed to accepting homosexuals in society and in church life—to support the rejection and vilification of people who find themselves to be same-sex attracted, alternatively gendered or practicing other than heteronormativity. On the one hand, same-sex couples seek to have their loving commitment to a life together honoured by a church that often sees them as incapable of love let alone commitment. On the other, many same-sex couples present as currently being persons of faith, people who have kept

---

1. Pew Forum, 'Gay Marriage and Homosexuality in America' at <http://www.pewforum.org/Topics/Issues/Gay-Marriage-and-Homosexuality> Accessed 11 July 2013. Pew Forum, *'a Survey of LGBT Americans'* at <http://pewsocialtrends.org/2013/06/13/a-survey-of-LGBT-Americans> Accessed 11 July 2013.

their faith in the face of secularisation, rejection, demonisation and being declared an abomination by their religious communities. This combination of requests—same-sex couples who are clearly persons of faith and seeking through marriage to honour and seek support for their commitment to each other—has produced a chink in the armour of homophobia, a crack in the pillar of puritanism, and dividing of the ways among many Christians including Evangelicals and Catholics.

While this chapter is largely an academic analysis of church responses to social and cultural change I will use case studies involving the stories of real people to enflesh what could otherwise be an abstract treatment of issues that daily shape and either enable or hurt the living of their lives.

Case study one

There are two men in a parish I serve who have been living together for over fifty years. They are fully accepted in this parish and have held leadership positions. Both their love and their faith are fully accepted. They are open about who they are and the parish is open about considering them normal members and valued parishioners. The regional bishop would have a fit, but at least they are not clergy. This is of course the Anglican way. Anglicans often first accept change among the laity and then later extend the benefits of change to clergy. The best example of this approach to managing change being the way most Anglican Dioceses came to accept the remarriage of divorced persons.

Increasing numbers of nations and many States of the United States have been passing legislation permitting same-sex couples the same rights as heterosexual couples, including the right to marriage. In some instances this is a result of court interpretations of a country's Bill of Rights or similar rights-affirming legislation. Yet, at the same time, often having been stirred to do so by non-resident evangelicals, some nations, particularly in Africa and Southeast Asia, are legislating to make homosexuality illegal and in some cases punishable by death. Indeed the providers of gay conversion programs in Australia, upon realising that their programs have failed here and made illegal elsewhere, have moved to set up shop in Malaysia, Uganda and other places where homosexuality is illegal, as a part of their campaign to enshrine heteronormativity as the only Christian way to be in relationship.² These views include a very masculinist gender stereotype as the model for Christian men based on male 'headship' in the family and church if not all spheres of life.³ Women of course are secondary and to be protected, and in order to be protected they must be controlled, violently if necessary.

The Anglican Church is a microcosm of this phenomenon of competing conceptions of intimate relations and gender roles.⁴ The tensions within the church reflect the debates and changes in the larger society, with some groups supporting and promoting the move to increased acceptance of diversity as part of an expansion of grace and fulfilment of God's redeeming work in the world, and others decrying change as satanic and contrary to the orders of creation and God's will.⁵ The church as ever is both reflective of and embroiled in the socio-cultural processes of the day. As the culture changes from rejection to acceptance of multiple forms of gender and sexuality, church groups that were once 'cultural' have become counter-cultural without themselves changing.

For example, in response to the legislation introducing marriage equality to the United Kingdom, the Archbishop of Canterbury, Justin Welby, announced that his church would not seek to stop this and that the duty of the church was to respond in love to all people.⁶ As an Evangelical, Welby had come a long way from condemning homosexuality to arrive at this position. His journey was partly assisted by conversations with young people who pointed out that the church's traditional stance on sexual issues was an embarrassment to them and stood in the way of spreading the good news. Welby, a former oil executive, got the message listening to young people. Opposition

---

2. 'Heteronormativity' is the term used to indicate the use of both 'soft power' and legislative or conventional reinforcement of sexual relationships as only normal and natural when between a man and a woman, frequently extended to the confines of (heterosexual) marriage.
3. Muriel Porter, *Sydney Anglicans and the Threat to World Anglicanism* (London: Ashgate, 2011), 113ff; Timothy Jones, *Sexual Politics in the Church of England, 1857–1957* (Oxford: Oxford University Press, 2013).
4. Stephen Bates, *A Church at War: Anglicans and Homosexuality* (London: Tauris, 2004).
5. Porter, *Sydney Anglicans and the Threat to World Anglicanism*.
6. John Bingham, 'Archbishop Urges Christians to "Repent" Over "Wicked" Attitude to Homosexuality' at <http://www.theage.com.au/world/christians-should-repent-over-treatment-of-gays-archbishop-of-canterbury-20130829-2ss28.html> Accessed 5 September 2014.

to equal rights for same-sex attracted people (and presumably other sexual minorities—GLBTIQ)[7] was bad for marketing and sales— read: it impedes evangelism. This is reminiscent of St Paul arguing with those in the Jerusalem church over the necessity of circumcision for converts to Christianity, as reported in Acts 15. St Peter, having been opened to the work of the Spirit among the gentiles, agreed with Paul that, while it was required by the Law, circumcision was a serious impediment for converts to the new way and failed to respect the fact that these new gentile converts were showing all the marks of faith seen among Jewish Christians. St James led the way and the church decided to make the change.

Even as refusing to re-marry divorced persons became unmarketable to an earlier generation, so today, refusing to recognise the love and the faith of same-sex couples is unmarketable to the under 40s.[8] Younger people see Marriage Equality as a social justice issue not a moral one. They also have a high rate of acceptance of LGBTIQ people, seeing sexual orientation as diverse, like most other aspects of their lives.[9] A recent Nielsen survey found that 72% of Australians and over 50% of Australian Christians supported Marriage Equality.[10]

As humans we seem to have a propensity to take hard and narrow interpretations of sins to which we are not tempted—for heterosexuals there is little temptation to homosexual relations—and more nuanced ones towards sins to which we are more likely not only to be tempted but to commit, like sex before marriage, remarriage after divorce, or lying, or heterosexual irregularities. One senior Baptist pastor, Rowland Croucher pointed out that he was tired of the totally unforgiving approach taken toward clergy who were discovered to be

---

7. GLBTIQ is the common anagram for 'Gay, Lesbian, Bisexual, Transsexual, Intersexual and Queer' sexual identifications.
8. Pew, 'Graphics Slideshow: Changing Attitudes on Gay Marriage', Pew, 'Gay Marriage and Homosexuality in America', Pew '*a Survey of LGBT Americans*'.
9. Natasha Bita, 'Marriage Equality Wins Support of Two Out Of Three', at <http://www.theaustralian.com.au/50th-birthday-news/marriage-equality-wins-support-of-two-out-of-three/story-fnmx97ei-1226990227810> Accessed 5 Sept 2014. Pew, 'Gay Marriage and Homosexuality in America'.
10. Bita, 'Marriage Equality Wins Support of Two Out Of Three'; Lisa Cox. 'Poll Shows Growing Support For Same-Sex Marriage', at <http://www.smh.com.au/federal-politics/political-news/poll-shows-growing-support-for-samesex-marriage-20140714-3bxaj.html> Accessed 5 September 2014.

gay when clergy who had had heterosexual affairs were re-admitted to ministry after a period of repentance.[11]

The combination of human and Christian compassion and understanding in the face of a request for recognition of love and faith and the clear evidence that negativity in this area was a hindrance to winning souls—especially souls likely to be able to support the church generously—is having an effect. Some might prefer that this acceptance had been arrived at theologically first. However, like the early church, theology is discovered to be a post-experience reflection on our relationship with a God of love and compassion. Those wanting theological clarification can be assured that the biblical and theological work has long been done.[12] This work just has not gone mainstream in the churches yet. But it is also true that young people, like most of us, did not get to this position theologically but experientially. Rather like the Peter and Cornelius scene in Acts which ends with Peter, after his experience of visions and an encounter with Cornelius, proclaiming the theology: 'God has shown me that I should not call anyone common [the word could be translated 'profane'] or unclean [or 'polluted']' (Acts 10:28b). While Peter's vision was about there being no division between clean and unclean food as there had been in Jewish law, Peter made the *a fortiori* argument to people! Similarly, the realities of the people we and others know and the relationships they are in or observe, do not fall into 'good' or 'bad' along gay versus straight lines. Again our experience is one of diversity and many are not prepared to call 'bad' what is patently working for the people involved. Nor are they prepared to deny the reality of the faith of those who continue in faith in the face of such denial, persecution and denigration.

---

11. Rowland Croucher, 'Homosexuality: Rowland Croucher's Views', at < http://www.jmm.org.au/articles/599.htm> Accessed 5 September 2014.
12. Compare *inter alia*: Marilyn Alexander and James Preston, *We Were Baptized Too: Claiming God's Grace for Lesbians and Gays* (Louisville, KY: Westminster John Knox, 1996); Kathy Rudy, *Sex and the Church: Gender, Homosexuality and the Transformation of Christian Ethics* (Boston: Beacon Press, 1997); Nigel Wright (editor), *Five Uneasy Pieces: Essays on Scripture and Sexuality* (Adelaide: ATF Theology, 2011).

Case study two
Tom has two mothers. He is seven and goes to the local state school and his family attends a local inner city Baptist Church. When the kids in Tom's class pinned up pictures of their families, they were told to put up pictures of their mother and father. Tom was made to feel 'different', not 'right', and not 'normal'; so did those kids with only one parent. Tom had become accustomed to managing the phone when the caller asked to speak to his mothers, he would simply ask, 'Which one?' He decided to tough it out and posted pictures of his two mothers. Fortunately, the teacher realised the dilemmas caused by the way the request was made. The 'mistake' provided an opportunity to discuss what 'family' and 'parents' meant to them. In sharing their stories, the classmates discovered that there was a wide diversity of family forms. When diversity was seen as normal, all the kids could fit in. Tom said he wished his mothers could be married to make clear their relationship and reduce the amount of 'explaining' he would have to do.

As this chapter will show, this opening light of hope is shining in a very dark sky. In Australia there is much distance to be covered before equal rights are guaranteed and become a reality for sexual and gender minorities. The shifting sand of religious diversity in Australia is a critical factor shaping the way recognition and rights will flow in both the society and in churches. A second factor is the government practice of channelling substantial health, social services and education funding through faith based organisations. This peculiar conflation of church and state does not auger well for the rolling out of rights in a nation that is virtually the only liberal democracy that does not have a Bill of Rights.

The changing shape of religious diversity in Australia

Understanding religious responses to same-sex marriage requires an understanding of religious diversity in Australia. There have been major changes in Australia's religious profile in the life-times of those born before 1960. While there are virtually three times as many Australians in 2011 as in 1947, the actual numbers of Anglicans and British Protestants—Methodists, Congregationalists, Presbyterian and Uniting are now just at or well below 1947 levels. Catholics have grown substantially with there being more than three times as many now as in 1947. A major contributor to the change has been the rise of those declaring that they have 'no religion' from negligible to twenty-three per cent in the 2011 census. Those born during the 1960s and those born after 2000 live in very different religious worlds. In the world of young people, there are more Buddhists than Baptists, more Muslims than Lutherans and three times as many Hindus as Jews.

In other changes since 1947 not only is Australia no longer dominated by British Protestants, but Anglicans ceded first place to Catholics in 1986, and in 2016 the next census is most likely to show that Catholics have ceded first place to those declaring 'no religion'. The same census is most likely to show that there are more Buddhists and more Muslims than Presbyterians. There are already three times as many Hindus as Jews. Not only have a number of significant 'new to Australia' religious communities emerged—Buddhist, Muslim and Hindu in substantial numbers—but the internal diversity of religious groups once perceived as voting blocs has increased. Some of this new diversity is due to migration bringing different ethnic groups to existing communities. Irish Catholics have been joined by Italian, Dutch, Philippine, and other migrants. Anglicans have been joined by Karen, Sri Lankan and East African newcomers. Indeed the Methodist and Congregational Churches may be revived by migrants from the Pacific Islands who have preserved these forms of the Christian church. There are now young Presbyterians, but they are quite likely to be Korean.

What appears to be happening is a growing divide between those Australians who are religious and those who are not. Those declaring no religion are comparatively strong in their support for Marriage Equality and in their acceptance of a diversity of genders and sexualities as normal.[13] There are also those among the religious who support Marriage Equality, indeed they are a majority of those Australians declaring to be Christian.[14] However, those who take more conservative theological positions and attend church more frequently are less likely to be so accepting although there is a strong age difference with younger Christians more accepting.[15]

---

13. Bita, 'Marriage Marriage Equality Wins Support of Two Out Of Three'.
14. Bita, 'Marriage Equality Wins Support of Two Out Of Three'.
15. Philip Hughes and Lachlan Fraser, *Life, Ethics and Faith: Facts and Figures* (Melbourne: CRA, 2014); Bita, 'Marriage Equality Wins Support of Two Out Of Three'.

When social and moral issues, like extending the right to marry to same-sex couples, are raised as policy issues these internal- and between-group differences become more evident. The primary division is one of age. Issues about sexual morality, contraception and abortion are often raised as issues of concern by those over forty years old. Ironically, these are the ones least likely to be personally affected by the policies requested. To them, opposition to homosexuality is more of an identity issue, that is, people like us oppose this and if you do not also oppose homosexuality and marriage equality you cannot claim to be one of us.[16]

Religious freedom

Religious freedom is guaranteed by Section 18 of the United Nations Universal Declaration of Human and Rights to which Australia is a signatory and The International Covenant on Civil and Political Rights which Australia ratified in 1980. It requires a commitment to promote and safeguard the rights listed including the right to freedom of religion and belief. This includes the holding and changing of beliefs, the conducting of religious practices, and manifesting religion in life. Although committed to promoting and safeguarding these and other rights Australia has done little to pass legislation giving effect to these commitments.

Section 116 of the Australian Constitution provides some limited freedom of religion. The constitutional guarantee in Australia is limited to the Commonwealth government and does not apply to the States. However it is rarely appealed to in case law.[17] Its wording limits the actions of the Commonwealth government such that it cannot establish a state religion or require a 'religious test' for positions. Both a state religion and a religious test for positions, for example admission to Oxford and Cambridge Universities, had of course been in effect in the United Kingdom at the time of the First Fleet, although never officially in Australia. In this Australia led the Empire

---

16. Gary Bouma, 'Religious Resurgence, Conflict and The Transformation of Boundaries', in *Religion, Globalization and Culture*, edited by Peter Beyer and Lori Beaman (Leiden: Brill, 2007), 187–202.
17. Carolyn Evans, *Legal Aspects of the Protection of Religious Freedom in Australia* at <https://www.google.com.au/webhp?sourceid=chrome-instant&rlz=1C1CHMO_enAU550AU552&ion=1&espv=2&ie=UTF-8#q=religion+in+the+australian+courts> Accessed 5 September 2014.

in not imposing a state religion or using religion to screen people for positions.

While Australia is a signatory to the several United Nations Declarations regarding freedom of religion, it has not enacted the relevant legislation to guarantee this freedom in Australia. As a result, there is no law to appeal to should someone's freedom of religion be denied. This is in stark contrast to the United States which has a Bill of Rights and a rich history of jurisprudence in this area. Canada adopted a Bill of Rights some years ago and is developing such a jurisprudence. While agencies such as the Australian Human Rights Commission and the several state level Human Rights and Equal Opportunities Commissions do hear cases of religious discrimination, they are limited to the attempt to reconcile the parties involved and have no investigative or penalising capacity. Although there is some debate about this, many argue that Australians who assert that they have freedom of religion do so on the basis of a very thin legal constitutional and jurisprudential base.[18]

Freedom from discrimination

Commonwealth and state legislation protects citizens from discrimination on the basis of race and several states have enacted protection from discrimination on the basis of sexual orientation. These laws do provide a basis for the redress of grievances in courts. The State of Victoria, for example, has a Charter of Rights that includes protection for all persons, hence including persons of diverse sexualities and genders.[19] If marriage were a matter for the states to manage, this Charter would have provided a legal base to challenge the limitation of marriage to heterosexual couples. The State of Victoria also tried to introduce a law that would have required religious groups to show how their objection to a freedom was indeed part of core beliefs and practices and to demonstrate the need for an

---

18. Paul Babie and Neville Rochow (editors), *Freedom of Religion under Bills of Rights* (Adelaide: University of Adelaide Press, 2012); Geoffrey Robertson, *The Statute of Liberty: How Australians Can Take Back Their Rights* (North Sydney: Vintage, 2009).
19. Victorian Human Rights and Equal Opportunities Commission, 'Victoria's Charter of Human Rights and Responsibilities', at <http://www.humanrightscommission.vic.gov.au/index.php/the-charter>. Accessed 5 September 2014.

exemption on a case-by-case basis. This failed. These freedoms have come under sustained attack by religious leaders, Catholic, Anglican and Protestant, in recent years as they seek the right to continue to discriminate in order to defend and promote their 'ethos'. They argue that their opposition to homosexuality and by implication to marriage equality is a core belief and ethical principle and essential to maintaining their religious integrity. I find the claim that this is a 'core belief' hard to justify. It has no creed that I know of but has become one of the boundary markers defining orthodoxy for an evangelical.[20]

Case study three

A state-funded organisation that aims to provide a safe environment for young people who have recently discovered that they are same-sex attracted, contracted to use a camp facility owned by the Exclusive Brethren. The Exclusive Brethren had regularly rented the facilities to a wide variety of secular and religious groups. However, when they discovered the aims of this group, they cancelled the reservation citing that to rent to this group would violate core religious values and beliefs. The agency went to the Victorian Human Rights and Equal Opportunities Commission who facilitated a case before the Victorian Civil and Administrative Appeals Tribunal. The State of Victoria does have a Charter of Human Rights which includes both freedom of religion and freedom from discrimination on the basis of sexual orientation. VACT found in favour of the agency and imposed a small fine on the Exclusive Brethren. Key to the case was the argument that the camp was being run for more than the purposes of the Exclusive Brethren and thus did not fall under the exemptions given to religious groups to discriminate in cases where their key beliefs and values were at issue. The court decided not to try to assess the centrality of anti-homosexuality to the belief system of the Exclusive Brethren.

As it stands with respect to Commonwealth legislation, religious groups are granted a blanket exemption to all human rights legislation. Yes, all. This exemption is defended by some Australians who declare

---

20. Gary Bouma, *Being Faithful in Diversity: Religions and Social Policy in MultiFaith Societies* (Adelaide: Australasian Theological Forum, 2011) and 'Religious Resurgence, Conflict and The Transformation of Boundaries', *supra*.

that their freedom of religion is an absolute freedom or a right that takes precedence over all others.[21] This claim is based on paragraph one of Article 18 of the International Covenant of Civil and Political Rights which declares that 'Everyone shall have the right to freedom of thought, conscience and religion. This right shall include freedom to have or to adopt a religion or belief of his choice, and freedom, either individually or in community with others and in public or private, to manifest his religion or belief in worship, observance, practice and teaching'. This Article is used by some church leaders to claim that there is an hierarchy of freedoms and rights and to argue that religious groups must be given permission to discriminate against same-sex couples, single mothers, and others. The blanket exemption from human rights legislation and this hierarchy of rights is extended from such issues as male-only clergy to defend the right of religious groups to discriminate in their delivery of social, health and educational services, even those paid for by the Australian Government. While this argument is accepted by Australian lawmakers, it flies in the face of Paragraph 3 of Article 18 of the ICCPR which states that, 'Freedom to manifest one's religion or beliefs may be subject only to such limitations as are prescribed by law and are necessary to protect public safety, order, health, or morals or the fundamental rights and freedoms of others.' Thus it is not a right taking precedence over all other rights but one which is held in tension with others. Many would find it hypocritical of religious groups which seem quite ready to call politicians and others to account for denying rights to, say, refugees.

None the less, this domain of 'religious' discrimination has become increasingly significant as Australian governments channel increasing amounts of tax-payers' money through faith-based organisations.

Case study four

Tom and Ron need housing and approached a Commonwealth-funded housing agency for accommodation to which they were entitled given their financial circumstances. The agency was a faith-based organisation which had won a contract from the Commonwealth for

---

21. Gary Bouma, Desmond Cahill, Hass Dellal, and Athalia Zwartz, *Freedom of Religion and Belief in 21st Century Australia* (Sydney: Australian Human Rights Commission, 2011).

the provision of this service. Tom and Ron's request was summarily dismissed with disgust by the person whose job it was to provide the service to Australians.

In a context of increasing religious diversity including a growing number of Australians who declare that they have no religion, the problems raised by the fact that both Commonwealth and State governments are providing increasing proportions of tax-payer-funded social, health and education services through faith-based organisations (FBOs). Forty percent of school education is provided by religious schools that receive the bulk of their funding from government sources. The major providers of social services are religious—for example, Anglicare, The Society of St Vincent de Paul, The Salvation Army, and Uniting Care. These groups compete with each other and a smaller group of non-religious providers to win government contracts to provide services. These contracts, unlike those in the United Kingdom, do not include clauses requiring services to be provided on a non-discriminatory basis. Religious leaders argue that they must be able to discriminate in order to maintain their motivational basis for these services and to ensure that the particular ethics of the religious group are not undermined by those who do not share them or by the provision of services that would violate such ethics. Australia stands out in giving religious groups *carte blanche* to discriminate.

Balancing freedoms and rights

The request for the extension of the benefits of marriage to same-sex couples raises the issue of how to balance freedoms and rights. Those in favour argue that an inclusive society that is respectful of diversities, including sexual and gender diversities as well as a diverse range of family styles, is a healthier one and they adduce evidence supporting this claim. Those opposed argue that their freedom to live in a 'moral and ethical' society would be eroded by the proposed changes.[22] Some argue that such family arrangements are necessarily injurious to children although the evidence increasingly demonstrates this not to be the case.[23] Some religious leaders argue that if marriage equality

---

22. Bouma, Cahill, Dellal, and Zwartz, *Freedom of Religion and Belief in 21st Century Australia*.
23. Ellen Perrin and Benjamin Siegel, 'Promoting The Well-Being of Children Whose Parents Are Gay or Lesbian', in *Pediatrics* 131/4 (2013): 1374–83; Simon

were legislated they would be forced to conduct such marriages. This is simply not true. First, Australia has a small army of 'Civil Celebrants' who would be able to perform them. After all, they perform more than 70% of marriages in Australia at this time.[24] Secondly, those churches who oppose the remarriage of divorced persons have not been forced to do so, even though such remarriages constitute about one-third of all marriages solemnised annually.[25]

The balancing of rights is not easy. Those who take their religious commitments seriously want to see them expressed in their own lives and often believe that it is their duty to so shape the larger society such that it conforms to their beliefs. Catholics not only refusing abortions in their hospitals, but seeking to make them illegal is a case in point. Evangelical Christians promoting anti-gay legislation in Uganda is another. We have little problem with those who shape their personal lives according to their religious or other code of ethics. But when the exercise of one person or group's rights impinge on the rights of others that is when issues emerge. These are often not easily resolved.

How are such differences to be resolved? Telling people to keep the religious private does not solve the problem. All religions have social ideals and ethics which followers seek to make real. To argue that 'the majority rules' threatens to run roughshod over the sensitivities of minority groups.[26] Courts provide one avenue. In the USA laws limiting marriage to heterosexual couples have been overturned by courts through appeals to the Bill of Rights and other legislation preventing discrimination on the basis of gender and sexuality. Not all of these approaches have succeeded. This approach has not been tried in Australia as we have no Bill of Rights and no legislation at the Commonwealth level preventing discrimination on the basis of sexuality.

    Crouch, 'The Australian Study of Child Health in Same-Sex Families (ACHESS) Interim report' at <http://mccaugheycentre.unimelb.edu.au/__data/assets/pdf_file/0008/786806/simon_report_.pdf> Accessed 9 October 2014.

24. Australian Bureau of Statistics, *3310.0-Marriages and Divorces, Australia, 2011*. (Canberra: Australian Bureau of Statistics, 2012).
25. Australian Bureau of Statistics, *3310.0-Marriages and Divorces, Australia, 2011*.
26. Gary Bouma, 'Diversity of religions and freedom of religion and belief', in *The Routledge International Handbook of Education, Religion and Values*, edited by James Arthur and Terence Lovat (London: Routledge, 2013), 55–61; and *Being Faithful in Diversity*.

Proposals to enable same-sex couples to enjoy the benefits of marriage challenge the moral beliefs of some and to others seem to be an appropriate next step in recognising and welcoming God-given diversity. The debates provide a window on church and society relations as well as different patterns of theological reasoning and ethical consideration. The trend in the resolution of conflicts like this has been to enact enabling legislation which permits those desiring to be married to be able to do so and to give space for those groups who oppose to do so among their members. It is not yet clear how this will play out in Australia.

Chapter Three
Marriage and the Sacred: Fragments Straight and Gay

Sarah Bachelard

I find myself conflicted about the question of same-sex marriage. On the one hand, taking for granted the existence of homosexual orientation as a God-given, biological fact,[1] I see no reason that committed same-sex relationships may not in principle be expressed in the form of marriage.[2] On the other hand, I am uneasy about aspects of the practice of marriage itself, particularly in a Christian context. It seems to me as though we have too often made an idol of marriage, and that it can bear all the hallmarks of the false sacred. And where that is so, then whether marriage is between a man and woman, or between persons of the same sex, it is hard to be excited about its practice or its defence. In this essay, I want to explore this unease of mine with a view to articulating an understanding of marriage for both straight and gay which is consistent with and expressive of

---

1. James Alison speaks of the growing recognition that 'there is a more or less regular minority of people of both sexes who ... simply are principally attracted to people of their own sex at an emotional and erotic level'. 'Is it ethical to be Catholic? Queer perspectives', in *Broken Hearts & New Creations: Intimations of a Great Reversal* (London: Darton, Longman & Todd, 2010), 1–16, at 12. The title of my essay alludes to the title of another of Alison's books, *Faith Beyond Resentment: Fragments Catholic and Gay* (New York: Crossroad, 2001).
2. This is a large claim which I will discuss in more detail. Objections to it range from the semantic claim that the word 'marriage' just means marriage between a man and a woman, to the more substantive claim that marriage is 'ordained by God' to be between a man and a woman, and that marriage must in principle admit of procreative potential even if in practice (as in the marriage of elderly or infertile people) procreation will not be an outcome of the marital union. On these kinds of accounts, despite the likeness of the commitment of same-sex couples to that of heterosexual couples, the very nature of same-sex union is incompatible with the possibility of what is called 'marriage'.

discipleship of Christ and the transforming journey towards holiness. I will begin by elaborating on the notion of the 'false sacred'.

Identifying the False Sacred

In an illuminating discussion of the Christian roots of secularism, James Alison has noticed that when the sacred is defined in opposition to the profane, then it is dependent for its meaning on what it excludes.[3] 'Sacred' boundaries are sustained by taboo, sacrifice, religious rules and distinctions between pure and impure, righteous and unrighteous, Jew and Gentile, and so on. By his indiscriminate hospitality towards those who were on the 'wrong' side of this boundary, the unclean and religiously unsatisfactory, Jesus challenged this kind of sacred-profane duality. His challenge proved threatening to the religious and political authorities and he was executed, on a charge of blasphemy. In the resurrection, God revealed that the religious condemnation of Jesus was mistaken. 'By raising Jesus Christ from the dead', Thorwald Lorenzen writes, 'God revealed, confirmed, verified, and enacted the mission of the life and death of Jesus. The resurrection is God's concrete and unconditional "Yes" to Jesus' life and death.'[4] The holiness of God turned out to be not what the religious establishment thought it was.

Critical here is the insight that God does not simply reject the content of the particular set of sacred-profane distinctions whose transgression resulted in the charge of sacrilege against Jesus. Much more radically, what is called in question is the divine sanction for the whole religious mechanism that sets up the categories of insider and outsider, sacred and profane, where the righteousness, identity and belonging of some is secured at the expense of others.

The subversion of this mechanism is signalled, not simply by God's vindication of Jesus and his way, but by the manner of his return to

---

3. In what follows, I am indebted to James Alison's work, particularly 'The Place of Shame and the Giving of the Spirit', in *Undergoing God: Dispatches from the Scene of a Break-in* (London: Darton, Longman & Todd, 2006), 199–219 and 'Sacrifice, law and the Catholic faith: is secularity really the enemy?', in *Broken Hearts & New Creations*, 73–91.
4. Thorwald Lorenzen, *Resurrection and Discipleship: Interpretive Models, Biblical Reflections, Theological Consequences* (Maryknoll, NY: Orbis Books, 1995), 242.

his disciples in the resurrection. For although the disciples came to understand the resurrection as God's judgement of the judgement Jesus suffered, it did not take the form of casting out or excising the transgressors. Rather, God's judgement offered forgiveness, healing and the invitation to renewed relationship (cf John 21; Acts 2:14-42). What becomes possible in its light is a vision of human belonging—to God and to one another—from which no-one need be excluded.[5] Henceforward, on the Christian understanding, holiness or sanctity is connected to our participation in and transformation by, not law-keeping, ritual or cultic observance, but this pattern of life characterised by mercy, forgiveness and reconciling love.

This means at least two things. First, as we see from the witness of the New Testament, increasingly the distinction between sacred and profane, maintained by notions of taboo, religious rules and ritual sacrifice, is subverted. This distinction is now seen to have much more to do with human identity formation and boundary maintenance than with the 'new' humanity being brought into 'one body', the body of Christ. We see the painful process of subverting the old distinction in various places as, for example, when Peter learns in his vision of unclean animals that 'What God has made clean, you must not call profane' (Acts 10:19). On this occasion, in a trance, Peter sees 'something like a large sheet' being lowered from above, and in it all kinds of animals. A voice tells him to 'kill and eat', and when Peter protests that he has never eaten anything profane or unclean, the voice tells him that he must not call profane what God has made clean. This episode is the immediate precursor to Peter's encounter with the Gentile Cornelius and his baptism by the Holy Spirit, leading to Peter's amazed confession that: 'I truly understand that God shows no partiality, but in every nation anyone who fears him and does what is right is acceptable to him' (Acts 10:34-35).

The slow undoing of the old sacred-profane distinction is also evident as the early Christian community grapples with questions

---

5. Rowan Williams writes, 'when God receives and approves the condemned Jesus and returns him to his judges through the preaching of the Church, he transcends the world of oppressor-oppressed relations to create a new humanity, capable of other kinds of relation—between human beings, and between humanity and the Father'. *Resurrection: Interpreting the Easter Gospel* (Cleveland, OH: The Pilgrim Press, 2[ed] ed 2002), 9.

of ritual purity in relation to circumcision and the eating of meat sacrificed to idols (eg Romans 14). This is the sense in which it is possible to understand secularism as having its roots in the Christian experience. Writes Alison,

> Phrases like, 'everything is permitted, but not everything is convenient', or 'to those who are pure, everything is pure', or 'the letter kills, but the spirit gives life', could be quoted by anybody, and sound the rankest of secularising remarks. And they are. They are all phrases by which St Paul sought to make the oddity of the un-religion which he was preaching available to people: the subversiveness of the pattern of desire, unleashed by the sacrificial death of Christ, proving God's goodness to us when faced with any 'sacred' religious observance.[6]

There is, in other words, no longer anything by definition that is profane or unclean, no food, no person, no nation or disease. There are instead ways of being, forms of life, that are consistent or not with God's merciful and all-embracing love for the world.

Second, then, true holiness, true sanctity is to be conformed to and expressive of this hospitable and unthreatened way of being. Its growth in us is perhaps most evident in the character of our relationships with those who are victims of the judgement, including the religious judgement, that casts out. This is why the criterion of God's final judgement in Matthew's gospel is in terms of relationship to those who are hungry and thirsty, alien and naked, sick and in prison (Matt 25:31–46). The true sacred, on this account, is intrinsically connected to catholicity, universality: 'the whole point of Christianity is to bring down the sort of wall of protective sacredness which makes universality impossible by having a necessary "other" over against whom we make ourselves "good"'.[7]

So, on this analysis, the hallmarks of the false sacred include the maintenance of taboos or laws that systematically or necessarily exclude, and that tend to require sacrifice and deal death of some kind. And the true sacred, the Spirit of God, works to subvert that within any culture which tends towards sacrifice and divinely 'legitimated'

---

6. Alison, 'Sacrifice, law and the Catholic faith', 81.
7. Alison, 'Sacrifice, law and the Catholic faith', 88.

violence at any level, inviting our participation in a larger, forgiving, more generous life.

Marriage and the false sacred

So how do aspects of our understanding and practice of marriage display signs of complicity with the false sacred?[8]

The first concerns the way that being married can function as a means of identity formation which implicitly excludes and devalues the 'unmarried', so operating as a criterion for full social belonging and even virtue. This is the experience of many gay people who have, by definition, been excluded from the possibility of marriage,[9] but it shows up among those who 'fail' to marry for other reasons as well. For women, until the fairly recent past, successfully marrying had direct consequences for economic security and social participation, and something of this aura of 'prize' or 'success' in achieving matrimonial status remains. Helen Fielding touched this nerve when

---

8. I hesitated over the words '*our* understanding of, practice and relationship to marriage' since that may seem to beg serious questions about the 'we' implied here. Contrary to the claim often made by defenders of 'traditional' marriage that marriage has 'always' been ordained by God as between one man and one woman, it is clear that understandings of, practices and relationships to marriage have a long and varied history, and so extrapolating universal truths from current experience is often fallacious. See, for example, Peter Brown, *The Body and Society: Men, Women, and Sexual Renunciation in Early Christianity* (New York: Columbia University Press, 1988), and Adrian Thatcher, 'Beginning Marriage: Two Traditions', in *Religion and Sexuality*, edited by Michael A Hayes, Wendy Porter and David Tombs; Studies in Theology and Sexuality, 2 (Sheffield: Sheffield Academic Press, 1998), 415–26. In this section, I am attempting to articulate what I believe is in the background of contemporary marriage debates in Australia, particularly in many Christian contexts, and so am relying on readers to recognise something of their own experience in my argument at this point.
9. Evidence to the Australian Commonwealth Parliamentary inquiry into the bills proposing 'marriage equality' claimed that the mental health of same-sex attracted people was adversely affected by their exclusion from marriage 'because it is recognised as an important institution' and that to 'be barred from it specifically on the basis of their relationship is harmful' and an experience of 'stigma'. House of Representatives Standing Committee on Social Policy and Legal Affairs, *Inquiry into the Marriage Equality Amendment Bill 2012 and the Marriage Amendment Bill 2012*, Official Committee Hansard, Public Hearing, Thursday 12 April, 2012, Sydney *Hansard*, 9.

Brigid Jones, the unmarried heroine of her novel, Brigid Jones' Diary, loudly protested her experience of being condescended to by the 'smug marrieds' of her acquaintance. But the protest is itself a sign of a (strongly internalised) experience of exclusion from the 'right' order of things. In the Anglican Church in my context, I experience the ascription of a special kind of 'virtue' to marriage and family in various though subtle ways: family photos prominently displayed in episcopal offices; new clergy appointments, diocesan employees or conference speakers introduced in terms of their being married and being parents as if that were significantly relevant to their professional competence or spiritual maturity;[10] the pressure on younger members of the church to marry early; and the stigma and sense of failure among the childless.

A second dimension of complicity with the false sacred concerns the entanglement of marriage with sacrifice, both in connection with its continuance and with the social and ecclesial punishment meted out to those whose marriages 'fail'.[11] On the one hand, 'the marriage' becomes an end in itself and, for the sake of 'the marriage', all kinds of sacrifice can be enjoined with scant regard for the quality or possibilities of the particular marital relationship. Few Christians would now maintain that a marriage must be preserved at any cost, with violence or abuse together with adultery constituting commonly agreed justifying reasons for ending a marriage. But what about other kinds of suffering, mutual destruction, lack or the experience of entrapment in the context of marriage?

Stanley Hauerwas argues strongly that considerations concerning personal fulfilment or happiness are rightly deemed more or less irrelevant in the Christian understanding of marriage. On his account, the proper end of Christian marriage is related to the building up

---

10. I have not heard any unmarried speaker being introduced as 'single' and 'childless', this being tacitly considered perhaps an incomplete state—a slightly shameful fact best passed over in silence.

11. This is evident, for example, in the heavier burden placed on pre-marriage preparation (for both the couple and officiating priest) in relation to those seeking re-marriage compared with those marrying for the first time, regardless of the relative maturity and self-awareness of particular couples. I have recent knowledge of a case where, in fact, the insistence on a requirement to undergo a formal rite of confession before being granted permission to re-marry in church, drove one couple to marry in a registry office instead.

of the Christian community, and 'romanticism', which considers marriage to be internally related to individuals' sense of satisfaction in a relationship, is to be resisted as a corruption of this larger, 'heroic' task.[12]

The church exists to witness to God's kingdom and here, he claims, both marriage and singleness 'are necessary symbolic institutions'.[13] Singleness signifies trust in 'God's power to affect lives for the growth of the church',[14] and the priority of belonging to the church rather than to the natural family. In marriage, by 'our faithfulness to one another . . . we experience and witness to the first fruits of the kingdom of God. Our commitment to exclusive relations witnesses to God's pledge to his people, Israel and the church, that through his exclusive commitment to them, all people will be brought into his Kingdom'.[15] 'For the Christian', according to Hauerwas, 'marriage cannot and must not be seen as a necessary means for self-fulfilment. Christians are not called to marriage for "fulfilment", but for the upbuilding of that community called church'.[16] This leads him to coin such aphorisms as: 'love does not create marriage; rather, marriage provides a good training ground to teach us what love involves', and 'You always marry the wrong person'.[17]

I see, at least to some extent, what he means. Of course, we want marriage to be about more than narcissistic self-gratification and the worst excesses of romanticism. The vowed life—whether it takes the

---

12. Stanley Hauerwas, 'Sex in Public: How Adventurous Christians Are Doing It (1978)', in *The Hauerwas Reader*, edited by John Berkman and Michael Cartwright (Durham, NC: Duke University Press, 2001), 481–504, at 500.
13. Hauerwas, 'Sex in Public', 499.
14. Hauerwas, 'Sex in Public', 499.
15. Hauerwas, 'Sex in Public', 499.
16. Stanley Hauerwas, 'The Radical Hope in the Annunciation: Why Both Single and Married Christians Welcome Children', in *The Hauerwas Reader*, 505–18, at 512.
17. Hauerwas, 'Sex in Public', 502fn. Hauerwas quotes approvingly from Rosemary Haughton who writes: 'the qualities that make people stick out a hard life together, not stopping too much to wonder if they are fulfilled, are the qualities people need if they are to develop the hero in marriage, which is what being married "in the Lord" is about' ('Sex in Public', 500). This injunction to 'heroism', however, seems more reflective of Stoic than Christian virtue, and causes me to wonder exactly what is so edifying or appealing about a community where self-sacrifice has been equated this closely with self-suppression.

form of marriage, celibate singleness, or ordination—constitutes a commitment that transcends the day-to-day feelings associated with the promises we make. In free consent to the discipline this requires, being schooled by fidelity to their commitments, people may witness to the fidelity of God and offer themselves to be transformed through the inevitable sufferings of their chosen way into selflessness and Christ-likeness. In this way, the church is edified and the counter-cultural kingdom of God made visible.

I am troubled, however, by the abstract generality of Hauerwas' argument, its over-realised eschatology and its assumptions about what it is in fact that builds up the church. Eschatologically speaking, marriage may indeed be a symbol of God's life-generating faithfulness to humankind, but it is not in itself God's faithfulness.[18] To make every actual marriage bear that weight of meaning risks crushing the human bearers of the symbol and, just as Jesus insisted that 'the sabbath was made for humankind, not humankind for the sabbath' (Mk 2:27), so I want to insist that marriage is a gift given for our flourishing, not a burden to be borne at any cost. There is a difference between a cheap romanticism, to which Hauerwas rightly objects, and costly and truthful engagement with the question of what actually is the state and the possibilities, not of 'marriage in general', but of any particular marriage and so, of what faithfulness (to God, oneself, and others) calls for in that context.

Yet because of his prior commitment to the 'sacred' character of marriage in and of itself, Hauerwas offers no possibility of discerning the particulars of when and how a marriage is truly sanctifying, and when it may instead be oppressive or infantilising. In the name of some generic notion of the edification of the Christian community, he ties up 'heavy burdens, hard to bear, and [lays] them on the shoulders of others' (Matt 23:4). What seems missing from Hauerwas's understanding of the church is the notion of our being not only a sacrament of the kingdom but also a community 'on the way', a people who are making the cruciform journey from falsity to truth, and from

---

18. Strikingly, the value of marriage is expressed as contingent in the gospels, both in Jesus' response to the Sadducees' question about marriage in the resurrection (Mk 12:18-27; Matt 22:23-33; Lk 20:27-40) , and in Jesus' undermining of any claim to the absolute nature of 'family values' in the context of discipleship (Lk 14:26; cf Matt 10:37).

alienation to wholeness. But if that is who we are, then what is more edifying for the church? That it consist of people who stick heroically to their first commitments without pausing to reflect on what fruit is being borne, or that it allow the space for authentic and responsible discernment of the movement of life, penitent recognition of wounds inflicted and suffered, and the gracious possibility of forgiveness and new life emerging from brokenness?[19]

A former religious sister told me that after years of struggling with her vows, she began to understand that she had undertaken them in the first place out of a need for security and the certainty of salvation.[20] In the deeply frightening process of asking whether this was the life God wanted for her after all, she faced letting go of everything on which she had relied. At that moment, she said, she finally understood St Francis divesting himself of everything to stand naked before the love of God. For her, the real poverty to which she realised she was being called was not the vowed poverty of religious life, but the deeper surrender and vulnerability of letting go her ecclesial strategy for self-protection.

It may have been, of course, that through her struggle she could have remained a religious, although on an entirely different footing. It may have been that her maturing could have happened within the framework of the vows she had made. In fact, however, that was not how she discerned her situation. May not the same kind of struggle

---

19. Hauerwas says that 'we as church rightfully will hold you to promises you made when you did not know and could not fully comprehend what you were promising . . . From the church's perspective the question is not whether you know what you are promising; rather the question is whether you are the kind of person who can be held to a promise you made when you did not know what you were promising. We believe, of course, that baptism creates the condition that makes possible the presumption that we might be just such people' ('The Radical Hope in the Annunciation', 517). I think it is true that the church will 'rightfully' hold you to such promises, in the sense that you cannot simply abandon them without responsible and responsive discernment, and acknowledgement or engagement with those to whom you have promised yourself. But I would have thought that baptism creates the condition precisely for being able to acknowledge the 'death' of pretensions to heroic self-righteousness, which might (in some circumstances) allow for the humble acknowledgement of failure or the possibility of being released from a promise sincerely made.
20. 'Needs' which are themselves symptoms of consciousness in thrall to the 'false sacred'. I tell this story in my *Resurrection and Moral Imagination* (London: Ashgate, 2014), 172.

be undergone in the life of discipleship in the context of a marriage? As certain 'sins' are recognised and the call to deeper integration and reconciliation is answered,[21] there may be the possibility of transforming the basis of one's first commitment. But will it necessarily be so? Sometimes a journey of deepening integration goes by way of a necessary disintegration.

On the other hand, if the injunction to self-sacrifice to 'save' the marriage is refused, then in a community enthralled by the false sacred, there remains the possibility of sacrificing the transgressor anyway. Those deemed guilty of ending the marriage are judged and shunned, no longer fit to belong to the community of the heroically hitched. A friend of mine who suffered this kind of rejection says that the church preaches the forgiveness of sin, but actually wants to be a community made up of people who never need forgiveness. In my ecclesial experience, if someone's divorce happened ten years ago or out of sight, we can cope. But if we are asked to bear with the painful, confronting, messy process of a marriage coming apart in our midst, then likely as not our church communities will leap to judgements of 'guilt' and 'innocence', and offer our brothers and sisters not patient solidarity and friendship, but condemnation and shame. And whether or not we happen to agree with another's discernment in any particular case, such willingness to sacrifice the one for the sake of the unruffled moral complacency of the many is an infallible sign of the false sacred.

I believe that marriage may indeed be a symbol of God's generous love poured out, a relationship in and through which we come to realise our fuller life and capacity for self-giving love, sometimes in joy and sometimes in sorrow and struggle. But its true sacred character and its gift to the wider community is realised, not by sacralising the institution of marriage and hedging it about with taboos and oppressive social rules, but only by deepening our practice of marriage as a way of sanctification.

---

21. By 'sins', I have in mind the deep defences that keep in place our self-possession and strategies for self-protection—fear and avoidance of pain, patterns of inauthentic self-denial or self-hatred, and so on.

Marriage and sanctification

We learn from Jesus' calling of his disciples that the process of transformation or sanctification involves embracing and embodying the risk of unconditional commitment or self-gift, together with a growing non-possessiveness or non-attachment. These are the necessary elements, I propose, of a practice of marriage which is actually capable of signifying and communicating God's reconciling love for the world.

The call to unconditional commitment and self-gift is about no safety net, no foothold or backdoor, leaving a way out for the fearful and controlling ego which constantly seeks to have life on its own terms. Jesus says simply: 'Follow me', and he gives short shrift to those who seek to hedge their bets or hang onto some piece of their life not yielded to the way.[22] The way of transformation is necessarily a way of vulnerability, openness and trust. This is because, as Jesus said, we must 'lose' our lives if we want to be healed (Lk 17:33; Mk 8:35); we must die to the self-sufficient, self-protecting, self-righteous self.

Marriage, like other forms of the vowed life, may be understood as a practice that particularises and incarnates that movement of self-gift and love for something beyond the self, risking the vulnerability of unconditional commitment in the face of the unknown.[23] That is the significance, I take it, in the Christian marriage service, of the unconditional nature of the vows—'for better for worse, for richer for poorer, in sickness and in health'. We yield ourselves to a life, a call that transcends us, in faith, hope and love.

Yet, as Jesus also taught, this unconditional commitment to any particular human relationship finds its proper place, character and freedom only as we receive our identity from God. It must therefore

---

22. Consider, for example, the story of the rich young ruler who went away sad because he was unable to let go his many possessions and follow Jesus (Mk 10:21), the injunction to 'Follow me, and let the dead bury their own dead' (Matt 8:22), and the 'hard saying' that 'No one who puts a hand to the plough and looks back is fit for the kingdom of God' (Lk 9:62).
23. Of course, marriage in many contexts has no such 'spiritual' meaning or potential but may be understood as no more than a contractual relationship for the begetting of heirs and securing of dynastic property. I note that such a 'contractual' relationship would fall within the definition of 'marriage between a man and a woman', but would not by itself constitute (I take it) the 'sacred' institution that many defenders of traditional marriage are concerned to uphold.

be characterised, for both lover and beloved, by non-possessiveness or non-attachment, and a sense of its being non-ultimate. Jesus said: 'If anyone comes to me and does not hate father and mother, wife and children, brothers and sisters—yes, even their own life—such a person cannot be my disciple' (Lk 14:26). Discipleship, in other words, is about letting go attachment to the old sources of one's identity and receiving one's life, one's self, as gift from God. As Rowan Williams has said,

> Only as this begins to happen will I be delivered from treating the gifts of God as yet another set of things I may acquire to make me happy, or to dominate other people. And as this process unfolds, I become more free . . . to 'love human beings in a human way', to love them not for what they may promise me, to love them not as if they were there to provide me with lasting safety and comfort, but as fragile fellow-creatures held in the love of God. I discover . . . how to see other persons and things for what they are in relation to God, not to me. And it is here that true justice as well as true love has its roots.[24]

Without this kind of 'freedom' and letting the other be, then our human love tends to be corrupted by possessiveness and fear. Rather than partaking of the gift quality of God's love, it becomes enmeshed with guilt, shame, obligation and self-deception. If our commitment to another is truly to be unconditional, then it must be characterised by the willingness to let the other go.

The love that is God's own Trinitarian life is a communion of persons in relation, and each person of the Trinity is fully themselves and liberated to be so through the self-giving, non-possessive love of the other. It is this dynamic of authentic and life-generating communion between persons which may give marriage its sacramental character and its sanctifying potential.[25] It is to the extent that our practice of

---

24. *The Archbishop of Canterbury's Address to the Thirteenth Ordinary General Assembly of the Synod of Bishops on The New Evangelization for the Transmission of the Christian Faith*, 10 October 2012, Rome.
    <http://rowanwilliams.archbishopofcanterbury.org/articles.php/2645/archbishops-address-to-the-synod-of-bishops-in-rome#sthash.ky9vuE1H.dpuf>, para 5.
25. I do not believe that marriage is the only kind of human relationship which may have such sacramental and sanctifying potential. In the gospels other

marriage leads into this kind of communion, that it may rightly be called 'sacred' and, like the love of God, a source of life for others.

Same-sex marriage

If a certain content is given by definition to the word 'marriage', then some relationships will fall outside its range. If 'marriage' just means the union of a man and a woman, then the possibility of same-sex marriage will be ruled out by stipulation. This might preserve what is called 'traditional' marriage, but it seems a cheap victory that fails to touch the heart of the marriage debate. Those who advocate for same-sex marriage seek acknowledgement of the depth, seriousness and life-giving potential of committed homosexual relationships as on a par with and as deserving of public recognition as heterosexual unions. Those on the other side of the debate seem to suggest that expanding the concept of marriage to include same-sex unions will undermine the very nature of heterosexual marriage.

The logic of this argument can be difficult to follow, but it seems to be connected to the sense that since heterosexual marriage is sacred because it has been 'ordained by God', allowing same-sex unions to count as marriage will compromise the intrinsically sacred, God-given character of any marriage. Responses to a survey conducted as part of the parliamentary inquiry into amendments to the marriage laws in Australia, for example, included the claims that,

> Having been married to my wife for 40 years, I find it repulsive and insulting that the people supporting this notion are trying to push this legislation through. If same sex couples wish to live together that is none of my business and I would not discriminate against them in any way. However, I feel that the people trying to legalise same sex marriage are trying to gate crash our sacred institution of marriage between a man and a woman.
>
> I do not agree that a same sex union is an equivalent relationship to a marriage between a man and a woman.

---

analogies for unconditional divine love include the parent-child relationship, and friendship (cf Jn 15:15). Notably, orthopraxis does not require us to hold that every parent-child relationship or every friendship actually communicates, or is apt for communicating, this reality.

> I have been married for nearly thirty years and raised five children to adulthood with my wife. I think maybe without intending this bill demeans the specialness of the relationship which has so defined my life by making it one of a number of 'valid' expressions of human relationship. Find other ways to deal with same sex and de facto relationships but don't make them equivalent to marriage with the stroke of a pen.[26]

In this paper, I have sought to explore what the notion of the sanctity of marriage amounts to. I have argued that, in the Christian context, claims concerning sacred or profane which function simply as taboos cannot be accepted unquestioningly. As they were for the New Testament communities, such claims must be tested in relation to the revelation of God's holiness in the life, death and resurrection of Jesus. As James Alison has pointed out, as this revelation unfolds, increasingly there is an 'undoing' of established taboos such that there

> will no longer be any good reasons for sacred rules concerning food, for particular sorts of food which may not be eaten, or for special cultic killing rites for meat, for religiously-required forms of dress, for beliefs of impurity or impropriety concerning women's menstrual cycles. It is not that these things will suddenly be abolished, but that in every case the same realities will gradually come to be looked at differently: is such and such a food good for you, or for us?; is such and such a form of dress appropriate?; might not we agree on such and such a communal fast for those strong enough to do so?[27]

It seems to me that we are at a point in the life of our community and our religious tradition, where something of the false sacred character of our practice of heterosexual marriage has begun to be visible. And

---

26. The survey was conducted as part of the *Inquiry into the Marriage Equality Amendment Bill 2012 and the Marriage Amendment Bill 2012*. It was not a statistically significant survey, and overall the number of respondents who supported the amendment bills (64% and 60.5% respectively) was greater than the number opposed (36% and 39.5% respectively). A selection of comments, from which I have drawn these two, was published on the inquiry's website <http://www.aph.gov.au/parliamentary_business/committees/house_of_representatives_committees?url=spla/bill%20marriage/survey.htm> accessed 22 September 2014).
27. Alison, 'Sacrifice, law and the Catholic faith', 80–81.

this means that we are being invited to let go of the old religious taboos that have scaffolded and enmeshed it, often hiddenly, with mechanisms of exclusion and quasi-violent sacrifice. And I sense that, contrary to much of the rhetoric surrounding these questions, this may signal not the end of Christian marriage, but the fuller liberation of its authentically sanctifying potential. For now that we have glimpsed the distinction between the false sacred conception of marriage, hedged about by fear and arbitrary rule, and the possibility of being opened through profound mutual self-giving to participation in the life of God, then our understanding of what are the truly Christian questions to be asked concerning heterosexual and same-sex marriage, as well as concerning divorce and co-habitation, will be different.[28]

Recall again what Alison said of taboos concerning food: 'It is not that these things will suddenly be abolished, but that in every case the same realities will gradually come to be looked at differently: is such and such a food good for you, or for us?' In the same way, the question has gradually come to be asked about same-sex unions: is the possibility of same-sex marriage, good for you or for us? Of course, part of what needs to be worked out is what 'good for us' actually means. Increasingly, however, it is difficult to disregard the ordinary, incarnate criteria for discerning the human good (vitality, compassion for others, joyful participation in the common life of the community) in favour of arbitrary claims about what is allegedly 'ordained by God'. For if, in the unions of our brothers and sisters who happen to be gay, we recognise the same possibility of non-possessive, self-giving, unconditional love which characterises the best of heterosexual unions, which transforms lover and beloved, and gives life to all, then these unions are equally sacramental signs of

---

28. I note here that there are those who choose not to marry precisely because they see in the institutional practice of heterosexual marriage something that is incompatible with their love (a false sacred character) and so potentially corrupting of their life together. I am thinking, among others, of a well-known Australian couple, David and Emma Pocock, who have formalised their relationship with a commitment ceremony but have refused to marry legally because 'we didn't want to participate in a ceremony that doesn't allow others to take part due to their sexual orientation'. *When David Met Emma*, <www.news.com.au/lifestyle/relationships/love-story/story-fnet09p2-1226645450501> (accessed 11 December 2014).

God's love for the world. As such, I believe, they exemplify what any of us, straight or gay, desire to practice as marriage.

Chapter Four
Friends and Lovers, Friends and Others

Duncan Reid

In the context of the current debates about the inclusion of homosexual people in the church, and specifically the extension of the church's sacraments of marriage and ordination to persons living in homosexual relationships, a discussion of friendship may seem a distraction. But the current situation does invite, within the church community, an exploration of relationships more generally, including friendship. A discussion of friendship may have something to contribute to the broader current debate, not least because, as Mark Vernon observes, 'the anxiety provoked by the idea of gay marriage… [may have] little to do with sexual acts and much more to do with forms of friendship that challenge tight notions of family'.[1] Vernon's book includes a chapter outlining the similarities between love, including sexual love, and friendship. A recent Australian publication advocating 'full inclusion of gay, lesbian, bisexual, transgender and intersex people in the life of the Anglican Church' included a sermon that makes the same point.[2] Two of the issues a consideration of friendship needs to address in this regard would seem to be: first, whether friendship is a closed, private and intimate arrangement, or a more open, public relationship; and second, the place of similarity and difference (and potentially of equality and inequality) within friendship.

---

1. Mark Vernon, *The Philosophy of Friendship* (Basingstoke: Palgrave Macmillan, 2005), 9. Vernon explores this idea on pages 128–141.
2. Christopher Tyack, 'Friendship is the Basic Form of Love', in *Changing Attitude Australia Newsletter*, Feb 2014 at <http://www.changingattitude.org.au/wp/wp-content/uploads/2014/02/CAA-Newsletter-Feb-2014.pdf>. Accessed 19 February 2014.

References to friends and friendship are prominent in the Bible. Abraham is twice called 'God's friend' (2 Chr 20:7; Isa 41:8), or three times if you count the New Testament gloss on these texts (Jas 2:23). God is said to have spoken to Moses 'face to face, as one speaks to a friend' (Exod 33:11). The human friendship of David and Jonathon is paradigmatic. David is loved by both Jonathon and Jonathon's sister, Michal (1 Sam 18:1-3, 20), and while Michal becomes David's wife, it is to Jonathon that his 'soul is bound'. Michal's relationship with David seems to have become embittered, and David chooses other wives, but his friendship with Jonathon seems never to have been supplanted: 'I am distressed for you, my brother Jonathan; greatly beloved were you to me; your love to me was wonderful, passing the love of women' (2 Sam 1:26). The implications of David's famous lament for Jonathon I leave open.[3]

Jesus tells his disciples that he has called them (that is, considered them, treated them as) friends (Jn 15:13-15), and the early Christian community seems to have taken this with utmost seriousness (Acts 4:32-5). It is an open question as to how these references to friendship relate to the frequent references to love, as when the risen Christ three times asks Peter (a disciple, and so now also a friend): 'Do you love me?' (Jn 21:15-17). The same question could be asked concerning the anonymous disciple (friend) of Jesus 'whom he loved' (Jn 13:23, 21:20).

There are, however, other undertones in the Bible we should not overlook. Psalm 88:18 laments the experience that God has caused 'friends and neighbours' (or should that be 'friends and lovers', as the *Authorised Version* and the *Book of Common Prayer* both have it?) to be far from the speaker. Psalm 41:9 accuses a 'bosom friend' of betrayal. In Luke 23:12, a rather unsavoury political 'friendship' is initiated between two erstwhile enemies out of a conversation on how to handle a popular local agitator whose behaviour has become a threat to public order.

In the history of the church, though not always a prominent theme, friendship has come to the fore at significant times. A notable example in the West was the twelfth century, when friendships were both cultivated and reflected upon among the literate ruling classes.

---

3. See James Harding, 'Opposite Sex Marriage a Biblical Ideal?', in *Pieces of Ease and Grace*, edited by AH Cadwallader (Adelaide: ATF Theology, 2013), 35-52.

This movement called forth a theological response from Richard of St Victor, a scholastic writer who, as Denis Edwards puts it, 'built his theology of the Trinity on the basis of reflection on the experience of human friendship'.[4] An essential element of Richard's thought was to assert that friendship is perfected in being open: it is neither simply an *amor privatus* (private love, of oneself) nor an *amor mutuus* (mutual love, of two), but must extend to being shared with a third; it cannot be simply *dilectio* (choice or delight) between two persons, but *condilectio* (shared choice or delight) shared equally by a third. It is this that makes friendship an open relationship. Although Richard's concern was to explicate a trinitarian theology, his thought process reflects back on the nature of friendship, especially in relation to our first issue, that of the openness of friendship. Friendship in Christ thus embodies a critique of the inevitably closed nature of one-to-one friendships—this being the insight that underlies the discouragement in the past of 'special friendships' within certain religious communities. But particularity is also a characteristic of friendship, as we shall see.

The role of friendship more generally in mediaeval and early modern Christian thought and practice has been explored by Mark Vernon. Vernon produces a great deal of evidence to indicate that it is not till the late seventeenth century that the binary structure of marriage replaced the more extended concept of household, with its multiple opportunities for friendships of various sorts. With this early modern transition, the binary structure of marriage thus becomes the basis of society.[5] With marriage privileged in this way, friendship undoubtedly suffers a privatisation and a diminution in civic importance.

One practical exploration of friendship—dating, significantly, from the time of this shift in public perception—is to be found in the

---

4. Denis Edwards, *Jesus the Wisdom of God: An Ecological Theology* (Maryknoll: Orbis, 1995), 93–101. Edwards follows Brian Patrick McGuire (*Friendship and Community: The Monastic Experience, 350–1250* [Kalamazoo: Cistercian Publications, 1988]) in seeing the twelfth century as uniquely 'an age of friendship' and Richard's thinking as a product of his age. A classic treatment of the twelfth century changes in the understanding of human relationships is to be found in Denis de Rougemont, *Passion and Society* (London: Faber and Faber, 1962).
5. Vernon, *Philosophy of Friendship*, 94–119, especially 113.

work of George Fox (1624–1691), founder of the Society of Friends or Quakers.[6] Theodore Zeldin, in a discussion of the possibilities of friendships between women and men, sees the community founded by Fox as 'probably the most successful experiment in mixed friendship', giving rise to a plethora of movements for social reform, though failing in its one attempt to provide the ideological basis for a whole society. Colonial Pennsylvania, settled by Quakers, soon demonstrated 'that friendship and the giving of orders were incompatible, and that friendship was not a system for large groups of people'. This suggests that even open friendship has its limits, and finds itself transformed into something else when faced with the exigencies of political power and economic need. But for Fox it was clear that friendships are possible in spite of dissimilarities of gender. What he was defending, in fact, was an older, pre-modern practice of friendship as a civic relationship, against the closing in of relationships represented by the emerging nuclear family.

Friends and lovers: closed, private and intimate, or open and public?

Ziyad Marar describes intimacy as 'the feeling of being uniquely understood',[7] and notes that, alongside couple relationships, friendship is a 'place of retreat that provides the possibility of an intimate relationship'.[8] Having said that, he also notes something distinctive about intimacy. It can exist in momentary encounters, without past or future; it has an 'elusive, paradoxical and transitory' nature.[9] Moments of intimacy can and frequently do occur between strangers. You pass a stranger on the street, and respond fleetingly to their momentary smile. That is intimacy: the smile is an unexpected gift—to you alone, and you respond. Such moments are not the only forms of intimacy, but are frequent enough not to overlook. It is worth noting that for Marar, while intimacy may entail sexual

---

6. Theodore Zeldin, *An Intimate History of Humanity* (London: Vintage, 1998), 329–31.
7. Ziyad Marar, *Intimacy: Understanding the Subtle Power of Human Connection* (Durham: Acumen, 2012), 12.
8. Marar, *Intimacy*, 7.
9. Marar, *Intimacy*, 8–9.

encounter, it does not have to and in any case this is not its main feature. The opposite of intimacy is the alienation of being in the company—perhaps for some time—of a person who does not share your 'values, idiosyncratic preferences, sensibilities, hopes, anxieties or sense of humour'.[10] The absence of any one of these will banish even the possibility of intimacy.

Marar sees intimacy as consisting of four characteristics: it is reciprocal, it is confidential or even conspiratorial, it is emotional, and it is kind.[11] Reciprocity means that intimacy is mutual, unlike sexual attraction, which may be unrequited or rejected. It is also by nature exclusive: mutuality is between two.[12] Confidentiality means it involves self-disclosure to another, but not more widely.[13] There is a degree of vulnerability in such disclosure. Emotions, which as Marar points out, 'are not easily deployed on the basis of reason',[14] depend upon a level of trustworthiness. Where emotion can be self-centred, in intimacy it is counter-balanced by kindness, 'an irresistible prejudice in your favour'.[15] This is not to be mistaken for 'niceness', for kindness does not override truth-telling. But the momentary person-to-person equality of intimacy is also the opposite of generalised equality, as a political principle or an ethical virtue, because intimacy—even the intimacy of fleeting moments—treats people unequally: it favours one over all others. 'Morality lumps while intimacy splits', as Marar puts it, or more abstractly, there is a distinction to be drawn between the 'nomothetic' (lumping) formulations of generalised laws or principles to cover all possible cases, and the 'idiographic' (splitting) focus on a single case in its own unique particularity.[16] Intimacy sees the particular.

Marar's treatment of intimacy allows us to posit some initial similarities and differences between intimacy and friendship.

---

10. Marar, *Intimacy*, 26.
11. Marar, *Intimacy*, 44.
12. Marar, *Intimacy*, 49–53.
13. Marar, *Intimacy*, 65.
14. Marar, *Intimacy*, 90.
15. Marar, *Intimacy*, 103–4.
16. This suggests, incidentally, why Christianity, with its scandal of incarnational particularity, can exert a hold on the imagination unmatched by more generalised 'philosophies of life': a relationship holds out the offer of intimacy, in which 'I will know fully, even as I have been fully known' (1 Cor 13:12).

Friendship also splits; it discriminates and favours. It may assert an equality between friends, but also an inequality in favouring the friend to all others. Friendship also involves emotion, which operates beyond the normal bounds of reason. It can be a matter of puzzlement why some apparently strong friendships dry up and wither, while others last for decades and grow stronger in spite of distance and even long periods in which no contact is made.[17] But this in itself is also an indicator of friendship's difference from intimacy. Friendship is most definitely not momentary; of its essence is its duration, its durability. Nor does it have to be purely reciprocal, one-to-one, as we saw with Richard of St Victor, and indeed as we know from common experience of friendship groups.

Friendship for Richard is mediated by Christ, in what Dietrich Bonhoeffer was much later to call a 'spiritual love' by which Christ is mediator not only between ourselves and God, but also between ourselves and others: such love knows 'no immediate access to other persons…Spiritual love recognises the true image of the other person which he has received from Jesus Christ'.[18] This, for Bonhoeffer, stands in contrast to human love, which 'constructs its own image of the other person, of what he is and what he should become.' Such self-reflection is of necessity closed in on itself; friendship that sees the other in Christ 'is from the spirit's choice and free desire, needing no oath or legal bond'.[19] It is fundamentally open to the future.

When Marar sees friendship as 'a place of retreat that provides the possibility of an intimate relationship', he is referring to a modern, privatised notion of friendship. Jürgen Moltmann, on the basis of a theological rather than a purely phenomenological approach, offers a robust critique of such an understanding. Moltmann describes friendship as 'an unpretentious relationship… [which] unites affection with respect'.[20] He then goes on to demonstrate that Jesus is pre-

---

17. The curious friendship in Patrick White's novel between Laura Trevelyan and Voss highlights this; see Patrick White, *Voss: A Novel* (London: Eyre & Spottiswoode, 1957). See also A C Grayling, *Friendship* (New Haven and London: Yale, 2013), 199.
18. Dietrich Bonhoeffer, *Life Together* (London: SCM, 1954), 22–3.
19. Dietrich Bonhoeffer, 'The Friend' in *Letters and Papers from Prison*, ed. E Bethge (London: SCM Press, 3rd edition 1967), 388.
20. Jürgen Moltmann *The Church in the Power of the Spirit: A Contribution to Messianic Ecclesiology* (London: SCM, 1977), 115. See also Jürgen Moltmann,

eminently a friend,[21] though not, significantly, after either the ancient Hellenistic or the modern romantic understandings of friendship, that is, neither as a relationship between free citizens with the time and leisure to cultivate it, nor as something private and concerned purely with the inner life. The friendship demonstrated by Jesus is open and public, breaking the bounds and asserting freedom from any closed circle of friendship, so that 'Christian friendship cannot be lived in the inner circle of one's equals but only in open affection and public respect for other people.'[22] This friendship does not require social equality as a prerequisite—on the contrary it demonstrates the possibility of building friendships in the face of dissimilarities and inequalities, and ultimately with God. But it does require freedom, the freedom of the children of God to challenge social norms. In our contemporary social context, Moltmann argues that 'Christians must remove friendship from the private sector, so that it may again acquire the character of public protection and public respect…Open friendship prepares the ground for a friendly world.'[23] Moltmann demonstrates, among other things, the difference between the many phenomenological approaches and a properly theological approach to our theme: phenomenology merely describes the world; theology claims the authority to change it.

A recent Australian Anglican reflection by Stephen Pickard extends this possibility, suggesting that the church's common tendency to professionalise relationships in ministry, though often done for very good reasons, also 'masks our failure to appreciate how to be a friend within relationships of unequal power.'[24] Pickard in other words recognises the everyday reality of inequalities in power, and

---

Neuer Lebenstil: Schritte zur Gemeinde (München: Chr Kaiser, 1977), 51–70.
21. This is not the sentimental notion embodied in the hymn 'What a friend we have in Jesus', which Robert Dessaix, perhaps with some superficial justification, finds such an easy target to lampoon (Robert Dessaix, *(and so forth)* [Sydney: Macmillan, 1998], 381).
22. Moltmann, *Church in the Power of the Spirit*, 120. The radicalism of this approach highlights the limitations of the purely secular consideration of the theme that we see, for example, in AC Grayling's otherwise very comprehensive history-of-ideas approach. See AC Grayling, *Friendship*, especially 69–75, 192.
23. Moltmann, *Church in the Power of the Spirit*, 121.
24. Stephen Pickard, *Theological Foundations for Collaborative Ministry* (Farnham: Ashgate, 2009), 234.

asserts the possibility and indeed the indispensability of attempting friendship even within such relationships of power difference.

Friendship does not require equality, but creates it. That is Moltmann's, and following him Pickard's, far-reaching reinterpretation of friendship from a theological perspective. Christian discipleship disrupts classical ideas of friendship based on social equality and opens it to the neighbour who may not be an equal in the eyes of society, and precisely at this point of inequality, creates—but without compromising the unlikeness of the neighbour—a new equality. But does this perspective in fact abolish friendship simply because it seems to rule out particular relationships of ongoing intimacy? Kierkegaard, basing his analysis on, and reacting against, Augustine's reflections on friendship, chose to reject friendship as such and substituted love of neighbour as the only possible authentic stance for a Christian.[25] This would be a consequence if it were not for the tradition highlighted by Mark Vernon of civic friendships within Christianity.[26] Another defence of the authenticity of friendship emerges, I believe, from the theological deliberations of John Zizioulas.

Friends and others: similar and equal or different and potentially unequal?

Is friendship compatible with difference, or does it require similarity? Does it require likeness, or is it a relationship that can occur (or even must occur) between participants who are unlike in some significant way? Moltmann, as we have seen, proposes an open view of friendship, of 'people who are like ourselves and the people who are different,'[27] and Stephen Pickard makes a similar point.

Lesley Chamberlain, in her study of Russian philosophy, playfully draws attention to a commonplace of Russian usage that has implications for our theme: 'By happy chance there is a cognate bond between the Russian word for "friend" and for "the other", *drug* and *drugoi*. The two belong together as the fundaments of any viable modern philosophy. They wait for a Russian philosopher to become

---

25. Vernon, *Philosophy of Friendship*, 78–80.
26. Vernon, *Philosophy of Friendship*, especially 108–119.
27. Moltmann, *Church in the Power of the Spirit*, 121.

their author."[28] I can claim to be neither Russian nor a philosopher, but Chamberlain's invitation to engage with these fascinatingly interrelated concepts is too good to pass. In following this train of thought I intend in no way to pre-empt what other, more qualified explorers of ideas may uncover. As it happens, there is a contemporary theologian who may help unravel this connectedness.

John Zizioulas has, more than anyone else, developed a theological ontology of otherness. Where Richard of St Victor had spoken of the Trinity on the analogy of (the otherness of) friends, Zizioulas reverses this procedure to move from an understanding of the Trinity on the basis of otherness to a consideration of human relationality, which can include friendship. Otherness is built into the nature of reality, and by extension, should characterise our human relationships.

Otherness, for Zizioulas, is a primary ontological category, constitutive—according to trinitarian thinking—even of divine being.[29] In God we see the eternal causation of personal otherness—the othernesses of the second and third persons of the Trinity. It is a causation of otherness that explicitly excludes subordination and asserts equality. The implications of a trinitarian affirmation about God is further underlined, for Zizioulas, by the Chalcedonian definition of Christ, in whom the two natures stand in a relationship of otherness to one another, 'neither confused, nor changed, nor divided, nor separated'. Zizioulas applies these trinitarian and christological insights to human relationships when he argues that the freedom of the human person implies a drive to otherness; to relate to others—whether to animals, or to other human beings, or indeed to God—not by seeking undifferentiated union with them but precisely as others.[30] God's words in Genesis 2:16 to *ha adam* (the human being) is indicative of this: God addresses *ha adam* (or Adam) in the vocative, as *Thou*.[31] This address, and the freedom of otherness it implies, is a gift.[32]

---

28. Lesley Chamberlain, *Motherland: A Philosophical History of Russia* (New York: Overlook/Rookery, 2004), 280–1.
29. John Zizioulas, *Communion and Otherness: Further Studies in Personhood and the Church* (London/New York: T&T Clark, 2006), 34–6.
30. Zizioulas, *Communion and Otherness*, 39.
31. Zizioulas, *Communion and Otherness*, 41.
32. Zizioulas, *Communion and Otherness*, 43.

God's address to Adam is a divine affirmation of otherness, and it implies a critique of three opposed possibilities. First, it opposes any totalitarian ontology of sameness, which is a form of death. Death, because it homogenises, is the enemy of otherness.[33]

Second, and perhaps less obviously, the ontology of otherness stands opposed to any ontology that prioritises self over other. The clearest example of such an ontology is the classic modern starting point of Descartes, *Cogito, ergo sum* (I think, therefore I am). This is also, for Zizioulas, the most succinct expression of the human tragedy of alienation, one from an other.[34] It is a tragedy because it locks a human being into a reality that is fundamentally at odds with his or her own deepest reality, and it signifies the death of otherness by collapsing all otherness back into the purportedly primary Cartesian subject, the *ego sum* (I am). It also prioritises this subject as a thinking subject (*cogito* [I think]), disembodied and separated from the wholeness of human experience. This classic modern understanding is, for Zizioulas, essentially a Manichaean otherness—a duality (similar to other modern dualities) of self and other that implicitly designates the self as primary, whole, normative and good; and the other as secondary, defective, abnormal and evil. In contrast, trinitarian otherness holds together both self and other, affirming both, and affirming them equally as constitutive of divine being and creative of created being. The relational nature of divine being is, for Christian theology at least, affirmed in the words spoken to Moses: I am who I am…the God of Abraham, the God of Isaac, and the God of Jacob' (Exod 3:14–15).

This passage is the subject of a dialogue between Karl Rahner and the Jewish scholar Pinchas Lapide, where Lapide asks rhetorically 'why the apparently superfluous triple of the divine name when there is only one God?' His answer is to refer to the rabbinic consensus that Abraham, Isaac and Jacob represent three quite different experiences of the one and the same God. We may push this differentiated experience of God further, I believe, and see here a dialectic of inter-relationality that goes beyond any simple, adversarial duality.[35] The

---

33. Zizioulas, *Communion and Otherness*, 41.
34. Zizioulas, *Communion and Otherness*, 43.
35. P Lapide and K Rahner, *Heil von den Juden? Ein Gespräch* (Mainz: Matthias-Grünewald-Verlag, 1983), 39.

promise to created being finds expression in 1 John 3:2: 'we are God's children now; what we will be has not yet been revealed'. The initially unequal relationship of parent and child will give way to the new relationship of friend and friend.

Third, Zizioulas is careful to define his understanding of otherness not only in opposition to the classic modern notion of otherness as secondary to self, but also in contrast to the post-modern notion of 'difference'. Although he applauds Buber's prioritising of the other, not simply as an extension of the self, Zizioulas finds he must go beyond the ensuing dialectic of 'answer and response' between other and self, as this leaves us simply with the relationship, the in-between, as the defining concept. Zizioulas is also dissatisfied with Levinas' notion of 'absolute alterity', as this, he argues, leaves us with an ontology of distance and separation. In its place Zizioulas looks for an ontology of communion. Distance and separation lead to death; communion leads to life.[36] Zizioulas notes that Levinas is aware of this problem, and—unsuccessfully in Zizioulas's opinion—attempts to escape it through a comparison of the stories of Odysseus, who journeys but with the aim of a final return to his known starting point, with that of Abraham, who journeys into an unknown land and an unknown future.[37] One story posits a return to the source and so closes the otherness of distance; the other story opens, but to an absolute otherness that cannot ultimately admit of communion. Neither story adequately establishes a communion that allows the other to remain itself, but within relationship.

Zizioulas then moves to consider the patristic thinker Maximos the Confessor, whose theology highlights the phenomenon of desire (*eros*),[38] with the movement of desire seeking and finding its rest in

---

36. Zizioulas, *Communion and Otherness*, 47–8. It is debatable whether Zizioulas is justified in this critique, especially in relation to Buber and Levinas, but this is a question I have to leave open here.
37. Zizioulas, *Communion and Otherness*, 49. We might also note that these stories incorporate very different attitudes to the figure of the child. The child, when brought into focus of each of these stories, is the 'other' to the main protagonist and also the symbol of hope for the open future. Odysseus' journey, which returns to its own starting point, has started with the sacrifice of Iphigenia; Abraham's open-ended journey into the new land climaxes with the definitive prohibition of child-sacrifice.
38. Zizioulas, *Communion and Otherness*, 50.

the other, in what is other than itself. In Maximos, 'otherness disrupts every present [moment],'[39] so that otherness is not suppressed as it was in the classic thinking of modernity. But is Maximos falling into the age-old western temptation to offer some sort of closure, some sort of final unity—which for post-modern thinking typically raises so much suspicion? Zizioulas refuses to address this question head on, but instead puts a question to the common post-modern understanding of otherness. The aim of this rhetorical manoeuvre is to draw a distinction between what Zizioulas sees as a post-modern understanding of otherness as difference, and Maximos' notion of otherness as constituted by relationality, and in which relationality (rather than difference) is primary. Zizioulas's argument is that a notion of 'difference' as the primary category generalises, while Maximos's notion of otherness is particular and specific. We have already seen this distinction when Marar asserts that morality 'lumps' while intimacy 'splits'.

Zizioulas's question is two-fold: Is otherness (as difference) primary and ultimate for post-modernity, and is it relational? His answer to both is negative. To the first, Zizioulas argues that it is because post-modernity is—justifiably—suspicious of identity, especially in the sense of any 'politics of identity' in which a constructed self is set over against anything or anyone defined as 'other', that post-modernity posits otherness. But it posits this generalised 'otherness' at the expense of the particular other. And because it is—justifiably—suspicious of the modern tendency to totalising violence towards others, the post-modern critique of modernity cannot bring itself to entertain any possibility of relationality, or of communion as Zizioulas prefers to call it. But otherness as difference alone fails to break out of the established pattern of dualities, and to move us on into a post-modern multiplicity—except when it allows for the particular other, the 'ontology of the particular'.[40]

By contrast, according to Zizioulas, Maximos, representing one strand in the patristic tradition, argues that otherness, or rather a particular other, is the cause and destination of particular beings. These particular beings are not fixed identities; rather they grow towards one another. 'Being is in becoming', as Eberhard Jüngel has

---

39. Zizioulas, *Communion and Otherness*, 52.
40. Zizioulas, *Communion and Otherness*, 53.

put it in reference to God's trinitarian being;[41] for Zizioulas this holds true just as much for our human and therefore creaturely being. It is love—the primary Christian 'theological' virtue—that generates otherness, by allowing the other to be,[42] in a way that does not threaten the otherness of the (particular) other.

Zizioulas goes on to discuss the centrality of the body for his proposed ontology of otherness: it is the vehicle both of otherness and of communion.[43] Body here means a particular body, so that the other presents her-/himself as a particular, human, personal other, not as a generalised abstraction (such as humanity).[44] Christian ethical life takes cognisance of the particular other, and of the generalised other only as a consequence of this. The particular other can never be treated instrumentally as a means to achieve the betterment of some generalised collective other. Particular otherness excludes generalisation; it posits uniqueness.[45] This is the point of Zizioulas's differentiation of otherness from difference: difference does not necessarily entail uniqueness; the unique being of the personal other most certainly does.

When we begin our understanding of friendship on the basis of otherness, this is more than simply difference. Difference is self-referential; it means different from me, where we have not escaped the Cartesian distinction between *res cogitans* (the thinking entity) and *res extensa* (the extended, or thinned-out and weakened, entity). Difference, in this context, is extension of the thinking self. Otherness, as posited by Zizioulas, avoids, or seeks to avoid, unity and closure, both of which tend to suppress the other. Here, by contrast, it is the other that 'disrupts every present', especially our own present state. Zizioulas acknowledges the post-modern suspicion of the totalising reduction that can lie inherent in the notion of 'communion', for communion may do violence to the other by assimilating it. But if we start from the other (not from the self), the starting point is neither

---

41. E Jüngel, *God's being is in becoming: the trinitarian being of God in the theology of Karl Barth* (Grand Rapids: Eerdmans, 2001).
42. Norman Habel, 'Geophany: The Earth Story in Genesis 1', in *The Earth Story in Genesis: The Earth Bible, 2*, edited by N Habel and S Wurst (Sheffield: Sheffield Academic Press, 2000), 34–48.
43. Zizioulas, *Communion and Otherness*, 61.
44. Zizioulas, *Communion and Otherness*, 67–8.
45. Zizioulas, *Communion and Otherness*, 69.

'I think, therefore I am' (Descartes); nor yet 'I love, therefore I am';[46] but rather 'I am loved, therefore I am'. Then the other does not have to threaten my otherness, but rather generates it and endorses it.[47] Otherness does not have to involve an abstract equality but it does involve reciprocity of one another (*drug druga*, in Russian). If this understanding of otherness were to undergird our approach to friendship, perhaps the aspect of friendship highlighted might be the availability to be disrupted.

Conclusions

The Christian imperative is to love the neighbour, which—in its best known iteration—leads to the question: 'Who is my neighbour?' (Lk 10:29). In other words, its context is the question of mutuality, or rather of relationality. It is also significant that this passage moves the reader from an ethical question, a question of general principles for action, '*What* (must I do)?' to the personal question of the particular, immediate other: '*Who* (is my neighbour)?' This transition, which moves the reader from the realm of general, ethical questioning to the realm of immediate, particular, personal, relational concern is of course to be found elsewhere in the gospels.[48]

With the help of Zizioulas, we have followed Chamberlain's suggestion of starting from the notion of otherness in the hope that this might both throw light on the phenomenon of friendship, and so engage with the issues posed: Is friendship an open or a closed relationship? Is friendship compatible with difference, or does it require similarity?

To some degree both these issues represent the same general area of discomfort around friendship. Vernon suggests there are 'forms of friendship that challenge tight notions of family'. Zeldin asks 'why friendship between men and women has been so fragile'.[49]

---

46. Associated with the theology of Sophrony Sakharov. See Nicholas Sakharov, *I love therefore I am: The Theological Legacy of Archimandrite Sophrony* (New York: St Vladimir's Seminary Press, 2002).
47. Zizioulas, *Communion and Otherness*, 54–5, 89.
48. Matt 22:34–46 offers another example, where a question to Jesus about the greatest commandment (a 'what should I do?' question) elicits a response about a person: 'who is the messiah?'
49. Zeldin, *Intimate History*, 314.

Can friendship only exist between like and like, in other words, and preferably without the unspoken subtext of possible sexual attraction?

With regard to our first issue, whether friendship is open or closed, Marar has established that intimacy is a closed interaction between two people, however fleeting. Friendship is different from intimacy at least in this regard: it has duration. If we follow a theological approach (even the very different approaches taken by Richard of St Victor and Jürgen Moltmann) friendship can at its best be fundamentally open and public.

To the second issue, our consideration of otherness would suggest the problematic nature of settling for either similarity or difference. Friendship is not just compatible with difference, but demands an appreciation of the particular otherness of the other, the friend. The semantic range of 'other' reaches from very similar (one or an other of twins) to very different (the absolute, ontological otherness of God), so there are various sorts of otherness. Friendship requires otherness—it is not self-referring—but some forms of otherness tend to work against friendship, even though they do not render it impossible. Friendships across age groups may be problematic— different generations have always involved different life experiences, and now more than ever inhabit different cultures to some degree. Differences in age can of course be productive in mentoring, and such a relationship may in time entail a transition to friendship. Sexual attraction and intimacy (irrespective of the sexual preferences involved) may also be problematic for friendship. The problem of difference (primarily in gender or social status) for thinkers from Aristotle to Montaigne and beyond, however, was that they could not quite imagine an equal relationship between men and women, or servants and masters, or that such differences could be compatible with the equality they saw as essential to friendship. Increasingly, otherness—not simply of gender, but all manner of otherness— refuses to allow itself to be made an obstacle to reciprocity.[50]

---

50. See Andrew Solomon, *Far from the Tree: Parents, Children and the Search for Identity* (London: Chatto & Windus, 2013), 44. This is an extended testimony to the theory of 'intersectionality', 'that various kinds of oppression feed one another', and that difference must never be allowed to stand in the way of reciprocity.

The theological contributions made independently by Moltmann and Zizioulas, at least as I read them, urge us to a practice of friendship that is open and based in free response to our others. This leads into what is in fact an ontology of freely chosen communion. Here my particularity, my uniqueness, is given to me as a gift, the gift of my own otherness in its particularity. Here my identity—like the identity of every other person—is no longer something achieved on the basis of asserting my difference from others, but something I receive within a network of relationships. In receiving it as a gift, it also becomes my gift to my others, in an ongoing relational dialectic. Here we no longer speak in the abstract of friendship or even friendships, but concretely, of friends—each of whom is in various ways both similar and different from myself, and to each of whom I stand in a public relationship of loyalty and commitment. In the end, for a Christian, such friends point us to the one who is wholly, ontologically, other from ourselves, and who—surprisingly and paradoxically—speaks to us, calls us by name, and calls us friends.

Do these reflections on friends and friendships go any way toward dispelling 'the anxiety provoked by the idea of gay marriage', attributable according to Vernon, to particular anxiety-producing 'forms of friendship'? Well, maybe not entirely. But they do suggest that friendships can be expected to come in all manner of forms, including between people of notable similarities and notable differences, and that while they will certainly entail experiences of intimacy, which may or may not mean sexual intimacy, they can also expect to be publicly and openly acknowledged.

Chapter Five
Making Decisions

Peter Sherlock

Imagine you are an Anglican bishop—a straight bishop, married only once, maybe male, maybe female—in charge of an Australian diocese. Now imagine what you would do when the woman in your office tells you she is gay and that her partner is fully supportive of her 'yes' to the church's call to ordination. She is a first-class student in her twenties. She has an evangelist's heart and the ability to communicate the gospel to the unchurched. She's everything you'd imagine for the future of the church's mission to spread the gospel.

You have no problem with the ordination of homosexual people in theory. But you also know over half your diocese has a huge problem with that fact. You know that to ordain this person could expose the church to unwanted media attention, and open up a huge fissure in the diocese that might impede the church's mission more than this one child of God could ever hope to advance it.

> What do you do?
> Will you be that much-sought courageous bishop, who pursues principle over pragmatism even at the risk of dividing the church?
> Will you simply ask her not to have sex with her partner and leave it at that?
> Will you hope she goes away?
> Will you tell her what your leadership team wishes you'd say: we would love to ordain you but I am asking you to step away from this for the sake of the church's wider mission at this time?
> It is a hard call, and if you think it's an easy one, you're either a fool or idealist—both honourable Anglican positions.

The great unstated assumption in Anglican debates over the place of same-sex attracted people in the church is that we know what it is that needs to be decided. Furthermore, we assume we know who or what it is that needs to make the decision. Behind these assumptions lie a wide range of questions that engage different types of authority and different kinds of decision-makers, from the individual exercise of conscience to the formal process of conciliar bodies.

> Is the decision a collective, international affirmation by majority vote of bishops, clergy, and laity gathered in a yet-to-be-created World Synod on the proposition that "persons in a monogamous same-sex relationship may be ordained as deacons, priests, and bishops"?
> Is the decision a change to civil or ecclesiastical statutes in each province of the Anglican Communion to provide for the blessing of same-sex relationships?
> Is the decision a change of heart and mind by individual bishops and their clergy?
> Is the decision the affirmation by congregations of the same-sex couples already in their midst through including them on the morning-tea and flower-arranging rosters?
> Is the decision the moment a person accepts sexuality as a gift from God and begins the journey of working out how to live in a community of Christian discipleship that observes Jesus' teachings?

We must acknowledge that all of these decisions matter, from the daily encounter in an ordinary moment to a solemn deliberation of a council of the church that does not and probably will never exist.

We must also acknowledge that undoubtedly the hardest decision of all is what each Christian person faces, to articulate a sexual identity and to determine the nature of sexual relationships in the light of the gospel. It means agonising over the scriptures. It means confronting the weight of hundreds of years of tradition. It means feeling intensely lonely. It means searching for the Spirit's leading, wondering and doubting, 'is this who I am truly called to be?', over and again. It means continuous challenge: daily revisiting old decisions, living with uncertainty, temptations to be dishonest or to tell partial truths, having to construct one's own moral and ethical framework directly from the scriptures because the church has not developed one that makes any sense of the present context, deciding whether to risk sharing that framework with others.

Finally, it must be acknowledged that Anglican decisions about sexuality are also made as often as not to oppress, subjugate, harm, murder, exclude and convert people who are not heterosexual to enforced celibacy, self-harm, and alienation from the church.

The category of sexuality is one on which all Anglicans must now take a stance. There is no neutral position. The category cannot be unimagined or decisions avoided or the issue forgotten, at least not for a few more decades. So we should reflect, then, on the decisions that Anglicans make for themselves and for others about sexuality and Christianity.

When we Anglicans are honest, when it comes to this tender, furious matter of sexuality and sexual expression, our future does seem to be a lost cause for there can be no winners or losers. Yet a struggle for the soul of our church is before us, no less a question than who we are called to be as God's elect, and how we are to live in tension with our differences.

For Christians, sexuality is crucial to who we are: on the one hand, there is the creation narrative of Genesis which describes humanity as male and female, made in the image of God, while on the other, there is the assurance of the resurrection of the body. Flesh is fundamental to Christian history, from creation to eschaton, and the biblical witness presents our bodies as no more nor less a cause of pleasure, passion, sin and pain than our mind, soul or spirit. Moreover, our faith is relational, and as human beings we cannot escape from the place of sexuality, one, although certainly neither the only nor the necessary element, in the forging or fracturing of relationships.

It is no surprise then that the Anglican Communion has for the past twenty years teetered on the precipice of internal combustion over the place of same-sex attracted people in its life.

We need a framework for thinking about these many types of decision. First, some decisions are made primarily about one's own sexuality and sexual behaviour. Closely related are those decisions individuals make about the sexual and religious identities and behaviours of others. Second, some decisions are made consciously and overtly, such as a vote in a synod or vows in a relationship, while others are made inwardly, privately, such as recognition of a spiritual or sexual awakening. Yet others are made semi-consciously, in the unthinking choice of who to talk to after a church service or when to smile or frown during a sermon. Third, some decisions are formal, born of long preparation and forethought, and some are spontaneous, both in the moment of passion or of the prompting of the Holy Spirit.

These categories—personal and public, formal and spontaneous—overlap. I know from personal experience, for example, how the compulsion to speak into a formal debate in a synod can suddenly push unconscious desires and interior thoughts into the harsh light of ecclesiastical scrutiny.

So then, how do Anglicans make decisions about sexuality? This is a deceptively simple question. I want to try and address it here primarily by reference to the context of twenty-first century Australia.

The Anglican debate about sexuality has been conducted in earnest for twenty years, beginning with successful conservative initiatives to shape the outcomes of the 1998 Lambeth Conference and inhibit the development of greater acceptance of same-sex attracted people by the Anglican Communion. The last fifteen years have been dominated by two issues: the ordinations to the episcopate of persons in same-sex relationships, and the blessing of same-sex relationships largely prompted by civil advances towards marriage equality.[1]

Anglicans have been theologising around sexuality and engaged in various forms of a listening process at a global level since at least the Lambeth Conference of 1978. Matters came to a head with the episcopal ordination of Gene Robinson, a priest in a same-sex relationship, as Bishop of New Hampshire in 2003. This ordination, or one like it, had been expected for years. While the ordination was in strict accordance with the meticulous and labyrinthine constitutional processes of the Episcopal Church, that assure United States Anglicans of a high degree of consensus, unsurprisingly it produced outrage in other parts of the world. The Primates warned that the fabric of the Anglican Communion would be torn at the deepest level. Typically, the Anglican response was to commission a report, known as the

---

1. For a chronicle of events to 2008, see Simon Sarmiento, 'From Lambeth 1998 to Lambeth 2008', in *Rebuilding Communion: Who Pays the Price?*, edited by P Francis (Hawarden: Monad Press, 2008), 1–25. For an analysis of the early twenty-first century debate, see Stephen Bates, *A Church at War: Anglicans and Homosexuality* (London: Hodder & Stoughton, rev ed 2005).

'Windsor Report', which based itself on the assumption that 'proper' behaviour could somehow be restored to a worldwide church: no more gay bishops, no more cross-border interventions, recognition of each other as Anglicans.[2]

Ten years on from Windsor, little has changed. Bishop Gene has now retired, but the consecration of a second bishop in a same-sex relationship, Mary Glasspool, has only served to confirm the Episcopal Church's stance. Meanwhile the Fellowship of Confessing Anglicans is continuing to evolve out of the Global Anglican Futures Conferences as an alternative Anglican Communion for the majority of Anglicans who do not accept that homosexual behaviour is compatible with Christianity. The experience of ordinary Anglicans has further polarised, with some nations including the United Kingdom providing for same-sex marriages, and others such as Uganda imposing harsher and harsher penalties on homosexual behaviour or same-sex associations.

In Australia there has been very little conversation in the national church about sexuality since 2007. In 2004 the General Synod of the Anglican Church of Australia, the national governing body, passed four resolutions on the matter of homosexuality by majority vote. These were fairly predictable statements, that affirmed the national church was aligned with the 1998 Lambeth Conference 'resolution I.10', noted that 'at this time' the Australian church could not endorse the ordination of homosexual persons or the blessing of same-sex relationships, and called for further discernment including a listening process.[3] That listening process came to fruition at the 2007 meeting of the General Synod, where four pre-recorded stories by current or former Anglicans were heard by members.[4]

While the General Synod would appear to be the logical place to begin an inquiry into what Anglicans think about sexuality, its

---

2. Lambeth Commission on Communion, *The Windsor Report* (London: The Anglican Communion Office, 2004) at <www.anglicancommunion.org/windsor2004/index.cfm>. Accessed 29 November 2014.
3. Resolutions 61/04, 62/04, 63/04, 64/04 may be found in Anglican Church of Australia, *Proceedings of the Thirteenth General Synod 2004* (Sydney: General Synod Office, 2004), 56.
4. Muriel Porter, 'Paying the Price: An Australian Perspective', in *Rebuilding Communion: Who Pays the Price?*, edited by P Francis (Hawarden: Monad Press, 2008), 42–48.

website politely reports that, 'The Anglican Church of Australia does not have a formal, official policy on the issue of homosexuality.'[5]

Indeed, there is no policy document. Sexuality is not mentioned in the Constitution of the Anglican Church of Australia. Nevertheless, clergy in same-sex relationships that included sexual activity could be held accountable by their bishop or diocesan tribunal on account of legislation defining ecclesiastical offences and because of the fact that they cannot marry their partners. Thus the *Offences Canon 1962* of the General Synod refers to 'unchastity' as an offence, along with drunkenness, neglect of ministerial duty, failure to pay debts, and disgraceful conduct.[6] Following on from this is the professional standards document covering all church workers, *Faithfulness in Service*, which states that:

> 7.2 Sexuality is a gift from God and is integral to human nature. It is appropriate for clergy and church workers to value this gift, taking responsibility for their sexual conduct by maintaining chastity in singleness and faithfulness in marriage...
> 7.4 You are to be chaste and not engage in sex outside of marriage and not engage in disgraceful conduct of a sexual nature.[7]

Advocates for change might therefore consider several approaches to the General Synod to ensure full recognition of the place of same-sex attracted Christians in the life of the Anglican Church. The General Synod could be asked to adopt new resolutions that embraced the ordination of same-sex attracted persons and the blessing of their relationships. The *Offences Canon 1962* could be amended to refine the definition of 'unchastity', and *Faithfulness in Service* altered to reflect a wider range of relationships besides heterosexual marriage. Yet, depending on how a bishop or a diocese chooses to interpret these documents, none of this may be legally necessary.

---

5. <www.anglican.org.au/home/about/social-issues/Pages/homosexuality.aspx>. Accessed 6 December 2014.
6. Anglican Church of Australia, *The Constitution, Canons and Rules of the Anglican Church of Australia* (Sydney: General Synod Office, 2010), 47–48.
7. Anglican Church of Australia, *Faithfulness in Service: A National Code for Personal Behaviour and the Practice of Pastoral Ministry by Clergy and Church Workers* (Sydney: General Synod Office, rev ed 2011), 35.

Synods are strange places indeed for talking about sex and sexuality. I have yet to meet an Anglican who is truly comfortable in discussing these matters in the odd context of a meeting of synod without descending into pointless platitudes. Nevertheless a major turning point in the history of Australian Anglican attitudes towards same-sex attracted people occurred in precisely the unlikely moment of a bishop's address to a synod. This was the presidential address of the late Bishop John McIntyre to the Synod of the Diocese of Gippsland in May 2012.[8] In the address, Bishop John held himself accountable before the Synod for his action in licensing a priest with a same-sex partner to a parish of the diocese. This act had been done without fuss or fanfare, but came to prominence when a picture of the priest and his partner was published in the diocesan newspaper.[9]

McIntyre articulated three key decisions he had made: the stance he would take, the theological basis for this position, and how he had been led to this theological insight.

He told his synod simply that, 'I will appoint to office in our diocese those whom I believe God is calling to minister among us.' Sexuality was not in itself a basis for withholding such an appointment.

McIntyre's promotion of the full inclusion of same-sex attracted people in the church flowed from the principle 'by their fruit you will know them' as set out in Matthew 7:

> Only in light of reflection on God's Word did I finally come to understand. Despite what I or others may believe is their worthiness, the fruit of the works of many gay and lesbian people has brought God's blessing to me and to many other people, both in and beyond the church. *That* is the measure of their worthiness to minister in the name of Jesus Christ in the life of the church, and in the community in the name of the church. *That* indicates their place in the life of God's people.

---

8. Anglican Diocese of Gippsland, 'President's Address to the 36th Synod Third Session 18–20 May 2012' at <www.changingattitude.org.au/wp/wp-content/uploads/2012/05/Presidents-Address-36th-Synod-3rd-Session-May-2012.pdf>. Accessed 6 December 2014.
9. *The Gippsland Anglican* (December 2011), 8.

He construed his change of mind as a revelation of his blindness and error:

> You might well ask why it took me so long to acknowledge this simple truth. I think it was the correctness of religious law that blinded me to this truth, a truth that is known only in the experience of grace. In the first place, I needed to be entirely honest with *myself* and realise God works in and through *me* only by grace, and not because I act correctly according to some established religious code.

Significantly, he also reflected on the church's attitude—globally and locally—to decision-making itself:

> For too long we have asked same-sex attracted people to wait outside the church, or at most in its wings, while we decide the basis on which they can be a part of the church's life. The thought seems to have been that when we have decided (and we certainly don't seem to be in too much of a hurry to do this) we will invite gay and lesbian people into the church on our terms; that is, if they still want to be a part of us.

In making reference to the marriage equality debate, he spoke further about the manner in which Anglicans should participate in decision-making:

> The way of the Gospel, in the end, is the way of persuasion by a godly life, and by godly words and actions. A godly life, and godly words and actions are marked by grace, and the truth on any matter will emerge as we live by the same grace with which we are met by God in Jesus Christ.

In contrast to the Gippsland experience, where the bishop brought the matter of human sexuality before the Synod, in Perth it was synod members themselves who put the issue on the diocesan agenda in 2012 through a motion. This motion became widely publicised in 2012 and again in 2013 when Perth's Archbishop, Roger Herft, in an extremely rare decision, dissented from the motion.[10] Just as McIntyre

---

10. See, for example, the extended ABC report <www.abc.net.au/news/2013-10-29/anglican-reject/5052642>. Accessed 6 December 2014.

had held himself accountable for his actions before his synod, so too did Herft, in the form of letters to synod members explaining the reasons for his dissent.[11]

The motion in question read as follows:

> That this Synod:
> 1 recognises diversity within the Diocese of Perth, both in our sexual identities and in our theologies of human sexuality;
> 2 notes the support from many within the Anglican Church for committed same-sex couples being able to register their relationships as 'civil unions' in Australia; and
> 3 acknowledges that legal recognition of committed same-sex relationships may co-exist with legal recognition of marriage between a man and a woman.

Herft pointed to three broad areas of disagreement with the wording of the motion: theology, global Anglicanism, and the Australian Church's constitution. He argued that 'the first part of the motion gives our sexual identity and theology on sexuality a place of prominence that is not theologically sound', claiming that instead the 'primary lens through which we recognise each other' is as 'children of the one heavenly Father and inheritors of the kingdom of God'.

He indicated that while it might be true that many Perth Anglicans supported the recognition of same-sex couples, the same was self-evidently not true for Anglicans in other parts of the world, including numerous nations that had criminal penalties for homosexual behaviour with the support of Anglican leaders.

Finally, Herft argued that the third part of the motion was in direct conflict with the definition of marriage as presented in the 1662 *Book of Common Prayer*. The BCP marriage service spells out in no uncertain terms that marriage is the union of a man and a woman, ordained by God before the Fall and sanctioned by Christ at Cana. The Fundamental Declarations of the Constitution of the Anglican Church of Australia mandate the *Book of Common Prayer* (including its marriage service) as 'the authorised standard in matters pertaining

---

11. The motions put before the Synod and copies of the relevant correspondence may be found in the Archbishop of Perth's 'Circular: Members of Synod' of 28 October 2013, at <www.archbishopofperth.org/assets/files/Latest%20News/Presidents%20decision.pdf>. Accessed 6 December 2014.

to worship and doctrine'. Herft therefore claimed that the Perth Synod had no authority to pass the motion as in doing so it would be at variance with the Fundamental Declarations of the Constitution to which it was bound.

Herft has continued to argue that whatever his own view may be, his diocesan synod cannot adopt a resolution supporting the principle of same-sex marriage without action by the General Synod or a ruling by the Appellate Tribunal.[12]

While Herft's response in 2012 and 2013 raises crucial theological questions about the construction of sexual identity itself, and points to his commitment to a global Anglican communion, the most important outcome is his focus on the limits of the Australian Anglican Constitution and its place in synodal goverance. Herft has not publicly suggested a way forward for Perth Anglicans on this matter. It appears that for the time being the debate in synod has stalled.

If one accepts Herft's argument, then decisions necessary to allow the ordination of persons in a same-sex relationship would need to include the General Synod, to revise the concept of 'unchastity' in the *Offences Canon 1962*, to alter the code of conduct *Faithfulness in Service*, or to supplement the definition of marriage as set out in the *Book of Common Prayer*. Yet the current composition of the General Synod, and its complex rules regarding constitutional change, means any agreement is highly unlikely. Alternately, a legal ruling could be sought from the Appellate Tribunal as to whether these were in fact prohibitions on action by a diocese. Most dramatically, a diocese could attempt to withdraw altogether from the General Synod and the Anglican Church of Australia to achieve these ends.

In light of this apparent stalemate, and the contrasting approaches of McIntyre and Herft to the role of synods and constitutions and the authority of a diocesan bishop, a comparison with the Anglican debates on the ordination of women is instructive. This can throw light on how theological decisions were made by the constituent

---

12. The Archbishop made these points clearly in referring to his 2013 decision in his address to the 2014 meeting of the Perth Synod. The Archbishop of Perth, 'President's Address to the Third Session of the Forty-Eighth Synod', 4 October 2014 at <hwww.archbishopofperth.org/assets/files/Synod/Synod%20Charge%202014.pdf>. Accessed 6 December 2014.

parts of the church. There are of course major differences between the two debates. Women had almost never been ordained to Christian ministries prior to the nineteenth century, whereas same-sex attracted men had probably always been in the ranks of the clergy. While gay men could attempt celibacy or hide their sexuality and sexual relationships, it was impossible or unacceptable for women to conceal their physiology. Women did not need to fight to have their marriages to men blessed or recognised by the church, though many who campaigned for the ordination of women did need to persuade the church that fresh interpretations of the scriptures regarding marriage were required. Nor did women have to prove that they existed, or that they were part of God's will for creation, although they did have to argue that their place in creation was not confined to universal subjugation to men and that a woman's capacity and creativity was equal to that of a man.

Theologically there are striking similarities in the emergence and testing of the very idea that a woman or a same-sex attracted person could be ordained and serve the church in divine ministry. The caricature of the 'woman priest' always existed in western Christendom, ready to be resurrected as an object of ridicule to show how preposterous an innovation or argument was.[13] By the late nineteenth century and the gradual, grudging admission of women into professional roles and roles outside the bounds of the Victorian domestic sphere, the possibility of a woman becoming a priest seemed less ridiculous. This was especially the case in places such as Germany, North America, and Britain where women became deaconesses or itinerant preachers or were called by independent congregations into pastoral leadership roles.

By the twentieth century, some Anglicans began openly agitating for the ordination of women, looking to the many women who had led the people of Israel or the early church in the scriptures. They began to read New Testament injunctions regarding the role of women with fresh eyes.[14] Much of this early debate centred on the deaconess, a role established in London in 1861. Was a deaconess a female deacon,

---

13. Gary Macy, *The Hidden History of Women's Ordination: Female Clergy in the Medieval West* (Oxford: Oxford University Press, 2008).
14. Brian Heeney, *The Women's Movement in the Church of England 1850–1930* (Oxford: Clarendon Press, 1988).

equivalent to men of the same rank, or was a deaconess an order all of its own?[15]

By 1930 the campaign for the ordination of women reached the Lambeth Conference itself. Most bishops summarily dismissed the idea of female priests, yet the arguments they raised seemed more based on careless, undiluted prejudice than scriptural, theological argument. As a result, Anglicans did what they most love to do, and appointed an Archbishops' Commission to examine the whole question in some detail. When the Commission reported in 1935 there were two surprises. First was a minority report from the Dean of St Paul's London arguing that there was nothing in the church's sacred texts and traditions that would prohibit the ordination of a woman as a priest, and that indeed there were many reasons to proceed with such a step. Second was the theological weakness of the arguments put forward in the majority report against the ordination of women. The report's main contention was that the idea of female priests was such an innovation in Christian history that ecumenical consensus would be needed before Anglicans could take such a step.[16]

In the Church of England, it took another eighty years for the debate to play out, through endless reports, books, conferences, and synods, and for the church to do the work of sharing theological insight until theological principle became reality. This was fully achieved in November 2014, when the General Synod and the Parliament changed the law of England to permit both women and men to become deacons, priests, and bishops on equal terms. The statutory process in England was always clear, for, as the Established Church, the change required agreement from the General Synod, the Commons, the Lords, and the Crown. The Church of England's process did include much debate about the obligations and exemptions for members of the church who did not agree with the decision to ordain women as well as men, but a course of action other than a change to the law was not seriously contemplated.[17]

---

15. Henrietta Blackmore (editor), *The Beginning of Women's Ministry: The Revival of the Deaconess in the Nineteenth-Century Church of England* (Woodbridge: Boydell and Brewer, 2007).
16. *The Ministry of Women: Report of the Archbishops' Commission* (London: Church Assembly, 1935); and see Timothy Jones, *Sexual Politics in the Church of England, 1857–1957* (Oxford: Oxford University Press, 2013).
17. On the English debates, see Sean Gill, *Women and the Church of England:*

In contrast, the decision-making process in Australia was far less straightforward.[18] The process began in 1977 with the decision of the Australian General Synod that the theological objections raised did not constitute a barrier to the ordination of women. Yet over the next thirty years, a bewildering variety of positions were adopted by Australian Anglicans on precisely what decisions were needed before a woman could actually be ordained. These initially focussed on synodical legislation and constitutional reform, processes which required large, repeated majorities to be attained in the General Synod and the diocesan synods. In 1985, a canon was successfully enacted by the General Synod to authorise the ordination of women as deacons. But in the late 1980s, as the necessary majorities were not forthcoming for the ordination of women as priests, theologians and lawyers began to question the moral or legal need for legislation of any kind, especially at a national level. After all, where was the law establishing that men could be ordained?

Eventually two decisions were taken that enabled the ordination of women. First, some diocesan bishops, backed by their synods, determined that they already possessed the power to ordain women using diocesan constitutional or legislative provisions. Second, in 1992 the General Synod created an opt-in national system that removed any real or perceived prohibitions in the inherited law of the church which would inhibit a bishop from ordaining a woman. This legislation would only come into effect in a diocese which adopted the enabling canon of General Synod.

Matters became yet more bizarre in the push for the ordination of women as bishops. A case tested by the church's highest court, the Appellate Tribunal, found that a change to the definition of canonical fitness (the requirements for a person to be made a bishop) meant that in dioceses which ordained female priests, there was no barrier to their appointment as bishops. The result of this peculiar, partial approach to the ordination of women is a patchwork quilt of

---

From the Eighteenth Century to the Present (London: SPCK, 1994); Jacqueline Field-Bibb, *Women Towards Priesthood: Ministerial Politics and Feminist Praxis* (Cambridge: Cambridge University Press, 1991); Harriet Harris and Jane Shaw (editors), *The Call for Women Bishops* (London: SPCK, 2004).

18. On the Australian debates, see Muriel Porter, *Women in the Church: The Great Ordination Debate* (Melbourne: Penguin, 1989); Muriel Porter, *Women in Purple: Women Bishops in Australia* (Mulgrave: John Garratt Publishing, 2008).

responses, one that has diminished the communion of the Anglican Church of Australia and legitimised theological and institutional discrimination against female clergy. Thus at the time of writing there is still one diocese which does not ordain female deacons, four which do not ordain female priests, and several which do not ordain female bishops.

It now seems likely that if the issue returned to a vote at the General Synod in the near future, that more than a third of the General Synod's members would oppose the ordination of women as priests or bishops. This is largely due to the formula used to determine the membership of General Synod, growth in the number of clergy in the diocese of Sydney, and increasing representation from conservative evangelical Anglicans from other dioceses.[19] That means further constitutional change is unlikely to be seen for some years to adopt a different legislative approach to the question of ordination.

Thus, whereas in England the General Synod (and Parliament) changed the law of the land to enshrine the principle that both women and men could be ordained as deacons, priests, and bishops, in Australia, the law has been altered in some places to remove any prohibitions which may have existed. This leaves the Australian Anglican Constitution devoid of positive affirmation of the ordination of women, and the use of the masculine pronoun in the *Book of Common Prayer* ordinal unchanged.

A critical development in the synodical debates over the ordination of women in Australia was the increasing participation of women themselves, first as lay women, then as deacons and priests. (It is noteworthy, however, that the church's Appellate Tribunal, so often called to intervene on this matter, has never had a female member.) This was the result of deliberate strategies on the part of dioceses such as Melbourne which came out strongly in favour of the ordination of women in the 1970s, and through the lobbying efforts of the *Movement for the Ordination of Women* in the 1980s and 1990s which recognised the powerful effect of having actual ordained women in the General Synod. By way of parallel, there has been no such move in the case of LGBTIQ inclusion, not least because this would require

---

19. See for example Muriel Porter, *Sydney Anglicans and the Threat to World Anglicanism: The Sydney Experiment* (Farnham: Ashgate, 2011).

candidates for election to the General Synod to 'out' themselves in the nomination process.

So what may advocates of the full recognition of same-sex attracted Christians learn from this brief history? First is that as Anglicans we still have much work to do to establish the relative weight of the global, provincial, and local church. Second is that we need to evaluate the experiment of government by synod, which has only been part of the global Anglican experience for a century. Synods have provided an obvious arena for debate about critical theological, ecclesiological, and social issues, but it is not self-evident that they have been or will continue to be the best ways of handling such matters.[20] Third is that in the present Australian context, the General Synod is probably irrelevant. There is very little the synod could do to inhibit or force change, while its procedures and inherited behaviours do little to foster agreement or consensus. A long, protracted debate could be launched to change the definition of marriage, or to establish the eligibility of same-sex attracted people for ordination, following the suggestion implicit in Herft's actions. But is this really necessary?

The real arena for public, formal change in the church's recognition and inclusion of LGBTIQ people is in the conscience, teaching, and acts of the diocesan bishop. It is for this reason that opponents of change spend so much effort attempting to intimidate bishops into silence, or at the very least, retreat into the private sphere. As McIntyre's example shows, while the bishop's decision-making power is much greater than that of the average Anglican, the role of theological reflection through the reading of the scriptures is critical, in the same way as it is for all Christians coming to grips with human sexuality, whether on their own account or to support their neighbours.

We are united by our common worship of the one God and in our common dependence on the saving grace of Jesus Christ who died for us and for our salvation from our sins. We are divided by our inability to reach one accord on the deep question of who we are. This is intensely painful as our division constitutes disobedience to the

---

20. On the need to evaluate synods, see Tom Frame, *A House Divided? The Quest for Unity Within Anglicanism* (Brunswick East: Acorn Press, 2010), 109–124. For a broader consideration, see Colin Podmore, *Aspects of Anglican Identity* (London: Church House, 2005).

New Testament injunctions to unite, and as our consciences cause us to shame, exclude, and persecute one another.

What would I do? If I were trying to win a contest, to achieve victory by seeing the church open its ordained ministry and extend the blessing of relationships to persons other than heterosexual men and women, then I would be running a campaign directed at synods. I would organise tickets to get the right people elected to synods, prepare in-principle resolutions leading to the minor legislative changes required, win majorities, then run tickets to get the bodies which elect bishops stacked with members who will ensure that 'pro-gay' candidates enter the episcopate, and organise pressure groups to ensure these bishops are accountable to their constituencies.

This approach seems wrong for this issue. Pragmatically, a global view suggests that it would be very difficult to win a battle on these terms. Theologically, this approach is based on a false premise, that Christianity is about a contest that aims to create losers as well as winners.

What would Jesus do? He probably wouldn't be found on the floor of synod at all, and if he were, it wouldn't be long before he was turning over the tables and being thrown out of the debating chamber by the President. He would certainly be found with the people most marginalised by the church and by the world, hurting, loving, dying with them on the outskirts of society.

What, then, should we do?

Acting with integrity and honesty would be a good start. This is where the actions of Archbishop Roger and Bishop John are to be commended, even if you disagree with them. Archbishop Roger's refusal to act, and Bishop John's refusal not to act, were accompanied by transparent theological statements written from the heart and deeply engaged with scripture and tradition. Their decisions were made in full knowledge of their likely impact on their hearers and readers and on the people of their dioceses. We need more bishops who are willing to make themselves vulnerable, not by towing the party line, certainly not by avoiding saying anything at all, but by speaking honestly and clearly, by opening up opportunities to create relationships. Even keeping the conversation alive is important, as synods increasingly put issues of sexuality into the 'too hard' basket, which serves only to silence same-sex attracted people and once more deny our very existence in the church and world.

The most positive thing the Anglican Church could do would be to put same-sex attracted people at its centre. Ask us to make decisions. Trust us to wrestle with the great questions of sexuality and theology. We've been doing it for a very long time, I can assure you. Invite us to offer our views on the high price of unity and the sometimes competing demands of theological conviction.

But whatever we do, all Anglicans must recall that the final, primary, greatest decision was made long ago for all time and for all people. Two thousand years ago, on that hill and in that garden just outside the city walls of Jerusalem, God decided for us. Ultimately all we need is to find the courage and the hope to say 'Amen' to God's 'Yes' in Christ Jesus.

Chapter Six
It Seemed Good to Us

Phillip Tolliday

Readers who are familiar with the Acts of the Apostles will recognise the title of this essay. However, they will also recognise that I have taken some liberty with my allusion to the Acts reference. The citation in the New Testament reads, 'For it has seemed good to the Holy Spirit and to us …' Acts 15:28. The implication is, I believe, that because a certain practice—in that case what may be said to constitute the 'essentials'—has seemed 'good to the Holy Spirit,' it has, consequently, seemed 'good to us.'[1] Readers are invited to endorse Luke's claim that the will of God was discerned, and the result of that correct discernment led to the consequent sense of 'rightness' felt by the community. In other words, that certain practices came to seem good to the community was the result of the practices having been discerned to be right, that is, approved by the Holy Spirit.

There come certain moments in the church's journey—the current debate in the Anglican Church of Australia about human sexuality and same-sex relationships in particular, is one of them—when people feel the urgency of the issue, wonder about the irrevocability of proceeding forward and look for some definitive clue as to whether saying Yes or No is right or wrong. Turning to the Bible they cast anxious eyes over the texts that seem to deal with homosexuality as well as those that address more general principles of how humans ought to relate to one another in friendship and love. At the end of the day, however, the Bible seems to yield a rather inconclusive result. For conservatives the answer seems clear-cut; same-sex relationships

---

1. In the context of the discussion in *Acts*, the essentials consisted of 'what has been sacrificed to idols and from blood and from what is strangled and from fornication.'

are sinful, while for liberals the response is more varied. Some argue many of the texts allegedly dealing with same-sex relationships are not addressing that issue at all, or certainly not from within the parameters within which we construe things today. Other liberals argue that yes, the conservatives are right in their reading of the relevant texts, but we must just march on and relegate these texts—like many others in the Bible—to a culture-bound background that lacks perennial relevance to Christian living. In short, the Bible doesn't solve the issue to the satisfaction—albeit perhaps the reluctant satisfaction—of all. The Bible, and not just the Bible, is the playground of hermeneutics. Whether we are talking about words on the pages of the Bible or about the history of the church we are never making neutral, objective statements uninfluenced by human interests. But because human interests are so much part of us it is often—perhaps always—difficult for us to observe ourselves.

My underlying assumption in this essay is that we carry out certain practices and abstain from others because it seems good to us. Note, not because it seems good to God, but because it seems good to *us*. I suggest that in the passage of time when the phrase, 'it seemed good to us', takes in many of us and is not simply restricted to what seems good to me, that we then begin to discern that this was perhaps the way things were *meant* to be and at this point we may say, 'it seemed good to the Holy Spirit'. Thus my theological approach here is based on human experience: though of course, not just, or even primarily, on my own experience, but upon a wider understanding of experience that we know by the name of tradition.

I will argue that the debate about same-sex relationships in the Anglican Church of Australia, while unique in its particulars is not unique in the structural terms of the debate itself. This will permit me to argue that history can provide a precedent for the way in which the church discerns or 'receives' practices once thought contrary to Bible and tradition. In particular, I will suggest that the debates about whether women in the Anglican Church of Australia could be ordained may provide an instructive precedent for discerning how the church may approach the current issue of same-sex relationships.

The Adelaide Synod of 2012 included on its agenda a discussion of several motions that had been proposed about human sexuality. In brief these motions requested the Synod to continue a process of education and openness around such issues as marriage equality and reception of openly gay couples within the church. These issues touched deeply held feelings and convictions and it is fair to say that there was an undercurrent of unease among some members of synod as the debate grew nearer.

Coincidentally at the same time as the Adelaide Synod was convened, a recently published set of essays celebrating the twentieth anniversary of the ordination of women as priests, entitled *Prophets, Preachers and Heretics*, was to be launched during one of the Synod breaks.[2] Several speakers lauded the book. They reflected on the struggles of those times leading up to the ordinations. The impression given by the speakers was that we as a church could be justly proud of the movement to ordain women; that despite the acrimony with which it was surrounded at the time, it was a truly prophetic event.

During one of the breaks I took time out to flick through some of the essays. Since I had lived through those times it was a journey down memory lane; what Eric Mascall had called with a completely different reference, 'emotion recollected in tranquility'.[3] A common theme in the essays was the bruising debates of successive synods that left the advocates of both sides battered. As I read the essays, I could not help noticing the structural similarities between the debates then and now. In both cases the Bible was appealed to and was found inconclusive. In both cases the assistance of church tradition was enlisted in order to show the rightness or wrongness of the case, and once again, the appeal to tradition proved to be inconclusive. Admittedly, in the case of women's ordination there were hints to indicate some precedent for the practice in the past, whereas in the current debate this precedent seems less forthcoming. However, my primary point is that in neither case did Bible or tradition produce an unambiguous answer and yet in both cases and from both sides people *did* believe that the essential nature of the church, to say nothing of its health and vitality, was dependent on having the right approach to these questions. Would the ordination of women to the priesthood somehow diminish the church or would it rather be diminished by not ordaining women?

---

2. E Lindsay and J Scarfe (editors), *Preachers, Prophets and Heretics: Anglican Women's Ministry* (Sydney: UNSW Press, 2012).
3. EL Mascall, *The Secularisation of Christianity: An Analysis and a Critique* (London: Darton, Longman & Todd, 1965).

Similarly now the question seems to be, will the church be diminished by blessing same-sex unions and advocating marriage equality, or will it be diminished by standing against them?

In the case of women's ordination we know that the ordinations took place because certain bishops 'broke ranks' and went ahead and did it anyway. To the conservatives of the day, this was interpreted as an act of betrayal that was in contravention of due process. Although they were heady days, it is necessary to note that those first courageous women were entering an environment that was often hostile and largely indifferent to their presence. Twenty years on things look different, but the first years were tough.[4] There is a real sense in which the prophetic move was not only, or even primarily, in the bishop ordaining women to the priesthood. Rather, the prophetic nature of this event was discerned more in the way in which the church lived out this reality in its life, yet even in this case the evidence proves contested.[5] Although women have been ordained for twenty years in the Anglican Church of Australia, they have hardly enjoyed the equality of opportunity afforded to their male counterparts.[6]

As what we will come to know as the present streams to us from the future it seems natural to regard the future as the locus of possibilities. However, possibilities take many shapes, not all of them desirable. Thus the 'space' as it were, between the future and the soon-to-be-present becomes a contested space. The question of what the church—or indeed any other significant institution—will be like in the nearly imagined future is never without its vested interests. In the determination of this question, 'discernment' is not simply a matter of

---

4. See, for example, the reflections of Kay Goldsworthy, *The 'almost' Fully Ordained Meat Pie*, a paper presented to the University of Manchester in 2006: <http://www.perth.anglican.org/download/Spirituality_Theology/The%20almost%20fully%20ordained%20meat%20pie.pdf>. Last accessed September, 2014. The title refers to an infelicitous remark made by Ian Herring about the impossibility of women priests.
5. See, for example, Muriel Porter, 'Backlash: The New Threat to Ordained Women', in *Preachers, Prophets & Heretics*, edited by E Lindsay and J Scarfe (Sydney: UNSW Press, 2012), 374–391.
6. See, for example, the special edition of *St Mark's Review* 228.2 (2014): 1–141, under the heading 'Taking Stock: The Joy and challenge of ordained women in the Anglican Church of Australia,' edited by Heather Thomson and Sarah MacNeil.

'taking a look,' but rather, of actively, if often surreptitiously, *shaping* the future.

To put it bluntly, there seem to me to be two diametrically opposed approaches to the shaping of the future, and thus to our disposition in regard to the present. The first of these seeks to take a snapshot of a particular portion of the past, which it then claims as normative and thus ideally determinative for all futures. The second perspective also looks to the past but does so in order to ascertain lessons from it. Among such lessons are observations from those occasions when a community was so certain that a specific course of action was right, for example, the decision not to ordain women as priests, and yet was later proven to have been mistaken. Of course not everyone who disagreed with the ordination of women changed their mind; some who opposed women's ordination then, remain of the same opinion today. But in the passage of time and, most importantly, with the change of circumstance brought about by a change in practice, the majority of those opposed *did* change their minds.

The past and the present are the twin frames out of which we discern the shape of the future. The hermeneutic that we choose to adopt about the past will be significantly determinative for our construal and thus shaping of future possibilities. I will suggest that there are significant structural similarities between the current debate on human sexuality and previous discussion that took place around the ordination of women. Certainly the debates that then surrounded women's ordination were no less acrimonious than their contemporary counterparts, and neither were the advocates for certainty, whether *pro* or *con*, any less sure then than they seem to be today.

The issue of human sexuality being debated presently in the Anglican Church is, I think, another example of what I will call a conservative hermeneutic over a liberal hermeneutic. A liberal hermeneutic might seem to conclude that 'Whatever is, is right'—the words are Pope's, the vision is Hegel's.[7] I will suggest that a comparison

---

7. Pope (1688–1744) was an English poet, while Hegel (1770–1831) was a German philosopher. Pope's words come from his poem *An Essay on Man* and are suggestive of fixed providential future. Hegel's take on this is different, for in his case it is more accurate to say, 'whatever is about to be, is right.' I owe this formulation of the difference between the two views to Peter Thorslev in his essay, 'German Romantic Idealism,' in *The Cambridge Companion to British*

of the structural similarities between the earlier debates on women's ordination and the present discussions about human sexuality can serve to show us that not only is hindsight a wonderful thing, but that Hegel's providential vision of 'whatever is, is right', could be as good as it gets. If it *is* as good as it gets, then it follows that the task to discern or shape the future is a supremely ethical one. In other words, if the future is not somehow 'fixed' in eternity, but rather is always about to be fixed by dint of human performance, then *how* we shape that future is of great importance.

Structural similarities

In the present debate on human sexuality, advocates are in favour of marriage equality, that is, the view that two people of the same sex might live together in marriage. Against this, some have argued that this is not only undesirable (and currently illegal) but also, from a semantic point of view, it is impossible. Marriage, they argue, is by definition, the union between a man and woman, not between two women or two men. Therefore, while some will allow that it is possible and perhaps even desirable for two men or two women to live together, it cannot be called marriage because it contradicts the present definition of marriage.

The argument is reminiscent of a similar one made more than twenty years ago. Then it was seriously argued by some opponents of women's ordination that women could not be ordained as priests because the very definition of the word *priest* entailed that it referred to and indeed could only refer to a male. If a woman were to be ordained, they argued, she would not be a priest but rather a priestess. Of course such a claim provoked legitimate outcries of rage, for the subtext was clear enough; it was that priestesses were typically associated with the cultic rites of various forms of paganism. To be a priestess was to be consigned to a place outside of Christianity.

In both cases the thinly veiled assumption is that the meaning of a word, 'marriage' or 'priest' has an invariable referent and meaning that, once stabilised, cannot be changed. Moreover, the meaning of the word now determines all future practice associated with the

---

Romanticism, edited by S Curran (Cambridge: Cambridge University Press, 2010^2), 90.

designated word. Hence, priests must always and only be men. Marriage must always and only be between a man and a woman. So what shall we say of those women acting to all intents and purposes like their male counterparts? Are they priests or not? What shall we say of those same-sex couples living together and sharing life as a married couple? Are they not married? History records that over time the church was able to say, in answer to the first question, yes, they are priests. The answer to the second question—but are they married?—has not (yet) been decided.

One thing to take away from these observations is the principle enunciated long ago by Wittgenstein who said, 'don't ask for the meaning, ask for the use'.[8] It is the way we use words that will, in the end, shape their meaning and indeed expand their meanings over time. Few would now argue that women ordained in the church should be referred to as priestesses. Such an argument would be revealed as demeaning. Might not the same come to be true of our current definition of marriage? Time, but more importantly, practice, will tell.

When it comes to the scriptural similarities, I will not rehearse the arguments and evidence adduced for the positions for and against the respective viewpoints. There is an avalanche of literature that deals with this. Suffice to say, that within this particular series of volumes from *ATF Press* essays have been proposed in favour of a positive interpretation of same-sex relationships. And two volumes comprising essays representing the opposing opinion have been offered in response.[9] The scriptural arguments are compelling to sympathetic readers, but only rarely, if ever, do they convince those of a contrary view.

---

8. Ludwig Wittgenstein, *Philosophical Investigations, The German Text, with a Revised English Translation*, (Oxford: Blackwell Publishing, 2003), 18, para 43: 'the meaning of a word is its use in the language.' [*Die Bedeutung eines Wortes ist sein Gebrauch in der Sprache.*]
9. See NMcI, Wright, (editor), *Five Uneasy Pieces* (Adelaide: ATF Press, 2011); AH Cadwallader (editor), *Pieces of Ease and Grace*. Adelaide: ATF Press, 2013; M Bird and G Preece, (editors), *Sexegesis: An Evangelical Response to Five Uneasy Pieces on Homosexuality* (Sydney South: Anglican Press Australia, 2012); MD Thompson (editor), *Human Sexuality and the 'Same Sex Marriage' Debate* (Sydney South: Anglican Press Australia, 2015).

In both cases—women's ordination and the debate on human sexuality—the terms in which the contemporary debates are framed and the questions that are asked, make the Bible ill-suited as a repository for answers. In the case of the ordination of women, as the debate unfolded, it came to be recognised that there was no single form of ministry in the New Testament; that what the early Christian communities knew and practiced as authorisation for various forms of ministry was not really what we would recognise or mean as ordination nearly 2,000 years later. Similarly, scholars have claimed that many of the texts that come under scrutiny in the human sexuality debate are framed within contexts that are very different from the parameters of the contemporary discussion. Of course, not all scholars believe that the differences are either so great, nor of such significance. But my point is that *some* do, and this, I think gives grounds for arguing that scripture is at present inconclusive in this debate just as it seemed to be in the debate about the ordination of women.

I have made a distinction between the so-called 'scriptural similarities' by suggesting that in the midst of discussions about whether women could or should be ordained, scripture could be appealed to equally by each side but with an inconclusive result that failed to convince the opposition. This is very similar to how the situation stands presently with the texts about human sexuality. However, something has changed, because now there would be relatively few people seeking to argue against women's ordination on the basis of scripture. So what *has* changed. The thing that has changed is practice. By way of comparison, this is the very thing that has not (yet) changed in the current debate about same-sex relationships in the church. A stronger example, perhaps, are the texts in the New Testament that proscribe divorce and remarriage.[10] These words, attributed to Jesus himself, have served throughout the majority of Christian history to signal a boundary that must not be transgressed. But in the latter part of the twentieth century, divorce and remarriage gradually came to be legalised, social ostracism was overcome and scripture scholars in many cases overcame what would have been an unbridgeable reserve to reinterpret these texts so as to conform

---

10. Matt 19:1–12; Mk 10: 2–12; Lk 16:18 and 1 Cor 7:10–13.

to what was becoming a new social norm. Practice was determining meaning.

An issue of hermeneutics

My focus upon practice, or the lack thereof, is not accidental. Key to my thesis is Heidegger's appreciation of 'the interpreter as the location of meaning'.[11] Heidegger famously made a distinction between what we translate as the 'ready-to-hand' (*Zuhandenheit*) and the 'present-at-hand' (*Vorhandenheit*). The first of these, the 'ready-to-hand' describes our 'pre-reflective familiarity with our environment and our intuitive practical knowledge'.[12] The latter category, that is to say, regarding something as 'present-at-hand', is what we do when we come to regard or apprehend a thing, or as I shall suggest later, a practice as something to be reflected upon. We know it better perhaps under the name of orthodoxy or doctrine.

Heidegger used the example of a hammer, and elsewhere of a table, in order to illustrate the difference between these two perspectives. He points this out in the example of the hammer that takes on handiness (*Handlichkeit*) in the act of being used as a hammer, that is, hammering. It is this very property of handiness or being useful for *Dasein*—the human being—that gives the hammer the quality of being ready-to-hand. 'No matter how keenly we just *look* at the outward appearance of things constituted in one way or another, we cannot discover handiness. When we just look at things "theorctically" we lack an understanding of handiness.'[13] Similarly, when Heidegger reflected upon the experience of looking at his kitchen table, he noted that what he called his 'primordial perception' of the table was based around its handiness or usefulness. The primary thing about apprehending or interpreting the table was to know whether and how it was appropriate for one's purposes. Thus Heidegger's perception of his kitchen table was primarily influenced by such factors as whether it was large enough to accommodate the family at meal times, and

---

11. BH McLean, *Biblical Interpretation and Philosophical Hermeneutics* (Cambridge: Cambridge University Press, 2012), 99–142.
12. McLean, *Biblical Interpretation*, 107.
13. Martin Heidegger, *Being and Time*, translated by Joan Stambaugh (Albany: SUNY Press, rev ed, 2010), 69.

whether its surface was sufficiently smooth to permit him to sit there and write letters. That the table was made of wood; that it was a little more than one metre high; that its shape was rectangular and that the edges were beveled—all these may have been true but they were not the primary constituents of Heidegger's experience of the table.

Heidegger suggested that our normal taken-for-granted experience of things in the world is this primordial apprehension of them as 'ready-to-hand.' Things are apprehended relationally, which in Heidegger's terminology means, as they are for *Dasein*—the human being. Apprehending or interpreting something as 'present-at-hand' is, according to Heidegger, a practice that is counter-intuitive to us. 'The simple seeing of things nearest to us in our having to do with . . . contains the structure of interpretation so primordially that a grasping of something which is, so to speak, *free of the as* requires a kind of reorientation.'[14]

McLean, reflecting on Heidegger's distinction between the 'ready-to-hand' and the 'present-at-hand' notes that the 'ready-to-hand' permits things to become familiar to our consciousness in a 'non-propositional way'.[15] Drawing the reader's attention to the study of the Bible, McLean uses Heidegger's distinction to show 'that in contrast to a purely academic study of the Bible, many people read the Bible as ready-to-hand, that is, as part of the totality of their existential world of involvements, in ever-widening circles of relations'.[16] Indeed, this is how most readers of the Bible apprehend what they read; formal study, the 'present-at-hand' comes later and is derivative from the primordial experience, the 'ready-to-hand'.

As far as I have been able to ascertain, Heidegger never commented on Acts 15:28. However, given his desire to situate the place of meaning with the interpreter, an aim he sought to achieve with his distinction between the 'ready-to-hand' and the 'present-at-hand,' it is, I think, a reasonable surmise that he would have been sympathetic to the view that some of the practices of the early Christian community as they are identified in Acts 15:28, *first* seemed good to them, and on *that basis*, were later said to have received the approval of the Holy Spirit. Performance and action were the levers that led to interpretation

---

14. Heidegger, *Being and Time*, 145.
15. McLean, *Biblical Interpretation*, 108.
16. McLean, *Biblical Interpretation*, 108.

and meaning and part of the meaning was the attribution of divine approval to the practice under consideration.

Grammar as orthodoxy, regulative but not constitutive

In an article on contextual theology, the Asian theologian Anri Morimoto uses a model of language acquisition from Noam Chomsky in order to illustrate the relationship between faith and orthodoxy.[17] In his model, Chomsky had made a distinction between competence and performance.

> Competence is the tacit, innate, almost biological ability we possess for language acquisition, and performance is the actual use of language based on competence.[18]

When this model was transposed into a theological register, language competence was represented by faith, while performance was 'the actual expression of faith in prayers, hymns, art, rituals, behavior, and intellectual activities like theology'.[19] Morimoto's distinction parallels the distinction made in theology between the *lex orandi*—the rule or law of prayer—and the *lex credenda*—the rule or law of belief—which understands that there exists an irreducible dialectical relationship between performance and reflection or theory.

In the case of language, we know it is possible with practice and maturity to produce a seemingly endless range of well-formed sentences. The reason why these sentences are well-formed is due to the fact that they follow the rules of grammar, though curiously, for the most part, we form these sentences without being explicitly aware of the grammatical rules. They just seem *right* to us, or, as sometimes happens, wrong! However, Morimoto's primary point is that grammar does not generate or produce language: instead it describes language. Moreover, the grammatical rules are not invariable; they describe

---

17. Anri Morimoto, 'Contextualised and Cumulative: Tradition, Orthodoxy and Identity from the Perspective of Asian Theology', in *Studies in World Christianity* 15:1 (2009): 39–55. Although this is the first explicit use of the word orthodoxy in this paper, it, together with its sinister cousin heterodoxy, has been a covert companion throughout.
18. Morimoto, 43.
19. Morimoto, 43.

language performance at a certain place and time in history. The rules of grammar, or at least certain of them, can 'be overruled and eventually overwritten by performance over a period of time'.[20]

Corresponding to grammar in Chomsky's model of linguistic acquisition is, in the theological schema 'the orthodoxy that stands between faith and its performance'.[21] Similar to the way in which grammar describes but does not generate or produce language, so here, in the theological register, orthodoxy does not generate or produce faith. Instead, orthodoxy is itself 'formed in response to and in interaction with the performance of the faithful'.[22] On this understanding, orthodoxy cannot be frozen. It provides stability but not a straitjacket, which is to say that it functions in a 'regulative rather than constitutive manner'.[23]

Applying this model to the issue of the church's response to same-sex relationships as well as to the debate about the ordination of women proves to be illuminating. Morimoto speaks of tradition as a 'buffer zone' and as a place in which the church may breathe as it continues 'to weave the creative tapestry of tradition…'.[24] Orthodoxy functions as the 'tentative guarantor of the tradition'—tentative, because the tradition itself is never static, but always in the process of evolving. In the case of women's ordination, the movement had begun in the face of incomprehension, which grew rapidly into entrenched and seemingly intransigent opposition. In the early years of the debate, *orthodoxy* functioned so as to guarantee the tradition by simply rejecting what appeared to be at fault according to the perception of the majority of people at the time. In other words, from an ecclesial and theological perspective, at that time in history, ordaining women did *not* seem good to us. Similarly, in the case of marriage equality and same-sex relationships, the *orthodoxy* or grammar of the Anglican Church in Australia is functioning so as to make it impermissible to go against the tradition of past practice. But tradition itself has proven to be far from inflexible.

---

20. Morimoto, 43.
21. Morimoto, 43.
22. Morimoto, 43.
23. Morimoto, 44.
24. Morimoto, 45.

As the movement for women's ordination gathered momentum, a process that took considerable time and many disappointments, there gradually came to be a change in practice. Admittedly, that required a bishop to step outside the boundaries of church law (according to one reading) and act unilaterally. Yet such a move could not have succeeded had it not been the case that there was by then a groundswell of support for women priests. The situation with marriage equality and same-sex relationships is not the same. At the moment, the churches sit waiting more or less uncomfortably to see what the Australian Government will do about changing the legislation to permit same-sex couples to marry. For as long as such legislation is not forthcoming the church will be 'safe', absolved from having to make a decision. However, I suspect that legislation for marriage equality is probably going to happen, at which point it will become largely a matter of indifference to the state as to what the church does in response to it; just as the state was unwilling to become embroiled in the debate about women's ordination. For the most part, it just couldn't see the problem. But once the legislation is passed, it will reinvigorate debate within the church. Once marriage equality becomes a reality in society it will, I think, be a case of 'the performance (*lex orandi*)' gradually working upon the orthodoxy (*lex credendi*) of the church to cause it to 'gradually shift its judgement and positioning'.[25] And so it will be that the orthodoxy will 'move *along with* the body of faith expressions'.[26]

At this point it might be objected that I can't possibly *know* that this is the way things will unfold. I agree. In the early days of the women's ordination movement, I didn't know whether it would be successful or not. When I entered theological college as an undergraduate I hoped it wouldn't be successful. By the time I had left four years later, I hoped that women would be ordained—and soon. By that time there was more reason to believe that the hope might be fulfilled. There is reason to hope that the church's stance on marriage equality and same-sex unions may undergo a similar trajectory in the minds of many Anglicans.

However, change doesn't come to pass just by thinking about it. What had once seemed unquestionably legitimate, for example

---

25. Morimoto, 45.
26. Morimoto, 45. Emphasis in the original.

slavery, is no longer considered to be appropriate today. Removed in time and space from such a decision, we may be inclined to take it for granted, but in its time it appeared to its contemporaries as momentous and shocking. Or closer to us in time, consider divorce and the way in which the church has almost routinely acclimatised itself to the sad reality that human love may bear the promise of 'forever' but sometimes, for all sorts of reasons, such love is unable to stay the course. It would no longer seem appropriate to many Christians to say that a divorced person must remain celibate until the death of his or her partner.[27] A hundred years before these decisions, no-one could have foreseen 'which of these changes would eventually receive the status of orthodoxy' in successive generations.[28] And that's my point: orthodoxy, Chomsky's 'grammar', changed because our performance, changed. Of course, there was a dialectical relationship between them in such a way that we may speak of a hermeneutical spiral. But there is a real sense in which performance, and faith are constitutive whereas orthodoxy, the grammar of performance is regulative.

Conclusion

I wrote earlier that the task of discerning the future is a supremely ethical one. The reason for this is that the future is not some quiescent sphere of unrealised actuality for which we wait, and search anxiously for a hint of what it may intimate to us. Instead, I have suggested that the future grows out of the present and there is a real sense in which we construct the future, we don't merely wait for it.

Some recent discussions in Anglican theology and ecclesiology have counselled patience and waiting as dispositions we should adopt at the present time. When Rowan Williams was Archbishop of Canterbury, he sought to dissuade those he feared might act precipitously. This attitude led Rupert Shortt, an incisive and sympathetic commentator

---

27. I am aware some Christians would not adopt this revised or liberal attitude, though I suspect they are probably in the minority, at least in the Anglican Church.
28. Morimoto, 45, makes the point that 'the doctrine of the Trinity in its Greek formulation has had the status of orthodoxy for the longest period of time, but slavery had indulged an almost equal period of the church's sanction, until it became repugnant quite recently.'

on Williams, to surmise that if the crisis facing the Archbishop had been the ordination of women rather than the issue of same-sex relationships, Williams' counsel of patience could have meant that the Church of England would still have been waiting for women to be ordained. It is, of course, not possible to conclude whether Shortt is right or not. Some may point out that Williams faced an Anglican Communion that was much more chaotic and liable to fracture than it had been twenty years previously. However, we should remember that we make that judgement with the wisdom of hindsight and to many contemporaries of the time, things did appear just as dire in the Communion as some think them to be now.

It is sometimes said—using the Niemöller principle—that not to act, is to act and not to speak, is to speak.[29] When it comes to the world and our involvement in it, we are, as Rowan Williams reminded us, always already involved. Moreover, we are always 'starting in the middle of things'.[30] There is no tidy, uncluttered sideline to which we can retreat and wait patiently for what the future will bring. For the future will bring to us in large measure the aggregate of our present performances—or, if not ours, then those of others.

My claim in this essay has been that we should see ourselves as being essentially involved in the world and its future, which is to say, our future. In Heidegger, we saw that our default position of perceiving or interpreting the world is not one of detachment and objectivity, but rather one that demands our involvement in such a complete and radical way that for the most part we don't even notice it until it is brought to our attention. The nature of the world cannot be disconnected from its usefulness to us. Discernment therefore becomes a matter of comportment; a way of taking up a position *vis-a-vis* the present situation.

---

29. Martin Niemöller reflected thus: 'When the Nazis came for the communists, I was silent because I was not a communist. When they came to arrest the Social Democrats, I was silent because I was not a Social Democrat. When they came to get the trade unionists, I was silent because I was not a trade unionist. When they came for the Jews, I was silent because I was not a Jew. When they came for me, there was no one left who could protest.' Quoted in Katharina von Kellenbach, *The Mark of Cain: Guilt and Denial in the Post-War Lives of Nazi Perpetrators* (Oxford: Oxford University Press, 2013), 47.
30. Rowan Williams, *On Christian Theology* (Oxford: Blackwell, 2000), xii.

In the model proposed by Chomsky and appropriated for theology by Morimoto, I suggested that orthodoxy may be regulative of faith performance rather than constitutive. We saw that tradition in Christianity has provided a 'buffer zone', but that the edges of tradition, so to speak, were somewhat durable, as opposed to brittle. We saw also that the constant 'nudging' of performance could open up the tradition in such a way as to accommodate a different shape of orthodoxy—often a shape that would not have been recognised by earlier orthodox Christian believers.[31] Finally we noted that it was not possible to 'second guess' the changing shapes that orthodoxy might take.[32]

In conclusion, I should note that I am aware, as I said in the introduction, that I am taking liberties with the phrase from Acts 15:28. It is not intended to be exegesis. I chose the phrase and isolated it deliberately because it suggested to me that our experience of bringing about change, or not, is something that *we* do. Moreover, we do it because it does or does not *seem good* to us. Perhaps some readers will object to this approach, judging that I've not made a place for the role of the Holy Spirit. In truth, I have to admit to being very wary of attempting to place the Holy Spirit in discussions of this nature. Long ago Austin Farrer warned us about the difficulties of trying to trace what he called the causal joint between God and the world.[33] However,

---

31. A previous reader of this paper has observed that I have defined orthodoxy as 'group-located, given that neither Roman Catholics or Greek Orthodox support women's ordination' and in this sense my take on orthodoxy differs from that espoused by earlier centuries. That's true. I think the changed view on orthodoxy is a necessary consequence of the rise of a plethora of Christian denominations, all of which claim to be orthodox, but all in slightly different ways. Though Christianity was never entirely monolithic, it could sometimes in earlier centuries pretend to be, whereas since the Reformation/s the pretence to a monolithic orthodoxy is harder to sustain, despite claims of what the *Church* alleges to be orthodox.
32. That orthodoxy could and did take changing shapes is shown in the historical trajectory of Christological debates. Some positions that had been judged orthodox in the second century had been ruled out as heterodox by the fifth century. Classically, the church has referred to this dynamic as the development of doctrine. Development is viewed positively, while change is judged negatively. It then becomes a matter of debate as to whether all developments, or just some of them, might really be changes after all.
33. Austin Farrer, *The Freedom of the Will: The Gifford Lectures in the University of Edinburgh 1957* (London: A & C Black, 1958).

I have been perhaps more aware of the inevitably political nature of theology, by which I mean the justification of human decisions that are given the divine imprimatur. Rowan Williams refers to this ever-present danger when he speaks of the necessity of theology to make universal claims from its always already particular, situated context. Can we make such claims without ideological distortion? Some distortion, human interests, power-plays—all these are inevitable and no doubt through all of them, in some mysterious indefinable way, God is present. But let us try not to enlist the Spirit too early. Let us not use the Spirit to somehow smooth out the wrinkles of the present time while we wait patiently for the clarity of the future to appear, for I suspect we plan our future as carefully as we can by 'performing the present' in ways we would like the future to be. If our performance should take root in enough minds and hearts, then the day will come when it 'seems good to us' and then the church may say of marriage equality and the blessing of same-sex unions, just as it now says of the ordination of women that, it 'seemed good to the Holy Spirit' because it 'seemed good to us'.

Chapter Seven
Situating Lambeth 1.10 as Discourse in the Life of the Anglican Church

Cathy Thomson

The 1998 Lambeth Conference passed a resolution (1.10) outlining the response of the bishops of the Anglican Church to homosexuality, homosexual persons and homosexual 'practice'.[1] This resolution emerged from a consideration of a document called the 'Kuala Lumpur Statement on Human Sexuality'[2] that was made accessible to the Conference. As it has proven necessary in the Communion-wide debates that followed Lambeth 1998 to employ hermeneutical processes to assess the claims about the Bible in section (d) of the resolution,[3] so it might now be instructive to employ hermeneutical principles to an evaluation of the significance of the resolution as discourse among the Anglican events and documents which both preceded and followed it.

This paper will trace the processes leading to the passing of the resolution, the content and provenance of the discourses that prompted it, and its influence on future events and further discussion within the Anglican Communion. The paper will then attempt in some small way to assess the importance of the resolution for the life and mission of the Anglican Communion.

---

1. Please see Appendix 1; <http://www.lambethconference.org resolutions/1998/-1-10.cfm> Date accessed 23/8/14.
2. Please see Appendix 2; <http://trushare.com/25JUN97/JN97SOUN.htm> Date accessed 23/8/14.
3. Section (d): '(This Conference) while rejecting homosexual practice as incompatible with Scripture, calls on all our people to minister pastorally and sensitively to all irrespective of sexual orientation and to condemn irrational fear of homosexuals, violence within marriage and any trivialisation and commercialisation of sex.' <http://www.lambethconference.org/resolutions/1998/-1-10.cfm>

It is necessary to identify a simple methodology for this work which is concerned with establishing contexts, both textual and historical, identifying nuances of texts, and evaluating the significance of the events and the Human behaviour that constituted them. In tracing the processes leading to Lambeth 1.10, and in evaluating its influence on the discourse which resulted from it, two hermeneutical (interpretative) categories will be brought into play. These are 'intertextuality'—here a strategy to examine a range of relevant texts to establish how they connect and 'inter-play' with one another. The second is 'interpersonal(ity)', which will explore the meaning of the interrelatedness of the 'players' at Lambeth 1998 and of the commentators who reflected on proceedings afterwards. (The latter term is a neologism of my own coining which suits the purposes of this project).

Lambeth 1.10: the narrative

Lambeth 1998 was not the first Lambeth Conference to give attention to the question of what constituted acceptable faithful and chaste relationships for Anglicans, nor was it the first to explore the meaning of this question for those who identify as homosexual. Lambeth 1978 had affirmed faithfulness and chastity inside or outside marriage respectively, and called for a communion-wide theological study of human sexuality.[4] Its final clause said,

> While we affirm heterosexuality as the scriptural norm, we recognise the need for deep and dispassionate study of the question of homosexuality, which would take seriously both the teaching of scripture and the results of scientific and medical research.[5]

It also called for ongoing dialogue with homosexual people, and affirmed their need for and right to the pastoral care of the church.[6]

---

4. See Appendix 3; <http://www.lambethconference.org/resolutions/1978/1978-10.cfm> Date accessed 23/8/14.
5. Appendix 3; <http://www.lambethconference.org/resolutions/1978/1978-10.cfm> Date accessed 23/8/14.
6. David Virtue, 'Archbishops Argue Over Lambeth Resolution1:10' <http://www.virtueonline.org/archbishops-argue-over-lambeth-resolution-110> 6. Date

The event that accelerated the creation and promulgation of Resolution 1.10 at Lambeth 1998 was the second meeting of a group of Anglican bishops in 1997, all drawn from the southern hemisphere and calling themselves the 'South to South Encounter'. It was from this meeting that the theologically conservative statement on human sexuality, commonly referred to as 'The Kuala Lumpur Statement', emerged, although, as we shall see, by a less-than-straightforward process.

This statement was presented to the 1998 Lambeth conference and, despite there having been significant reluctance at the conference formally to debate issues of sexuality without further research, resolutions relating to it were drawn up and placed on the conference notice paper by representatives from the 'South to South Encounter' group, supported by some conservative bishops from the Church of England and from the Episcopal Church of the United States of America (ECUSA), now The Episcopal Church (TEC).

Resolutions IV.26 and V.23, which both sought reception and recognition of the Kuala Lumpur statement, were passed over and not voted on. Resolution V.1—which affirmed the primary authority of scripture, reaffirmed traditional church teaching on marriage and equated homosexual practise with both promiscuity and sin—and V.35 (which had similar imperatives) were proposed as amendments to Resolution 1.10, but were defeated. Resolution V.10, which affirmed the general categories of 'Christian Family values' and 'Anglican Sexual Ethics', was withdrawn by the mover.

This left Resolution 1.10 which upheld 'the teaching of Scripture' and interpreted it as 'faithfulness in marriage between a man and a woman in lifelong union' and abstinence 'for those who are not called to marriage'.[7] It recognised the experience of those who identified as homosexual persons, rejected homosexual practice as incompatible with scripture, and advised against the blessing of same-sex unions and against the ordination of those in active homosexual relationships. Resolution 1.10 also affirmed the full membership of homosexual persons in the body of Christ, and called for a commitment from the Bishops of the Communion to listen to them and learn from the

---

accessed 22/8/14.
7. 'Resolutions from 1998' from the Anglican Communion Website, <http://www.lambethconference.org/resolutions/1998/-1-10.cfm> Date accessed 23/8/14.

sharing of their experiences. However, against the background of the impact of the rejection of homosexual practice as incompatible with scripture, it was unlikely that the pastoral affirmations included in the resolution would find much traction. Indeed, so it proved to be.

The Resolution also commended the appended 'Report on Human Sexuality: "Called to Full Humanity"'. The report in this subsection had been created at the Conference by the human sexuality working group. It acknowledged that the bishops of the Anglican Church were 'not of one mind about homosexuality'[8] and outlined the range of understandings among the bishops from 'those who believe homosexuality is a disorder' to 'those who believe that the Church should accept and support and bless monogamous covenant relationships between homosexual people and that they may be ordained.'[9]

Arguably, Resolution 1.10 went against the inherited instinct of Lambeth Conferences not to be directive or magisterial in their pronouncements. Thus, with respect to both its content and tenor, its impact was hugely polarising and the implications of it are still being experienced throughout the Communion today.

Intertextuality

The meanings of a range of texts circulating within the Anglican Communion in the nineteen-eighties and -nineties intersected and 'played off' one another. The texts that should be included for consideration are: Lambeth Resolution 10, 1978; the South to South Encounter Statement of 1997; the Kuala Lumpur Statement; Lambeth Resolution 1.10; subsection 3 of the Report on Human Sexuality—'Called to Full Humanity'—which accompanied Lambeth 1.10; and 'A Pastoral Statement to Lesbian and Gay Anglicans from Some Member Bishops of the Lambeth Conference' (August 5, 1998).

A detailed examination of these documents is beyond the scope of this article. Instead I will present a summary of their textual interplay. Firstly, it is clear that Lambeth 1978, Resolution 10, although affirming what might be called traditional teaching on marriage and sexuality, nevertheless recognised with humility deficiencies in the church's

---

8. 'Resolutions from 1998'.
9. 'Resolutions from 1998'.

understanding of the mystery of sexuality and displayed an openness to learning about homosexuality taking into account Scripture and the findings of scientific medical research.

> While we reaffirm heterosexuality as the scriptural norm, we recognise the need for deep and dispassionate study of the question of homosexuality, which would take seriously both the teaching of Scripture and the results of scientific and medical research. The Church, recognising the need for pastoral concern for those who are homosexual, encourages dialogue with them.

Here, although heterosexuality is affirmed as the scriptural norm, there are no condemnatory statements about homosexuality. This careful, pastorally sensitive, albeit partial, statement about human sexuality is deeply respectful of the personhood of those identifying as homosexual. It is a far cry from the tone of censoriousness and condemnation which pervades the Kuala Lumpur statement, to which we now turn our attention.

The Kuala Lumpur statement was promulgated at Lambeth 1998 as the product of the Second South to South Encounter (SSSE). It therefore claimed to be a document whose appearance at Lambeth was legitimated by its already having been supported by eighty bishops of the Anglican Communion. However, it was not in fact a product of the SSSE meeting. The Statement emerging from that meeting was called 'Trumpet II The Encounter Statement' which was largely concerned with the centrality of Scripture and which had one five-point paragraph on sexuality (Paragraph six).[10] There are two of the five clauses in this paragraph, which, in upholding marriage as the only and sacred expression of sexuality, can be read as implying disapprobation of homosexuality. There is only one explicit reference to homosexuality as follows:

---

10. Anglican Encounter in the South, 'Second Trumpet from 2nd Anglican Encounter in the South, Kuala Lumpur 10–15 February 1997' in Global South Anglican Online. <http://www.globalsouthanglican.org/index.php/blog/comments/second_trumpet_from_2nd_anglican_encounter_in_the_south_kuala_lumpur_10_15> Date accessed 23/8/14. (See Appendix 4).

> 6.5 We are aware of the scourge of sexual promiscuity, including homosexuality, rape and child abuse, in our time. These are pastoral problems, and we call on the Churches to seek to find a pastoral and scriptural way to bring healing and restoration to those who are affected by any of these harrowing tragedies.[11]

Although these words referring to homosexuality, which equate it with rape and child abuse, are undoubtedly of an offensive and condemnatory nature, it would appear that homosexuality *per se* is not the focus of the SSSE statement, as the subject is mentioned explicitly only once in the above sub-clause of section six, one of eight sections on Scripture. And there is no evidence to support the claim that The Kuala Lumpur Statement was formally adopted by the SSSE. It appears to have been created by a working committee of the Encounter gathering, after the meeting.[12] Certainly it was then circulated widely during 1997. The Standing Committee of the Province of South East Asia endorsed it 'unanimously', and there is correspondence from six bishops of the Episcopal Church in the US, who designate themselves 'orthodox believers' and bishops in 'continued communion with the Province of South-East Asia and other like-minded provinces.'[13] It is, however, difficult to track down the levels of acceptance of the document throughout churches in what has become known as the 'Global South', namely those in nations in the southern hemisphere which are characteristically, if not exclusively, poorer or developing nations.

Interperson(ality)

The above section on intertextuality may seem unimportant because the details of the process leading to the development of the Kuala Lumpur Statement have been overtaken by subsequent history. However what the above does indicate is that Lambeth 1998 became the focus of tensions within the Anglican Communion which may have

---

11. Simon Sarmiento, 'Lambeth Perspective—Two Kuala Lumpur Statements' in <http://justus.anglican.org/newsarchive/lambeth98/sjn16.html> Date accessed 23/8/14.2 .
12. 'Lambeth Perspective', 3.
13. <http://trustshare.com/25JUN97/JN97SOUN.htm> 2–3.

preceded any concern about homosexual practice. The introduction of the statement of the SSSE actually betrays the self-consciousness of a section of the global Anglican Church as a new force in a world where demographic change had concentrated more than 80% of Anglicans in eight developing nations,[14] no longer referred to as 'third-world' nations but as belonging to the 'two-thirds world'.[15] On another website supportive to the Global South and called 'Soundings from the South', it is suggested that 'Anglican reconstruction' was discussed at that meeting because of 'serious strain on the internal unity of the communion' and that this reconstruction might involve the giving up of provincial autonomy of churches across the communion in order to ensure 'mutual accountability and interdependence'.[16] It is clear that not only was the business of the SSSE not centrally concerned with sexuality, it was also contemplating schism before Lambeth 1.10 was ever thought of, thus belying any suggestion that homosexuality is the one pivotal cause of division in the Communion.[17] Indeed, the contribution to the situation of 'crisis' in the Anglican Communion, which on a simplistic reading appears to find its origins in Lambeth 1.10, may well have deeper roots in global tensions and grievances inherent in colonisation.

Intertextuality (second)

It is important now to turn to the text of Lambeth 1.10 itself, but to read it in the context of yet two others texts: Subsection 3 of the Report on Human Sexuality—'Called to Full Humanity'—which accompanied Lambeth 1.10; and 'A Pastoral Statement to Lesbian and Gay Anglicans from Some Member Bishops of the Lambeth Conference' (August 5, 1998).

It is interesting to consider the uncountenanced state of panic that emerged at Lambeth 1998. It soon became clear that strategies

---

14. <http://www.globalsouthanglican.org/index.php/blog/comments/second_trumpet_from_2nd_anglican_encounter_in_the_south_kuala_lumpur_10_15> Date accessed 23/8/14.
15. Kevin Ward, *A History of Global Anglicanism* (Cambridge, UK: Cambridge University Press, 2006), 308.
16. Ward, 309.
17. 'Soundings from the South' in <http://trushare.com/25JUN1997/JN97SOUN.htm> Date accessed 23/8/14, 3

that had worked at past conferences to discourage the forcing of resolutions in order to defuse heightened feelings were not going to be successful this time around. The result was acrimony and confusion around the Standing Orders, as rulings by the Conference Chairs allowed the 'passing over' of two of the motions promoting the Kuala Lumpur Statement. There was also great confusion about group processes so that there were questions about whether any resolution about sexuality would be put and whether the groups that met were to create resolutions, reports or statements about sexuality.[18]

It is fascinating to compare the recollections of two bishops (Archbishop Ndungane of South Africa and Bishop Colin Bazley of the Southern Cone) each of whom was involved in the preparation of materials on human sexuality.

Bishop Bazley alleges in a tone of clear anti-'liberal' polemic that Archbishop Njongonkulu Ndungane, the Primate of the Anglican Church of South Africa, tried to dissuade his (Bishop Bazley's) working group from seeking (or creating the words for) a resolution. He then alleged that the first resolution that his group did indeed submit to the chair was altered without the permission of the mover and seconder, and that this had to be redrawn to satisfy the working group. It was this redrawn resolution that formed the basis of Resolution 1.10.

The aforesaid Archbishop Njongonkulu Ndungane reflected that while being responsible for all sub-groups dealing with issues of human sexuality, he nevertheless chaired one particular working group of seventy bishops who were charged to prepare a report on human sexuality named 'Called to Full Humanity.' These bishops worked on this document for an estimated 800 'bishop hours', and it was this that formed the basis of Subsection 3 referred to in Resolution 1.10.[19]

On the day of the debate of Resolution 1.10 the atmosphere had deteriorated as tensions heightened. Gareth Jones reports thus,

---

18. 'Archbishops Argue Over Lambeth Resolution 1.10' in <http://www.virtueonline.org/archbishops-argue-over-lambeth-resolution-110> Date accessed 23/8/14.
19. 'Archbishops Argue Over Lambeth Resolution 1:10' in <http://www.virtueonline.org/archbishops-argue-over-lambeth-resolution-110>. Date accessed 23/8/14.

> Accounts of that day remain disturbing: the manipulation, the emotional blackmail, the desperate bargains struck the night before, the apparatchiks and their cell phones pacing the hall. Some have described the atmosphere as akin to a political rally.[20]

In the end Resolution 1.10 was affirmed by 526 bishops, opposed by 70, with 45 abstaining. Bishop Bazley commented on the fact that, as 750 were registered for the conference, over 100 bishops must have stayed away to avoid voting.

Kevin Ward notes that Resolution 1.10 departed from previous Lambeth practice which had been to work slowly for a consensus rather than force a resolution.[21] He also notes that this Lambeth resolution has come to be regarded as 'a touchstone of orthodoxy, a way of defining the limits of change and of curbing provincial autonomy'.[22] This too is a departure from the norm for resolutions or reports from Lambeth. Mark Chapman agrees, suggesting that this resolution 'in many quarters was regarded as a magisterial teaching of the Anglican Communion'.[23] He acknowledges that this is a significant departure from the understanding that the Conference's role is nothing more than an 'advisory' one, albeit with 'moral authority'.[24]

The most controversial part of Resolution 1.10 was its Clause (d), whose opening words are the most absolutising of the whole Resolution.

> (d) (This Conference) while rejecting homosexual practice as incompatible with Scripture, calls on all our people to minister pastorally and sensitively to all irrespective of sexual orientation and to condemn irrational fear of homosexuals, violence within marriage and any trivialisation and commercialisation of sex.[25]

---

20. Gareth Jones, '"Thy Grace Shall Always Prevent. . . .", in *Gays and the Future of Anglicanism*, edited by A Linzey and R Kirker (Hants, UK: John Hunt Publishing, 2005), 116.
21. Ward, 307.
22. Ward, 307.
23. Mark Chapman, *The Anglican Covenant: Unity and Diversity in the Anglican Communion: Responses to the Windsor Report* (London: Mowbray, 2008), 17.
24. Chapman, 17.
25. 'Resolutions from 1998', from The Anglican Communion Website

While it is interesting to consider this resolution in the light of a changed 'balance of power' at the 1998 conference, it is nevertheless important to ask why so many people identified with the liberal wing of the church (must have) voted for a resolution containing such an absolute denunciation and blanket rejection, to allow it to pass with such a large majority.

It is likely that the Bishops felt they had done all they could to come to a compromise. It is also possible they believed that by surrounding the Lambeth 1.10 (d) with other texts which attempted to lessen the hurt for gays and lesbians and their families and supporters, the Communion would maintain openness towards issues of sexuality and particularly homosexuality and that this would afford some consolation.

Within the resolution itself, there is a call to the church to commit to 'listen to the experience of homosexual persons.'[26] Richard Kirker writes that if only that process had begun, there would still be hope for a church which is in some senses a 'disappointment'.[27]

And the resolution has appended to it subsection 3 on Human Sexuality—'Called to Full Humanity.' This affirms human sexuality as a gift of a loving God, and characterises the fullest expression of sexuality as that between a man and woman in the 'covenant of marriage'. But this is coined in the words and tone of vocation not prescription. The report then goes on to affirm those who experience themselves as homosexual as full members of the body of Christ and strongly opposes homophobia. This document does not equate homosexuality or homosexual expression with sin. And what is arguably most remarkable about it, is that it expresses honestly that the bishops at Lambeth 'are not of one mind about homosexuality'. It then suggests the range of understandings of the bishops as stretching from those who believe homosexuality is a 'disorder', to those who would support the blessing of monogamous same-sex covenant relationships and the ordination of gays and lesbians.

<http://www.lambethconference.org/resolutions/1998/-1-10.cfm> Date accessed 23/8/14.
26. 'Resolutions from 1998', 1.
27. Richard Kirker, 'Afterword: Why Gays Refused to be Unchurched', in *Gays and the Future of Anglicanism*, 329.

The report then calls for unity. This is followed by a short Christian anthropology that states that homosexual persons share the humanity that God has called all into, and which it pleases God to transform constantly into a redeemed humanity. The intention here is pastoral, although the words (probably inadvertently) could be read to suggest that homosexual orientation has no reality.

> At the deepest ontological level therefore, there is no such thing as 'a' homosexual or 'a' heterosexual; therefore they are human beings, male and female, called to redeemed humanity in Christ...[28]

In the midst of these positive and supportive statements of openness and support, it is a great pity that the one statement that stands out and is remembered and referred to in discourse about Lambeth 1:10 is the rejecting section. But such is the negative power of absolutising and 'othering' language that sadly no additional text has been able to ameliorate for Christian gays and lesbians the hurtful impact of section (d).

Gareth Jones suggests that Lambeth 1.10 was the result of moral cowardice.

> Here was an opportunity to say unequivocally that judging people on their sexuality was wrong and immoral, and that being part of the body of Christ was not determined by the gender of one's partner. There was an opportunity to tell people who hated others for being gay that they were not Christians, and never would be Christians as long as such hatred was in their hearts. There was an opportunity to say once and for all that the bishops of the Church taught a gospel that transcended the bigotry that is evident in every town in England, and that they stood for God's passionate and inclusive embrace of everyone, irrespective of their sexuality. There was an opportunity in short, to speak of the gospel as truth rather than church expediency: to affirm love and reject hatred, once and for all.[29]

---

28. 'Resolutions from 1998', from The Anglican Communion Website <http://www.lambethconference.org/resolutions/1998/-1-10.cfm> Date accessed 23/8/14.
29. Gareth Jones, 'Thy Grace Shall Always Prevent...' in Andrew Linzey and Richard Kirker, *Gays and the Future of Anglicanism* (Hants, UK: John Hunt Publishing,

Interperson(ality) (second)

The last text to look at that is interdependent both historically and hermeneutically with Lambeth 1.10 is 'A Pastoral Statement to Lesbian and Gay Anglicans from Some Member Bishops of the Lambeth Conference'.[30] This statement was the initiative of the Rt Rev'd Ronald Haines, bishop of Washington. It was circulated on 5 August, 1998, and by November of that year had been signed by 188 bishops, nine of the signatories being primates.[31]

This document is both heartfelt and heartbreaking. It is clearly written (and signed) sincerely. It is deeply respectful:

> Within the limitations of this Conference, it has not been possible to hear adequately your voices, and we apologise for any sense of rejection that has occurred because of this reality. This letter is a sign of our commitment to listen to you and reflect with you theologically and spiritually on your lives and ministries. It is our deep concern that you not feel abandoned by your Church and that you know of our continued respect and support.[32]

It is also redolent of the brokenness of bishops who have striven to prioritise a notional 'unity' and now have to confront personally the people who have actually borne the cost. It is speculation on my part to suggest this document might also have been a vehicle for regret for institutional collusion (intentional or otherwise) and perhaps, for some, a recognition of personal lack of courage.

There is a slight suggestion of irony in Richard Kirker's assertion that,

> This (the passage in 1.10 about 'listening' to gay and lesbians people) may help to explain why the primates of North America and others whose provinces ordain lesbian and gay people can continue to assent to Lambeth 1.10, and how so

---

2005), 118.
30. See Appendix 5.
31. Ronald Haines *et al*, 'A pastoral statement to lesbian and gay Anglicans from some member bishops of the Lambeth Conference' <http://changingattitude.org.uk/resources/key-church-documents/pastoral-statement> Date accessed 23/8/14.
32. 'A pastoral statement to lesbian and gay Anglicans'.

many were able to vote for resolution 1.10 and, then, almost immediately sign the Pastoral Letter to Lesbian and Gay Anglicans which called for their 'full inclusion' in the life of the Communion.[33]

If I might introduce a little irony of my own (I am disposed towards this), Resolution 1.10 can be found in the account of resolutions of the Lambeth Conference following from Resolution 1.1 in upward progression. 1.10 with its absolute rejection of the validity of gay relationships is set in the proximate context of other resolutions that would make any socially concerned Anglican proud: 1.1: Affirmation and Adoption of the United Nations Universal Declaration of Human Rights; 1.2: Religious Freedom and Tolerance; 1.3: Justice for Women and Children; 1.4: A Faithful Response to Aggression and War; 1.5: Uprooted and Displaced Persons; 1.6: The Plight of the People in Northern and Western Uganda; 1.7: The Plight of the People of the Sudan, Rwanda and Burundi; 1.8: Creation; 1.9: Ecology; 1.11: Nuclear Weapons; 1.12: Calling for a Commission on Technology and Ethics; 1.13 Landmines etc . . .[34] These texts together promote human rights, religious freedom and tolerance, justice for women and children, and the sacredness of the environment; and condemn war and violence, ecological degradation, the production of nuclear weapons and the proliferation of landmines. There seems little consciousness of the irony that no apparent application of principles of human rights, freedom, tolerance and justice was present in the discourses of Lambeth 1998 around the issue of homosexuality. Interestingly, none of these socially-concerned resolutions is present in the memory of global Anglicanism today to anything like the same extent as is Lambeth 1.10.

In the wake of Lambeth 1.10: the response

In the years following Lambeth 1.10 there have been a range of responses to the resolution, the Lambeth experience and the ongoing

---

33. Kirker, 'Afterword', 329.
34. Simon Sarmiento, 'Lambeth Perspective- Two Kuala Lumpur Statements (6 Aug, 1988)' <http://justus.anglican.org/resources/Lambeth1998/LC98res/sec1.html> Date accessed 23/8/14.

discourse about sexuality. The responses which have been situated in the official discourse of the church and particularly in the *Windsor Report* and in proposals for an Anglican Covenant have skirted the moral debate about homosexuality, which nevertheless remains the 'elephant in the room'.

Intertextuality (third)

Conservative church writers were quick to support Resolution 1.10 and somehow to see the events leading to it as a 'campaign by liberal bishops for the ordination and marriage of practicing (*sic*) homosexuals' which 'suffered a striking setback'.[35] This is a strange interpretation as most liberal bishops at Lambeth 1998 were keen not to have a confrontation about homosexuality.

Liberal critics of 1.10 included Scottish Bishop Richard Holloway who said he was 'gutted, shafted and betrayed' but swore 'the struggle will go on'.[36] There were also some considered critiques of Lambeth from within Church of England clergy, such as that of Dr Jeffery John, who was rejected for the post of Bishop of Southwark on the grounds of being a homosexual, though celibate. Johns now claims that the church is 'the last refuge of prejudice'. He goes onto say that

> Same-sex monogamy seems to me to be spiritually indistinguishable from a marriage between two people who are unable to have children. The fact that fifty years on [after the decriminalisation of homosexuality] the Church is seen as enemy No 1 of gay people, is a disaster, both for our own morale and for our mission to the country. We have become the last refuge of prejudice.

Dr Johns continues,

> In the Church of England we readily bless the second and even third marriages of couples who never darken our doors, yet

---

35. Timothy C Morgan, Robert Nowell and David Virtue, 'Anglicans Deem Homosexuality "Incompatible with Scripture"', in *Christianity Today*, September 7, 1998, <http://www.christianitytoday.com/ct/1998/september7/8ta032.html?paging=off> Date accessed 23/8/14.
36. Morgan, *et al*, 'Anglicans Deem Homosexuality "Incompatible with Scripture"'.

we reject hundreds of our own faithful clergy and laypeople who long to bring their love and commitment before God and ask His blessing.[37]

The 'Church Society,' an Evangelical Church of England group, set about encouraging English parishes to pass resolutions at their Parochial Church Councils to endorse Resolution 1.10, and pressure their diocesan bishops into compliance.[38] On their website they denounced the 'revisionist theology' of those who support the acceptance and ordination of gays and lesbians 'practicing' (sic) or otherwise, and expressed their grievances against what they saw as an inheritance of colonial power in the global church, as well as the underrepresentation of evangelical clergy at the Church of England Synod (which, following the Lambeth Conference, prevented them getting through a Synod motion endorsing Lambeth 1.10).

Evidence that Lambeth 1998 and the covenantal process following on from it can lead to misunderstanding and overstatement is exemplified in an unpublished 'online' article by Paul Sullins of the Catholic University of America. Sullins says,

> Formerly an amalgam of Catholic and Protestant elements, Anglicanism today appears to be following the path of Protestant sectarianism...One may observe that Anglicanism is today instantiating the extended dynamics of this signal failure to maintain unity in the church, and is experiencing, albeit perhaps more belatedly than other denominations have done, the organizationally fissiparous tendencies of Protestantism.[39]

Undoubtedly concern for the unity of the Anglican Communion which became the dominating principle as an Anglican Covenant began to emerge in the wake of the *Windsor Report* of 2004, was already implicit in the Lambeth 1998 discussions of homosexuality.

---

37. Ruth Gledhill, 'Church is the last bastion of prejudice, says gay Priest', in *The Times* (London (UK)) 13 Mar 2012.
38. The Church Society, 'Resolution 1.10 of the Lambeth Conference of Bishops 1998'<http://churchsociety.org/issues_new/ethics/sexuality/Iss_ethics_sexuality_lambeth-1-10 > Date accessed 23/8/14.
39. Paul Sullins, 'Homosexuality and the Crisis of Anglicanism', <http://www.tandfonline.com/loi/rrel20> Date accessed 23/8/14.

In fact the two issues of church unity and homosexuality have become so intertwined that the former seems posited on postponing a resolution of the latter; and the latter is unlikely to be resolved in the political context of the former.

Interperson(ality) (third)

As the immediacy of responses to the Lambeth Conference of 1998 lapsed, the Church moved on into the aforementioned proposed Anglican Communion Covenantal phase which has been no less disputed than Resolution 1.10. Interestingly though, in that time there has been some considered work done to evaluate the 1998 Lambeth Conference decision and the various alliances it forged and dis-alliances it brought about, against the background issue of colonialism.

Ward suggests that the strong stand against homosexuality in some quarters of the Communion could be an indirect stance against colonialism and deep-seated resentment against what have been experienced as unequal power relations.[40] He points out the danger that post-colonialism can become a neo-colonialism as Anglican Churches in the southern hemisphere seek to build relationships with, or are sought out by, richer conservative churches particularly in the UK and US.[41] (Clearly the power to wield the overseas aid dollar is significant in the making and breaking of these alliances.)

Ward identifies the 'early twenty-first-century crisis of Anglicanism' in terms of 'a dominant "southern Anglicanism", in alliance with northern allies, imposing its rigorous version of Christian orthodoxy on the North.'[42]

---

40. Ward, 308–9.
41. Ward, 309.
42. Ward, 316. An article by Christopher Craig Brittain and Andrew McKinnon of the University of Aberdeen supports Ward's view. 'Homosexuality and the Construction of "Anglican Orthodoxy": The Symbolic Politics of the Anglican Communion', in *Sociology of Religion* 72.3 (2011): 351–73.

Conclusion: the legacy of Lambeth 1.10

The picture of the Anglican Communion post-Lambeth 1.10 that has emerged from this exploration is that the issue of homosexual 'practice' has become a symbol of unresolved grievances and resentments that preceded Lambeth 1998, and sixteen years later are unlikely to go away. For faithful gay and lesbian Anglicans in our churches who were directly 'smacked' by Lambeth 1.10, there has been no addressing of some crucial hermeneutical issues within the document itself.

The following questions still need to be struggled over: Can the Bible be said to function as a moral guidebook for complex twenty-first century issues? Why does it seem a simple matter to characterise 'the' biblical vocation as heterosexual monogamy or celibacy, and then to elevate this putative biblical vocation to the status of moral prescription? When will the church find ways to respect homosexuals not only as persons, but also as homosexual persons? When will come the 'full inclusion' of gays and lesbian members of our churches that they, their loved ones and their supporters long for?

Because the homosexuality issue, unfairly, and due to a coalescence of various historical circumstances, has become the symbolic representation of division in the Anglican Communion, (though clearly it is not its pivotal cause), it is unlikely to be resolved in the near future. Colonialism and global demographic change within the Communion find themselves playing out in new theological orthodoxy. In this context Lambeth 1.10 has become value-loaded: the touchstone of orthodoxy and the definition of the limits of change for the churches of the global south.

Clearly the failure of Anglicanism to resolve the issue of the full inclusion of gays and lesbians in the life of the church alienates those Christians from the Communion. Clearly, it is less than appealing to the section of our contemporary world, which is more and more embracing gay rights, that the church is unable to do so. Clearly the fact that the church is still divided and seems set to remain so for a long time, is discrediting and affects our credibility as a church and a denomination.

The absolutising and value-loaded document that is Lambeth Resolution 1.10, although 'strangling' any official changes in the Anglican Communion's response to gay and lesbian Christians is coming under strain within some national churches because of social changes. In 2005 England legalised same-sex civil unions, and in 2014 England, Wales and Scotland have legalised same-sex marriage.

The Pilling Report, which was finalised in November 2013 and thus preceded the 2014 government legislation confirmed that in principle, the Church of England is still committed to the belief that sex outside of a traditional marriage between a man and a woman is a sin. It confirmed that it might be appropriate for clergy to make pastoral response to a request for a prayer from a same-sex couple living in partnership (though later consideration by the Church of England bishops has ruled out the development of a liturgy of blessing for same-sex civil partnerships).[43] It is also tacitly understood within the Church of England that, if gay or lesbian clergy are part of a same-sex civil union, there is no barrier to ordination (even to the episcopate) if the clergy member assures their bishop that they are celibate.

These issues are unable for obvious reasons to be 'played out' within Anglican Communion forums. They clearly do not represent 'emancipation' for gay and lesbian Anglicans. They do however indicate perhaps a glimmer of hope that national churches might be allowed gradually to respond to societal changes with integrity, sensitivity and love.

Appendix 1

Lambeth 1998: Resolution 1.10

This Conference:

(a) commends to the Church the subsection report on human sexuality;

(b) In view of the teaching of Scripture, upholds faithfulness in marriage between a man and a woman in lifelong union, and believes that abstinence is right for those who are not called to marriage;

(c) recognises that there are among us persons who experience themselves as having a homosexual orientation. Many of these are

---

43. Belinda Goldsmith, 'Church of England rules out blessing for gay marriage' in <http://uk.reuters.com/article/2014/02/16/uk-britain-religion-marriage-idUKBREA1F0NE20140216> Date accessed 23/8/14.

members of the Church and are seeking the pastoral care, moral direction of the Church, and God's transforming power for the living of their lives and the ordering of relationships, and we commit ourselves to listen to the experience of homosexual people. We wish to assure them that they are loved by God and that all baptised, believing and faithful persons, regardless of sexual orientation, are full members of the Body of Christ;

(d) while rejecting homosexual practice as incompatible with Scripture, calls on all our people to minister pastorally and sensitively to all irrespective of sexual orientation and to condemn irrational fear of homosexuals, violence within marriage and any trivialisation and commercialisation of sex; (e) cannot advise the legitimizing or blessing of same-sex union, nor the ordination of those involved in same-gender unions;

(f) requests the Primates and the ACC to establish a means of monitoring the work done on the subject of human sexuality in the Communion and to share statements and resources among us;

(g) notes the significance of the Kuala Lumpur Statement and the concerns expressed in resolutions IV.26, V.1, V.10, V.23 and V.35 on the authority of Scripture in matters of marriage and sexuality and asks the Primates and the ACC to include them in their monitoring process.

Appendix 2

The Kuala Lumpur Statement

Statement on Human Sexuality (2nd Anglican Encounter in the South, 10 to 15 February 1997).

God's glory and loving purposes have been revealed in the creation of humankind (Rom 1:18; Gen 1:26, 27). Among the multiplicity of his gifts we are blessed with our sexuality.

1. Since the Fall (Gen. 3), life has been impaired and God's purposes spoilt. Our fallen state has affected every sphere of our being, which includes our sexuality. Sexual deviation has existed in every time and in most cultures. Jesus' teaching about lust in the Sermon on the Mount

(Matt 5:27–30) makes it clear that sexual sin is a real danger and temptation to us all.

2. It is, therefore, with an awareness of our own vulnerability to sexual sin that we express our profound concern about recent developments relating to Church discipline and moral teaching in some provinces in the North - specifically, the ordination of practicing homosexuals and the blessing of same-sex unions.
3. While acknowledging the complexities of our sexual nature and the strong drives it places within us, we are quite clear about God's will in this area which is expressed in the Bible.
4. The Scripture bears witness to God's will regarding human sexuality which is to be expressed only within the lifelong union of a man and a woman in (holy) matrimony.
5. The Holy Scriptures are clear in teaching that all sexual promiscuity is sin. We are convinced that this includes homosexual practices between men or women, as well as heterosexual relationships outside marriage.
6. We believe that the clear and unambiguous teaching of the Holy Scriptures about human sexuality is of great help to Christians as it provides clear boundaries.
7. We find no conflict between clear biblical teaching and sensitive pastoral care. Repentance precedes forgiveness and is part of the healing process. To heal spiritual wounds in God's name we need his wisdom and truth. We see this in the ministry of Jesus, for example his response to the adulterous women, ' . . . neither do I condemn you. Go and sin no more.' (Jn 8:11)
8. We encourage the Church to care for all those who are trapped in their sexual brokenness and to become the channel of Christ's compassion and love towards them. We wish to stand alongside and welcome them into a process of being whole and restored within our communities of faith. We would also affirm and resource those who exercise a pastoral ministry in this area.
9. We are deeply concerned that the setting aside of biblical teaching in such actions as the ordination of practicing homosexuals and the blessing of same-sex unions calls into question the authority of the Holy Scriptures. This is totally unacceptable to us.

10. This leads us to express concern about mutual accountability and interdependence within our Anglican Communion. As provinces and dioceses, we need to learn how to seek each other's counsel and wisdom in a spirit of true unity, and to reach a common mind before embarking on radical changes to Church discipline and moral teaching.
11. We live in a global village and must be more aware that the way we act in one part of the world can radically affect the mission and witness of the Church in another.

Appendix 3

Lambeth 1978: Resolution 10

Human relationships and sexuality

The Conference gladly affirms the Christian ideals of faithfulness and chastity both within and outside marriage, and calls Christians everywhere to seek the grace of Christ to live lives of holiness, discipline, and service in the world, and commends to the Church:

1. The need for theological study of sexuality in such a way as to relate sexual relationships to that wholeness of human life which itself derives from God, who is the source of masculinity and femininity.

2. The need for programmes at diocesan level, involving both men and women,

> (a) to promote the study and foster the ideals of Christian marriage and family life, and to examine the ways in which those who are unmarried may discover the fullness which God intends for all his children;
> (b) to provide ministries of compassionate support to those suffering from brokenness within marriage and family relationships;
> (c) to emphasise the sacredness of all human life, the moral issues inherent in clinical abortion, and the possible implications of genetic engineering.

3. While we reaffirm heterosexuality as the scriptural norm, we recognise the need for deep and dispassionate study of the question of homosexuality, which would take seriously both the teaching of Scripture and the results of scientific and medical research. The

Church, recognising the need for pastoral concern for those who are homosexual, encourages dialogue with them. (We note with satisfaction that such studies are now proceeding in some member Churches of the Anglican Communion.)

Appendix 4

Trumpet II The encounter statement

6. Scripture, the Family and Human Sexuality

Reflection on our Encounter theme has helped further deepen our resolve to uphold the authority of Scripture in every aspect life, including the family and human sexuality. Therefore:

6.1 We call on the Anglican Communion as a Church claiming to be rooted in the Apostolic and Reformed Tradition to remain true to Scripture as the final authority in all matters of faith and conduct;

6.2 We affirm that Scripture upholds marriage as a sacred relationship between a man and a woman, instituted in the creation ordinance;

6.3 We reaffirm that the only sexual expression, as taught by Scripture, which honours God and upholds human dignity is that between a man and a woman within the sacred ordinance of marriage;

6.4 We further believe that Scripture maintains that any other form of sexual expression is at once sinful, selfish, dishonouring to God and an abuse of human dignity;

6.5 We are aware of the scourge of sexual promiscuity, including homosexuality, rape and child abuse in our time. These are pastoral problems, and we call on the Churches to seek to find a pastoral and scriptural way to bring healing and restoration to those who are affected by any of these harrowing tragedies.

Appendix 5

A pastoral statement to lesbian and gay Anglicans from some member bishops of the Lambeth conference August 5, 1998

Dear sisters and brothers,

The Lambeth Conference has spent nearly three weeks deliberating issues of human sexuality, among many other vital issues facing our worldwide Communion. We have met in a climate of enormous diversity and have attempted both to articulate our views and listen carefully to those of others.

Within the limitations of this Conference, it has not been possible to hear adequately your voices, and we apologise for any sense of rejection that has occurred because of this reality. This letter is a sign of our commitment to listen to you and reflect with you theologically and spiritually on your lives and ministries. It is our deep concern that you not feel abandoned by your Church and that you know of our continued respect and support.

We pledge that we will continue to reflect, pray, and work for your full inclusion in the life of the Church. It is obvious that Communion-wide we are in great disagreement over what full inclusion would mean. We ourselves have varied views and admit, as the report of the Human Sexuality Sub-section of the Conference says, that there is much we do not yet understand. But we believe it is an imperative of the Gospel and our faith that we seek such understanding.

We call on the entire Communion to continue (and in many places, begin) prayerful, respectful conversation on the issue of homosexuality. We must not stop where this Conference has left off. You, our sisters and brothers in Christ, deserve a more thorough hearing than you received over the past three weeks. We will work to make that so.

Faithfully, as of November 26, 1998.

Total: 188 (including 9 Primates)

Chapter Eight
Innovation, Undecidability and Human Sexual Diversity: an Anglican Ecclesial Perspective

Stephen Pickard

Setting the scene: A recent Anglican episode

In 2003 the *Inter Anglican Theological and Doctrinal Commission* (IATDC), at the invitation of the Archbishop of Canterbury, wrote to the Primates of the Anglican Communion regarding 'the blessing of same-sex unions, the ordination of non-abstinent homosexual persons to the diaconate and priesthood and the appointment of such a person to the office of Bishop and related issues of Church order'.[1] The Commission posed the following questions to the Primates: How is the church to make right judgments in relation to such matters? What weight ought to be given to such innovations? How significant for Christian faith and practice is the Episcopal Church of the USA's decision to appoint a non-abstinent homosexual person to the office of Bishop within the Anglican Communion?[2]

These were the questions on the table so to speak a decade ago and the history of the Anglican Communion with respect to these and related matters has been highly conflictual and divisive. The context has changed significantly over the past decade. For example in July 2012 the General Convention of the Episcopal Church in the United States authorised provisional use of a rite for same-gendered couples, 'Witnessing and Blessing a Lifelong Covenant'. More generally, same-gendered marriage ('gay marriage') is now legal in a number of countries (including the United Kingdom and New Zealand) and

---

1. The letter can be found on the Anglican Communion website: <http://www.anglicancommunion.org/media/107645/IATDC-Inter-Anglican-Theological-and-Doctrinal-Commission.pdf>.
2. This was a reference to the decision of the Episcopal Church to consecrate the Rev'd Gene Robinson as a bishop.

is on the agenda of others. And while the matter of same-gender marriage remains controversial within the churches,[3] in Western societies there appears to be in the community, media and political life a growing acceptance of gay, lesbian and transgendered persons and gay marriage.

In 2003 the Commission noted that, 'If conservative voices are not to be driven out, it must be possible for an admonition about recent issues to do with homosexuality to be delivered, clearly argued from biblical sources . . . On the other hand, if progressive voices are not to be ignored, new knowledge has honestly to be confronted.' The Commission went on, 'Though there is still much uncertainty, it is evident that the existence in some people of homosexual inclinations has to be understood in a way not available to biblical writers. It has to be recognised as a cost of the engagement of the Gospel with the world, that Christians remain open to changing ideas with their attendant uncertainties and controversies.' The tensions in the now long-running discussion on human sexuality are evident in the above remarks of the Commission and, of course, are felt keenly and painfully among those 'who live the life'. How then are we to respond to such matters that have become the subject of an even more wide-ranging discussion and conflict both within the church and in wider society?

At the time that the Commission wrote to the Primates, the discussion turned not so much on the question of matters of sexuality *per se* but on how the church made judgments regarding controversial matters. In this respect, it was recognised that 'the Church, for good reasons, consistently renews its understanding of the substance of the faith, by which it lives and prays for the coming kingdom. As it does this, it has to wrestle with the fact that not all features of the life of the Church are of equal importance; some lie closer to the heart of the Gospel than others'. The Commission thus posed a question:

How crucial to Christian faith and communion is the blessing of same-sex unions, the ordination of non-abstinent homosexual

---

3. For arguments both supporting and opposing greater acceptance of and understanding of human sexual diversity see Ellen T Charry (editor), 'Same-Sex Relationships and the Nature of Marriage: A Theological Colloquy', in *Anglican Theological Review* 93.1 (2011). The literature of a biblical and pastoral kind on this matter is significant and increasing.

persons to the diaconate and priesthood and the appointment of such a person to the office of Bishop?

The Commission stated that if these matters were deemed of crucial import to the communion of the churches then they ought to be dealt with beyond the local level of the Communion's dispute-settling processes, that is, by those who have responsibility for the 'care of the churches' of the Communion. On the other hand if the matters of the above question were deemed not essential to Christian faith and communion, the Commission posed a second question:

How significant is the nature of the disputes regarding these matters?

With respect to this second question the Commission made a threefold distinction concerning a dispute, being:

> (a) *intense* for example that which generates a high degree of sustained and unresolved debate that threatens the unity of the Anglican Communion; or that requires urgent attention;
> (b) *extensive* for example, not confined to one section or region of the church; has significant implications for mission and ecumenical relations; has a wider social impact; and
> (c) *substantial* that is, concerning an actual issue, and not, for example, simply being generated by the media.

If a disputed matter was deemed of such significance with reference to its intensity, extent and substance that it makes for the disunity of the church, then the matter needed to be addressed at the higher levels of the Communion, that is, beyond the local diocese. The Commission's approach was an attempt to focus on the nature of ecclesial communion, authority and decision-making in the context of tensions and conflict.

Very soon after the above advice was offered the Commission's work was placed on hold for a number of years while the Windsor Group undertook some very specific work on the matter of the blessing of same-sex unions and ordination of non-abstinent homosexual persons to the offices of the church. This culminated in the *Windsor Report* which recommended—not without controversy —the adoption of an Anglican Covenant by the churches of the Communion. This was in effect a two-tier system of belonging in the Communion.[4] The fortunes of the proposed Covenant and its current 'limbo land' status offer, among other things, an insight into some of the challenges of an ecclesial kind concerning matters of great controversy and conflict in the church: problems to do with new developments and their reception; the nature and status of innovations; problems of undecideability and authority; challenges concerning the unity and catholicity of the church. I want to consider some of these issues because greater clarity regarding such matters might assist the people of the church to develop a sympathetic imagination with one another amidst the current conflicts and confusions about homosexuality in the church.[5]

An ecclesial lens

At the outset, I note the paucity—indeed neglect is not too strong a word—of discussion of an ecclesiological nature on matters to do with human sexual diversity in general;[6] specific issues concerning homosexuality in the church; and more recent issues conerning same-sex unions, gay marriage and ordination. Understandably there is quite a deal of scholarly work of a biblical and pastoral kind on such matters. And this draws significantly on modern understandings of human sexuality from the social sciences and anthropology. But what is the ecclesial status of such work? What are we to make of continuing disagreement, controversy and conflict among the people of God over such issues? There is of course no general consensus on such matters in the church considered as a whole and it would be naïve to expect this to be otherwise given the fact that there are other matters

---

4. The Report and Covenant proposals can be accessed via the Anglican Communion Website: <www.anglicancommunion.org>. The two-tier nature of the report arises from section four which contains provisions for signing up to the Covenant or not with the result that parts of the Anglican Communion of Churches (at provincial and diocesan levels) might not endorse the Covenant.
5. Martha Nussbaum examines the need for a sympathetic imagination in the multi-faith contexts of the West. See her book, *The New Religious Intolerance: Overcoming the Politics of Fear in an Anxious Age* (Cambridge, Mass: Belknap Press, 2012), 146.
6. The works of James Alison are an exception to this, for example, *Faith Beyond Resentment: Fragments Catholic and Gay* (London: Darton, Longman & Todd, 2001/New York: Crossroad, 2001); *On Being Liked* (London: Darton, Longman & Todd, 2003/New York: Crossroad, 2004).

of a doctrinal and ecclesial nature that have proved divisive within churches and between churches that go back over a millennium. Does that mean that the discipline of ecclesiology is an inherently contested domain of Christianity? I suspect so. If that is the case, then how might the people of God live together with contentious issues? How might Christians listen to and behave towards one another in a Christian manner?

I want to offer a brief sketch of some of the issues of an ecclesial kind that do not usually arise in debates and conflicts in the church about homosexuality, same-gender unions and gay marriage.[7] I am interested in finding more satisfactory and respectful ways of engaging in difficult and contested matters that resist quick solutions. In this sense, the discussion remains open regarding homosexuality and same-gender unions and gay marriage. Or rather my approach is an indirect one with the aim of facilitating more intelligent and thoughtful dialogue and dispute and at the same time exploring what ecclesiological wriggle room there might be for local variation regarding practices with respect to such matters. In pursuit of this goal, my discussion seeks to uncover some neglected aspects of the nature of controversy in the church and hopefully to lead us to a deeper appreciation of why we hold fiercely to very different positions on matters to do with homosexual practice. Personally I believe there is much more room for latitude on such matters than is presently recognised, but my purpose in this essay is to invite a more careful consideration of some critical foundational issues affecting the ecclesial significance of our disagreements, issues which are usually ignored or not given due weight.

In the discussion that follows I identify two themes—innovation and undecideability—that rarely appear as topics of conversation and/or inquiry in church controversy in relation to the matters being considered in this Chapter. Yet I want to argue that the church's processes for discusing and deciding on difficult and controversial issues that affect the life of the people of God requires a more mature and theologically informed appreciation of the reasons for disagreement;

---

7. This discussion is indebted to an earlier article 'Innovation and Undecidability: Some Implications for the Koinonia of the Anglican Church', in *Journal of Anglican Studies* 2.2 (2004): 87–105. I have developed the basic frame of that argument and applied it to the particular subject of this chapter.

reasons that encompass not only biblical, pastoral, emotional, ethical and moral considerations but also often overlooked concerns about the nature of innovation; the fact that some matters prove resistant to decision-making and consensus; that reception of new developments is a necessarily long process in which the outcomes are more often than not far more complex than might be anticipated. Moreover such innovations have to do with the identity and character of the church. The purpose of this essay is thus to offer a more informed and less naïve account of controversy in the church in relation to current matters concerning human sexual diversity.

Innovation

The matter of human sexual diversity and homosexuality in particular are hardly new matters requiring a response from the Christian church. Nor is the matter of same-gender unions or the ordination of practicing homosexual persons. What is new is the fact that the church is now wrestling with such matters in an open and public manner. In other words what is new is that certain matters, for a long time neither acknowledged or addressed, or simply taken for granted—in terms of what was accepted and acceptable—are now being discussed, and decisions are being made regarding the official acceptance of such practices signifying formal endorsement by the church. While the moral and ethical weight of such discussions is not lost on the church, what is often ignored or dismissed as secondary is the fact that such innovations as identified above are significant for the being of the church. My point is that ecclesiology is not a secondary matter for consideration once the biblical and pastoral concerns have been clarified. The question of human sexual diversity is primarily an ecclesial matter; it concerns our life together as the visible body of Christ even as it remains a deeply personal matter.[8] Whatever bibical, ethical, moral, legal, psychological or pastoral issues arise through examining human sexual diversity, homosexuality, same-gender unions, gay marriage and related matters, eventually they will have to

---

8. Rahner's communitarian emphasis for human personhood was succinctly stated some years ago when he pointed out that Christianity is intrinsically an ecclesial matter. See Karl Rahner, *Foundations of Christian Faith: An Introduction to the Idea of Christianity* (London: Darton, Longman & Todd, 1997), 345.

pass through the filter of the church and accordingly be re-calibrated in relation to the life of the body of Christ. The innovations lie in the area of ecclesiology; this is where the rubber hits the road, so to speak. But it oversimplies the matter when the ecclesiality of such controverted matters remains on the periphery of the discussion, functioning as an afterthought of a practical and often annoying kind.

So how do we approach innovations in the church? Innovation derives from the Latin *innovare*, meaning to renew or alter; essentially to bring in or introduce something new. Hence we may speak of novel practices and/or doctrines. It is a controversial feature of the life of the Christian church. Innovation is almost endemic to Christianity. The very nature of the gospel suggests that notions of surprise and novelty belong to the life of discipleship because they first inhere in the very character and action of God. The great surprising act of God in the incarnation and resurrection of the Messiah sets the pattern for the emergence of novelty at the heart of Christianity. However, as is well known, novelty and innovation have been, from the outset, highly contentious in the Christian community. The reasons are related to the need and importance felt by the early Christian movement to discover its own particular identity in relation to its roots in Judaism and also as it moved out into the Gentile/Roman world developing its particular apologetic.

The controversial nature of innovation covered both doctrine (for example Christology, Trinity) and practice (ethical domain, organisation/ecclesiastical matters). The controversies that occurred usually had important practical and pastoral dimensions. For example, the Apostle Paul attempted to adjudicate regarding meat offered to idols. (See for example, Romans 14 and 1 Cor 8 and 10). Evidently faith in Christ gave a certain flexibility regarding what was eaten which might not otherwise have been considered possible. Of course when we think of innovation and controversy in the early church, the Arian question usually comes to mind. This controversy is an early example of the church's attempt to preserve a theological innovation regarding the doctrine of God. This heresy involved a failure to appropriate the innovation of the incarnation into a doctrine of God founded on a traditional philosophical account of Divine simplicity.[9] Innovation

---

9. The Roman Catholic theologian, William Hill, suggests that the early centuries of trinitarian and christological reflection can be understood as an attempt to

concerning the doctrine of God was an implicate of the Christian community's fidelity to the gospel. Yet securing and maintaining this trinitarian innovation was a drawn-out and highly conflictual process that divided Christian communities, fractured relationships between church leaders and altered political alignments for generations. The Arian dispute endured for well over a century and had significant pastoral and practical effects of an ecclesial kind.[10]

With the emergence of a 'normative' doctrinal consensus, expressed through the great ecumenical creeds of the early church, the question of doctrinal innovation had the appearance of being settled. As a result, it was not unusual until relatively recent times for novelty to be considered as essentially antithetical to Christianity. Novelty was thus a feature of heretical movements and a sign of unfaithfulness to the established theological tradition. Tertullian encapsulated the ideal: 'Look, whatsoever was first, that is true; and, whatsoever is latter, that is corrupt.'[11] Constancy and fidelity to the past rather than innovation became the great virtue. The appeal of such an approach is security. But it is more imagined than real. The actual history of Christianity is one of constant eruption of new and surprising elements in the community of faith, in both beliefs and practices. What are we to make of the last 1500 years of faith and practice? What response might be possible to novel beliefs and practices? Historically, one option (in line with the appeal to antiquity) has been to charge those who proposed such new things with introducing novelty. The charge itself did not necessarily resolve the matter but it set the framework for the ensuing debate. This forced proponents of an alleged novelty

---

show how 'neither the Incarnation of the Word nor the real distinction of divine persons is in any way injurious to God's simplicity', 'Simplicity of God', in *New Catholic Encyclopedia of Theology* edited by State Catholic University of America (Washington: McGraw-Hill, 1967), volume 13, 230. Tom Torrance argues that the doctrine of the *homoousion* represented the Christian reinterpretation of Divine simplicity. See Torrance, *The Trinitarian Faith* (Edinburgh: T&T Clark, 1988), 132–35.

10. For example, excommunications, multiple bishops of single sees, interference of the emperors.
11. For this translation of Tertullian's *Prescription Against the Heretics*, see John Jewel, *Apologia Ecclesiae Anglicanae: An Apology of the Church of England* and *Defence of the Apology*, in *The Works of John Jewel*, edited by J Ayre, 4 volumes (Cambridge: The Parker Society, Cambridge University Press, 1848), volume 3, 106.

to defend their position as something entirely consistent and faithful to the gospel tradition.

Another option involved making a careful distinction between those parts of Christianity that could admit of change and novelty, and the parts that had to remain constant, not subject to change and innovation. Hence, the traditional Anglican appeal to fundamentals in the faith compared to non-fundamentals—and the associated concept of *adiaphora*[12] became important. Such a distinction was not unique to Anglicanism. (It is found, for example, in Lutheranism.) Indeed, it is an unavoidable distinction in Christianity even in the corpus of belief associated with Roman Catholicism.[13]

The historically contingent character of innovation is a matter that has become more clearly recognised in recent centuries. In his famous *Essay on the Development of Doctrine* of 1845[14] John Henry Newman offered an account of how some novelties (for example, the cult of the saints, purgatory) could be received as part of the 'homogenous evolution' of doctrine and practice. His seven tests for authenticity and legitimacy of doctrinal development as opposed to corruptions were not uncontroversial but they had the merit of providing a reasoned framework for disagreements in the church concerning the status of new developments.[15]

To move from disagreement to a more settled acceptance of an innovation could be a long and arduous process of reception in the church. In this respect, Newman drew attention to the importance of the wider faith community as an essential criterion for assessment and judgments regarding innovations in belief and practice. The *consensus fidelium* becomes fundamental in the process.[16] Here the critical

---

12. *Adiaphora*: things neither commanded nor forbidden.
13. This has been developed in the wake of Vatican II through the concept of the 'hierarchy of truths'. See 'The notion of "Hierarchy of Truths": An Ecumenical Interpretation', Joint Working Group between the Roman Catholic Church and the World Council of Churches, Sixth Report (Geneva: WCC, 1990), Appendix B, 38–46.
14. *An Essay on the Development of Christian Doctrine* (Hammondsworth, UK: Pelican, 1974).
15. Preservation of the essential idea; continuity of principles; power of assimilation of true developments; definite anticipation at an early period in the history of the idea to which development belongs; gradual and orderly logical sequence; an addition which is conservative of what has gone before it; chronic continuance.
16. Paul Avis has commented that '*Consensus fidelium* has now established itself

factor is the existence of communities of interpretation in which change occurs, is assessed and in turn transforms the ecclesia. Where such communities of interpretation lack coherence and adequate interconnectedness, the notion of *consensus fidelium* retracts into ecclesiastical enclaves.[17] This is a feature of the contemporary context of the churches and impacts upon dialogue, discussion and debate about controversial issues to do with human sexuality and, in particular at this time, about homosexuality, same-gender unions, gay marriage and related matters. Responses to such matters tend, now, to define an enclave. In the short term, this default may appear attractive for both advocates and opponents but in the longer term it only ensures loss of capacity to exercise a sympathetic ecclesial imagination for one another's position/perspective—indeed 'plight' might be appropriate.

What is the impact of the loss of coherence and increasing fragmentation of the church in response to conflicts concerning human sexuality? For example, it could mean that innovation in the area of sexuality becomes a much more unwieldy occurrence and subject to premature, top-down decisions at provincial, diocesan and parish levels. An alternative view would suggest that this new development is worthy of a measure of local freedom that would not be binding beyond the local or regional level. What capacity do the churches now have to decide in matters of innovation? Perhaps genuine wide-spread consensus is impossible. Maybe the churches are fated to perpetual division and controversy about human sexuality? Perhaps some things are essentially undecidable!

Undecidability

It may seem odd, and certainly it may seem to run counter to Christianity, to refer to some things as essentially undecidable in the

---

as one of the key concepts of contemporary ecclesiology'. See Avis, *Ecumenical Theology and the Elusiveness of Doctrine* (London: SPCK, 1986), 60.

17. Sociologist Bryan Turner refers to the evolution towards 'the enclave society' as a feature of society and organised religion. He states, that 'With the emergence of enclaves, ghettoes, diasporas and walled communities, society as a whole is divided and fragmented'. See Bryan Turner, *Religion and Modern Society: Citizenship, Secularisation and the State* (Cambridge: Cambridge University Press, 2011), preface, ix.

church. The fact is that churches have decided (eventually!) about a myriad of controversial matters and practices in the course of its history.[18] It is also the case that the decision-making processes have been exceedingly conflictual and the process of reception of new practices has been long and painful.

The relevance of the notion of undecidability to our discussion is fairly clear: while some sections of the church may firmly believe that a matter is decidable in a particular way (for example, acceptance of gay marriage), another section may firmly believe that the matter is decidable, in a manner directly at odds with the former approach. An example of this is the ordination of women to the priesthood and episcopate in the Anglican Church. This issue has been determined in some parts of the Anglican Communion in the affirmative; in other parts in the negative and in some parts it has simple not been addressed in any meaningful way. The result is that there is no consensus within the international Anglican community. Evidently the matter cannot be resolved simply by recourse to Scripture. This necessary and indispensable reference in conflict resolution nevertheless remains insufficient, by itself, to decide the matter.[19] Local context and cultures of interpretation add further layers of complexity. The status of the innovation remains essentially contested and undecidable, particularly if the *consensus fidelium* is important in the determination of decidability. Precisely because the ordination of women is a deeply ecclesial matter—as most innovations are in the church—the manner of resolution cannot be easily separated into prior questions regarding truth and secondary questions concerning ecclesiology. The two are interwoven and the honouring of this symbiotic relation between the truth of things and their ecclesial significance for the life of the body of Christ is integral to the decision-making process.[20] This also means that any decision regarding such matters is always provisional and limited in scope pending a wider

---

18. Slavery and apartheid are examples that come to mind. The date of Easter was a controversial issue in the early church.
19. Not least because there is no consensus about the nature of Scripture authority (for example, normative, informative, or participative).
20. In Anglicanism, at least, the truth we can carry together is the truth that binds us. We have never had the luxury of splitting questions of truth from the social/ecclesiological context—which is always more than mere context, but, rather, the essential condition for the emergence of truth.

consensus. This certainly gives more scope for experimentation than might normally be realised.

Inevitably, consensus as a thoroughly contingent process will be slow, often painful and will retain a certain provisionality. On this account, we can argue that undecidability is related to the eschatological nature of the church. The *ecclesia* is essentially an open system which admits of innovation but this very openness ensures that many matters cannot finally be decided upon, or, even if they are, a decision can never be more than provisional at best. In this context, living truthfully as the people of God and making difficult decisions as a church requires the cultivation of a certain habit of life, and an approach to holiness shaped by just practices, humble attitudes and patient forebearance with those with whom one disagrees. Yet recognition of this does not dispense with the need to make difficult decisions. A question remains: how then can the church make decisions regarding innovations when many of these innovations appear practically undecidable within the *ecclesia*, regardless of how theoretically decidable (abstracted from the *ecclesia*) we might like to think such matters are?[21] Perhaps, in this context, the issue of undecidability deserves further exploration.

The immediate horizon for the discussion of undecidability is the recent philosophical contribution of Jaques Derrida who introduces the notion to highlight the essential disjunction between preparing for a decision and the actual decisions we make.[22] There remains, argues Derrida, an elemental risk, requiring a leap of faith. No amount of prior preparation or consideration can provide a guarantee of a hoped-for or anticipated outcome. Derrida invokes Kierkegaard:

---

21. The fact that many secular states have made decisions regarding contentious issues on human sexuality raises questions about the work of the Spirit in the world (not just in the church). How ought the church attend to movements in society that seem to run counter to its own teaching and practices? This is a much-vexed issue. Put bluntly perhaps, the world is making a contribution to the church. Exactly what that contribution is, remains highly contested!
22. For a useful overview and discussion of Derrida's scattered references to undecidability in relation to moral decision, see John Llewelyn, 'Responsibility with Indecidability', in *Derrida: A Critical Reader*, edited by D Wood (Oxford: Blackwell, 1992), 72–96. I am grateful to Dr Winifred Lamb for references and discussion on this issue and a copy of an unpublished paper by Jack Reynolds, 'Habituality and Undecidability: A Comparison of Merleau-Ponty and Derrida on Decision' (Australian National University).

'The instant of decision is madness'.[23] The decision is thus 'something one can neither stabilise, establish, grasp [prendre], apprehend, or comprehend'. Derrida is reflecting at this moment on the sacrifice of Abraham.

Derrida has been criticised for the way in which his appeal to undecidability avoids the necessity of responsibility in the public sphere.[24] His 'philosophy of hesitation' seems to offer little assistance for facing the practical realities that confront us in our public, political and ethical life. This may or may not be the case, though it is hard to deny that the philosopher has identified something quite fundamental in relation to the contingent and provisional nature of the decisions we make. We are unsure of our footing; it is not always, if ever, clear what course of action to follow. More particularly, there exist significant disagreements in our communities regarding the ethical and moral dilemmas we face. Furthermore, the dilemmas actually look quite different depending upon our context. If we hesitate, we might not be lost; we might simply be bearing witness to our very humanity. Undecidability may be a given of our existence. If this is the case it points to the importance of a degree of faith and 'courtesy' being extended to others when we make our decisions.[25] From this perspective, undecidability points to the impossibility of control over outcomes and scenarios. Innovations generate a variety of responses and the hesitant society may be a natural outcome though of course not necessarily the wise or only possibility.

Undecidability may have deeper roots than Derrida supposes. Perhaps there are elements in the nature of Christianity itself—alluded to earlier—that generate a 'natural undecidability' about many matters of faith and morals. Here we are in the region of ontology and specifically that which has to do with the being and

---

23. Jacques Derrida, *The Gift of Death*, translated by D Wills (Chicago: University of Chicago Press, 1995), 65–6.
24. See the discussion by Simon Critchley, *The Ethics of Deconstruction: Derrida and Levinas* (Oxford: Blackwell, 1992).
25. 'Courtesy is the style of interaction with the "other". It is characterised by thoughtfulness, respect, graceful speech and attentive listening'. George Steiner refers to both the 'yearning' and 'fear' of the other necessarily involved in courtesy. For discussion see Graeme Garrett, 'Open Heaven/Closed Hearts: Theological Reflections on Ecumenical Relations', in *Faith and Freedom, A Journal of Christian Ethics* 6 (1998): 18.

action of God in the Christian tradition. As Richard Hooker said centuries ago, the essential character of the Divine might be identified as 'riches', 'abundance' and 'variety'.[26] When it comes to the Christian doctrine of God we have to do primarily with a theology of divine abundance—for example, creativity, grace, forgiveness—that is shaped and substantiated by the life of Jesus and the Spirit in the world and the people of God. The characteristic theme might be overflow or abundance.[27] Much could be said here but the basis is laid in the Christian tradition for recognition of God's plenitude that remains elusive, resistant to comprehension and endlessly dynamic.

Minimally, this points to a profound creativity that belongs to the Divine life. Few have explored this with such insight as the Orthodox philosophical theologian, Nikolai Berdyaev.[28] Such creativity is not necessarily to be equated with 'a cult of the future and of the new'. Rather 'true creativeness is concerned neither with the old nor with the new but with the eternal. A creative act directed upon the eternal may, however, have as its product and result something new, that is, something projected in time'.[29] Berdyaev notes that creativeness, always the work of the Holy Spirit, does not necessarily bring 'bliss and happiness', but has its own pain and suffering. His reflections are most apposite, for they draw attention to the necessary distinction between creativeness *per se* and the domain of human innovation. The relation is not one of direct correspondence; innovations as human deeds may simply instance the emergence of something new but without reference to 'the eternal'. The need for practical judgment and discernment arises precisely because human innovations and creativity does not directly and unambiguously bear witness to the creativeness that flows from divine abundance.

---

26. *Of the Laws of Ecclesiastical Polity* (London: Dent, Everyman edition, 1907 [1593]), 1.1.4.
27. See, for example, Col 1:19, 2:9 *pleroma*; Jn 10:10b *abundance*; 1 Tim 1:14 *superabundance*. In the same vein Ricoeur refers to Paul's letter to the Rom 5:15-21 as 'the "odd" *logic of superabundance*' wherein an 'ordinary "logic" collapses and the "logic" of God ... blows up'. See Paul Ricoeur, 'Biblical Hermeneutics', in *Semeia* 4 (1975): 138.
28. See *The Destiny of Man* (New York: Harper, 1960), chapter 3. Berdyaev develops a trinitarian approach to Christian ethics moving from the ethics of law to redemption to the ethics of creativeness, the last being the work of the eternal Spirit.
29. Berdyaev, *The Destiny of Man*, 151.

However, the foregoing discussion of the pleroma and creativity of the triune God in the world does provide a foundation for a more peculiarly Christian understanding of the roots and logic of undecidability. It has ontological weight. Diversity of understanding, multi-perspectives, and possibilities for new and surprising responses—all of these things may in fact belong to the character and ways of God in the world. Therefore, if the church finds new problems and moral and ethical dilemmas, it should not be surprised that this is accompanied by an inability to reach consensus. Nor should it be too quick to dismiss out of hand what appears as new and even confronting. It may be that the significant differences of interpretation of divine intentions and desires are precisely what one *should* anticipate in the Christian tradition. This also suggests that the church urgently requires an ethic of creativeness in order to practise wisdom and discernment in the practical affairs of its life and mission. And this applies to issues concerning human sexual divsersity as much as anything else today.

Of course, there are a variety of other reasons for undecidability connected to issues of cultural mores, social life, different value systems and human sin. However, it is not so easy to disentangle these and one wonders whether it is ever finally possible or appropriate. What it does mean is that our ecclesial life is often messier than we would wish. This is difficult for us to tolerate and we mostly desire clarity and sharpness of boundaries as a means to preserve and nurture personal and communal identity. Being vague and unsure are hardly virtues that we hear our leaders extol. However, when dealing with the difficult terrain of innovation in the church and the undecidables that seem to haunt us, we are in urgent need of resources that enable us to live with ambiguity and vagueness.[30] This is quite difficult given the strong views increasingly voiced these days by those of the Christian churches who call for sharper delineation

---

30. While we seek plain and clear texts, doctrines and ethical standards, perhaps the reality is quite different. We have difficulty dealing with the 'irremediable vagueness' and indefiniteness that seems to lurk within the plainest of statements and positions. Yet this very 'vagueness' provides the conditions for diverse and new interpretations and responses. Charles Peirce's (1839-1914) notion of 'irremediable vagueness' is interesting in this regard. See Peter Ochs, *Peirce, Pragmatism and the Logic of Scripture* (Cambridge: Cambridge University Press, 1998), 161-245.

of moral, ethical and doctrinal boundaries. The legislative impulse is powerful.

The dualisms that prevail in our present culture and church contexts are often quite uncompromising. We are often assailed by the either/or which leaves little room for positions that occupy what may be termed the excluded middle ground. This in-between place can appear unattractive to many. Voices from this place are significantly silent in many of the debates of the church today. The error of the 'undecided' is usually identified as their inconsistency. There are rigorists on both sides of the divide who share a common aversion to perceived inconsistency. Their systems and ideologies are tight, consistent and uncompromising. Those unsure and the vacillating display many of the opposite tendencies—divided minds, inconsistent positions, apparent double standards, essentially vague in their habitation of the fast receding middle ground. The virtue of the former position is internal coherence and consistency but the price is high. The system is notoriously incomplete and essentially closed.[31] There seem to be only two options. One can accept the either/or approach and argue for the rejection of all views save the preferred one. Alternatively one can reject the either/or approach and recognise the possibility of various perhaps unreconciled viewpoints. The merit of the latter is that it does give those who occupy the undecided place—the middle ground—the opportunity to be recognised and heard in the debates of our times.

This discussion of undecidability highlights a critical reason why issues surrounding human sexuality and in particular debate in the church about homosexuality, same-gender unions and more recently gay marriage have proved so divisive and intractable. Of course, there are other reasons for this state of affairs that often betray crass prejudice and fear and can be traced to psycho-sexual domains of individuals and indeed cultures. No amount of careful biblical scholarship, theological argument nor appeals for gentle and respectful pastoral sensitivity seem to dent such strong reactions.

---

31. If a system is internally consistent it will not be complete; if it aspires to completeness, it will invariably contain inconsistencies. This, in essence, is Thomas Torrance's interpretation of Godel's theorum in *Theological Science* (Oxford: Oxford University Press, 1969), 255. Torrance points to the inevitability of open systems containing 'undecidable or extrasystematic propositions'.

However, the matter of undecidability—for whatever reasons it emerges in any given context—cannot be quickly dismissed or ignored. As the foregoing discussion has highlighted, the fact of undecidability has traces back to fundamental issues about the nature of God, and is associated with the inevitable openness, richness and range of possibilities for interpreting and living our lives christianly. In other words undecidability and the puzzles it generates has a primary theological logic which grounds biblical, pastoral and psychological considerations. Undecidability appears to be a condition of our humanity as such.

While the fact of undecidability often appears in the Church as an annoying irritant that prevents us getting on with things, making decisions, and authorising new practices, the reality is . . . it is here to stay; it cannot be otherwise. From an ecclesial point of view, recognition of innovation and undecidability illuminates the essential contestability of so many issues that present for decision making and new practices in the church. We should not be surprised and nor should we attempt to ignore or bracket out such realities in the interests of more pressing pragmatic concerns. From an ecclesial point of view, the critical issue is how the body of Christ might continue—throughout its tensions and controversies about undecidable ethical and moral issues—as the one body bearing the fruits of the Spirit of Christ. What kind of koinonia is possible and how might that be sustained?

Human sexual diversity and Anglican polity

Article 20 of the Anglican Thirty-nine Articles of Religion states in part: 'The Church has power to decree Rites or Ceremonies, and authority in Controversies of Faith: And yet it is not lawful for the church to ordain anything that is contrary to God's Word written . . . '. This article points to a responsibility of the church to exercise appropriate authority in matters pertaining to faith. Innovations in teaching, doctrine and morals would seem to fall within the ambit of this article and thus issues concerning human sexual diversity are relevant. However, part of the problem today (quite different from the sixteenth and seventeenth centuries) is that Anglicanism is now an international communion spanning the globe. Structurally it is a complex organisation operating at a variety of levels of existence: Diocesan, national, provincial, international—a communion of churches bound by certain moral, theological and ecclesial ties that trace their heritage to common origins. When such a Communion of churches decides in matters of controversy what does this mean? Who is it that is deciding?

In matters of innovation affecting fundamental issues of church life—both in doctrine and morals—does it matter at what level or degree of organisational complexity the decisions are made? Is there a case for differentiating between different levels of ecclesial structure in relation to Article 20? For example, innovations that might be inherently difficult or impossible to reach consensus about at a meta-level might be resolvable (at least in a provisional sense) at a less complex level of organisation such as the diocese. This approach accords with the well-known principle of subsidiarity by which 'every "higher" authority ought to encourage the free use of God's gifts at "lower" levels'.[32] The implication is that a central authority should only undertake those tasks that cannot be effectively handled at more local levels. This principle points to a view of authority in the church that is focused in particular bodies at particular levels of national church life (vestry, diocesan synod, general synod). Recognition of this state of affairs was the basis for the international theological Commission's letter of advice to the Primates of the Anglican Communion discussed at the outset of this essay.

A multi-foci and layered approach is very different from a centralist approach to authority. Within the arena of international Anglicanism, the common mind of the Church is sought through discussion and consultation. The exercise of authority occurs in informal and powerful but indirect ways through, for example, allocations of funding and representation within committee structures. Whether it is possible and appropriate for the Anglican Communion to develop an international system for decision-making that is binding throughout the communion and thus able decisively to rule on innovations in a province(s) is a critical issue for contemporary Anglicanism. It was a matter considered in the *Windsor Report* and took shape in the proposed Anglican Covenant designed specifically in response

---

32. For a discussion of subsidiarity, see *The Virginia Report*, Anglican Consultative Council, 1997, chapter 4 and paragraph 4.10 for the present reference.

to controverted issues to do with homosexuality and same-gender unions in the church. For some, the attraction of a binding authority at the international level is that it appears to provide a simple solution to the problem of undecidability in the Anglican Communion. For others, such a solution would jeapodarise something fundamental to the Anglican idea of a fellowship of independent churches.

However, at present the situation is quite different. Within the Communion, it is possible to have a variety of innovations that remain undecided and undetermined at higher levels of the ecclesial organisation but are settled *for the moment* at lower levels of complexity. Their essential (practical) undecidability at one level does not preclude decisions made at other levels. Indeed, it could be argued that some matters, for example, practices concerning diverse human sexual expression, ought to be decided precisely in this way. Decisions at one level do not bind the church at higher levels of koinonia, nor do they provide grounds for rejection or fragmentation of the koinonia at lower levels. Conflicts between ecclesial bodies at similar levels across the globe would undoubtedly persist but this would simply witness to the fact that what might be regarded as essentially undecidable at a meta-level remains provisional, even at those levels at which decisions have already taken place.

This approach is attractive for a number of reasons. Firstly, it provides a way to ensure oneness with freedom, two basic ecclesiological principles of Anglicanism. This suggests a koinonia that has reached a level of ecclesial maturity. It does this by properly differentiating the church, refusing the tendency to create a monolithic entity which cannot respond to the very different cultural and religious contexts in which it exists. In other words, it enables the church to take account of the different communities of interpretation (ecclesial, theological and cultural) of text and tradition that coexist in the one worldwide Anglican Communion. And this can be observed in the different approaches to questions of homosexuality, same-gender unions and gay marriage in Anglicanism.

Secondly, it endorses a notion of the *consensus fidelium*, which is fundamentally of an emergent quality rather than a top-down process. In truth, consensus is usually occurring from both directions at once—a top-down causality and a bottom-up emergence. However, a ground-up emergent process allows time for decisions over contentious issues to be tested and practised at levels of church life that remain open to critique and revision, and at the same time able to contribute to a top-down wisdom. An expanding and deeper consensus is thus a product of time and requires a certain level of intensity in commitment by all parties to the koinonia of the church. Without that commitment the consensus cannot expand nor, importantly, can it be tested beyond the local. It remains an innovation within an ecclesiastical enclave that easily falls prey to a postmodern tribalism. This compromises both the catholicity and the apostolicity of the local church.

A ground-up approach to decision-making seems to be an Anglican way of living out the gospel. It is enshrined in the variety of canon law and constitutions of the Communion.[33] Yet such a decentralised approach to the exercise of authority cannot ignore the relationship between the level of decision-making and the nature of a proposed innovation. This requires some explanation, for it has an important bearing upon some of the disputes and conflicts in the Anglican Communion today. On the one hand, there are powerful voices that point to the importance of the independence of the provinces of the Anglican Communion. As autonomous provinces, each has a certain independence and responsibility to order its own ecclesial life in response to local needs for mission and witness. Thus, it is not unusual for there to be strong reaction over perceived interference from the wider communion over local decisions. Disagreements and controversies over issues of human sexuality discussed above are a case in point. However, there are a number of matters that significantly impact upon the claim of provincial autonomy. To open this area up is simple enough. For example, no province or local church—within an Anglican ecclesiology—would ever claim that it had the authority to introduce innovation in doctrine or practice that undermined the divinity of Christ. This is a matter that has the widest possible consensus in the Christian tradition and is not open to renegotiation—at least in a manner that denied the ecumenical consensus through time and space. Here the claim for provincial autonomy does not work, if it is meant in the sense of freedom to change something so substantive for Christianity. The example raises the importance of a fundamental relation that is singularly missing

---

33. See Norman Doe, *Canon Law in the Anglican Communion* (Oxford: Clarendon Press, 1998).

in much of our current debate regarding homosexuality, that is, the relation between the nature of the matter in dispute and the level of ecclesial life at which the dispute is handled and determined. We might posit a fundamental relation here: the level of dispute-settling in the church is correlated to the nature of the issue in dispute. This correlation is axiomatic for the life of the Anglican Communion and the appropriate exercise of authority.

This leads to a number of important issues regarding the way Anglicans deal with conflict and make decisions regarding innovations including decisions about matters to do with human sexual diversity touched on in this essay. First, a theological judgment is called for concerning the substantive matter in dispute. This is a fundamental activity of the church. It is a sign of a lack of wisdom to avoid or devalue the need for practical theological judgments in the church. For example, exactly how important is the issue of ordination of openly homosexual persons or the blessing of 'same-sex unions' by the church? Judgments here are notoriously difficult but nonetheless critical. The fact that the church is in dispute about these very matters is a sign that it finds consensus extremely difficult if not impossible. The matter may be practically undecidable. However, as argued above, this fact does not mean that the church can avoid making decisions about such matters but it does mean that (a) that there may be a degree of freedom for a local church to determine such matters and that (b) such decisions will nonetheless have a certain provisionality about them and be subject to critique and revision.

The difficulty of coming to a settled view about such matters often generates moves to avoid the theological task by opting for more immediate practical and politically expedient outcomes. This is understandable but it has the effect of closing down the numerous conversations and face-to-face engagements required to maintain the catholicity of the church. There are a number of possible scenarios. One familiar approach is to appeal to a traditional authoritarianism. This can occur either through appeal to a top-down leadership that decides on matters without recourse to a wider consensus (typical of some characteristic expressions of action in the Roman Church) or a not unfamiliar appeal in Protestantism to the so-called facts or plain sense of Scripture—though who exactly claims authority in this case is itself contested. Nonetheless, both these options lie within a top-down authoritative mode of action and both marginalise the theological task of the church. The other option appears under a more democratic model of polity and process where the top-down appeal cannot be invoked. This has more of the flavour of a bottom-up approach but the outcome is similar in principle to the former approach. A decision is made by majority—in lieu of the possibility of a consensus—which settles the matter politically. Again, the theological task is studiously avoided. In both approaches, the accent is on law and its processes and in both cases the substantive matter remains essentially undecided.

Now there may be a good dose of Anglican pragmatism here which recognises the impossibility of a theological consensus (at least in the short term) and seeks solutions to conflict and division through political and constitutional processes. But this only draws attention to the matter of who makes decisions in the church. In Anglicanism, the answer might be that such decisions are made at all levels of the Communion. This means that in contested and controversial matters, the more local the decision, the more provisional it is, the more open to revision, the more open to criticism from 'outside', and the more fragile the outcome. This at least is on the agenda from an ecclesiological point of view and it is curious how little in the disputes of the church in relation to its calling and mission, the specifically ecclesial significance of its life is recognised in the decisions it makes. Provincial autonomy ought not to operate without reference to the wider ecclesia in precisely those areas in which a wider consensus would be appropriate.

This discussion highlights the importance for the church of determining the nature of an innovation in faith and practice; primarily its significance in relation to the gospel. A guide in such matters is Article 6 of the Thirty-nine Articles, which confirms the principle of subsidiarity; decisions ought not to be taken at higher levels that are properly the province of lower levels. But it also calls attention to the importance within the principle of subsidiarity of the necessity of a theological judgment as to the nature of the subject matter in dispute in deciding at what level decisions ought to be made. A ground-up approach to decision-making, while the natural ecclesial default position in Anglicanism, does not have an absolute claim. This would be most un-Anglican! It is informed by and proceeds on the basis of a recognition of the correlation that obtains between the level of decision-making and the substantive matter under consideration. Determining the weight of any particular matter requires a theological judgment in relation to the nature of Christianity. This points to the crucial importance of an informed and discerning church in which theological education is not only vigorously encouraged but also seen as one of the critical means for the enrichment of the koinonia of the Church. Current debates and conflicts about human sexuality would benefit greatly from a more informed and dialogical approach to difficult areas of life.

On patience and trust: the long day's journey of the Saturday

It is clear from the above discussion that living as the body of Christ is not a simple state of affairs but a dynamic and restless reality. As a church our koinonia is fostered and nurtured by constant innovation— new responses in new contexts that seek faithfulness to the tradition and relevance in the modern world. In other words, innovation belongs to the dialectic of the gospel. Yet koinonia is also constantly threatened by innovation as many of our current controversies about human sexuality indicate. Innovation is thus inherently conflictual and unavoidable. For these reasons, innovations appear in the life of the church as undecidable yet at the same time they require determination (albeit provisional) for the sake of our discipleship in the world. This suggests that a key thing for Anglicanism might be how it engenders a Christian ethos in its life together and in the way it deals with controversy and difference. Perhaps there is a moral vision of the kind of ecclesial life we are called to be which provides the framework and substance of our shared life. It cannot be one that seeks simple default solutions through authoritarian top-down or democratic majority bottom-up approaches. It will necessarily be one that constantly struggles with allowing freedom and space for all yet strives to include others in decision-making about difficult issues.

This discussion also highlights the fact that koinonia requires patience and long-suffering. There are no short cuts through political or legal manoeuvres that do not also include a moral vision of what it means to be a communion that travels, in the words of George

Steiner, 'the long day's journey of the Saturday'.[34] Steiner's invocation of the Holy Saturday tradition at the end of his remarkable *tour de force* of the cultural and philosophical condition of the twentieth century provided a powerful reminder that we find ourselves in times of immense transition and uncertainty. In such a context of radical innovations and so many undecidables, a cultivated waiting that brims full of vigour, life and resilience becomes paramount. Steiner counsels neither the despair of Good Friday nor the triumphalism of Easter Sunday but rather a hopeful waiting. It is a theme picked up by Rowan Williams' meditations in the aftermath of 11 September 2001.[35] In closing, Williams reflects on Jesus' writing in the dust recorded in chapter 8 of John's Gospel. In this strange and enigmatic gesture Williams senses hope:

> He [Jesus] hesitates. He does not draw a line, offer an interpretation, tell the woman who she is and what her fate should be. He allows a moment, a longish moment, in which people are given time to see themselves differently precisely because he refuses to make the sense they want. When he lifts his head, there is both judgement and release. So this is writing in the dust because it tries to hold that moment for a little longer, long enough for some of our demons to walk away.[36]

An Anglican Communion that provides resources for the long day's journey of the Saturday will be a church that fosters a particular fruit of the Holy Spirit; the spiritual discipline of patience (Gal 5:22). It was Tertullian in the third century who considered disharmony and conflict in the *ecclesia*—the family of siblings—as a sign of impatience.[37] He saw the archetype of this present in the Cain and Abel story wherein Tertullian argued that 'Therefore, since he [Cain] could not commit murder unless he were angry, and could not be angry unless he were impatient, it is to be proved that what he did in

---

34. See George Steiner, *Real Presences* (Chicago: University of Chicago Press, 1989), 231–32.
35. Rowan Williams, *Writing in the Dust: Reflections on the 11 September and its Aftermath* (London: Hodder & Stoughton, 2002).
36. Williams, *Writing in the Dust*, 81.
37. Joseph Hellerman, *The Ancient Church as Family* (Minneapolis: Fortress Press, 2001), 173–82.

anger is to be referred to that which prompted the anger'.[38] Tertullian's exegesis may be unconvincing but his appeal to the sibling metaphor for the ecclesial family and his emphasis upon harmony and discord revolving around the theme of patience may yet prove instructive in our present context. It may be precisely through this ancient discipline that the church is enabled to find a richer and resilient koinonia informed by God's Spirit. And such patience is a double-edged sword. It is a patience enjoined on all; it is not a virtue required of some but not others. Enough has been said in this essay to suggest that there is room for a measure of local ecclesial variety of practices in the area of human sexuality towards which the wider ecclesia can be patient in order to allow time for the process of reception to be worked through.

A koinonia that emerges out of patient and hopeful waiting in troubled and unsettled times cannot be one that can be artificially manufactured and managed. It comes as gift but requires fundamental trust between people, and across boundaries of cultural and ethnic differences within, as much as beyond, the boundaries of contemporary Anglicanism. Trust is not an easy matter in our present situation, though the giving and receiving of trust is basic to shared lives and genuine community. Trust has a somewhat troubled history and is difficult to establish and sustain in modern society.[39] However, koinonia based on trust and associated mutual respect and recognition is precisely what the gospel invites us to embody in our life together. Such trust includes face-to-face relations, interdependent lives, openness to correction and willingness to offer and receive wisdom. The richest context for such trust and the critical referent in all our disputes is our common worship in which the ultimate Other, who addresses, re-forms and raises creation, can be encountered. Maximal openness to God in the eucharistic life is thus at the heart of all our engagements and the cauldron in which our innovations and undecidables have to be continually placed. In this context we do not capitulate to a happy pluralism nor can we take the road of a rigorist legalism. Rather we are enjoined to find our common life in Christ in the koinonia of the Spirit in the 'long day's journey of the Saturday'.

---

38. Hellerman, *The Ancient Church as Family*, 178.
39. For a discussion see Anthony Giddens, *The Consequences of Modernity* (Cambridge: Polity Press, 1990), especially chapter 3.

Chapter Nine
The Fear of Being Wrong: a Conversation with James Alison

Nikolai Blaskow

'Hypocrite lecteur, mon semblable, mon frère'[1]

Misplaced fear in turbulent times

The imperative of re-learning our values and thinking in the context of the seismic social changes that are taking place in the world has never been more important. Equally, never has it been more critical to embrace the subversion of our patterns of thinking implicit in the life, death and resurrection of Jesus. The Son of Man himself foresaw a day when people would faint from fear and foreboding of what is coming upon the world, as the powers of what has always been perceived as secure, are shaken (Matt 21:26). But he adds this reassurance, '[It is then] that they will see the Son of Man coming . . . with power and great glory. Now when these things begin to take place, stand up and raise your heads, because your redemption is drawing near' (Matt 21:27–28). Fear is a precursor to new life.

The writings of the theologian Fr James Alison, based on his reading of the theorist René Girard,[2] present us with a perspective that confronts head-on the fear that comes with the destabilizing effects of the upheavals that shake the very foundations of our social certainties. These upheavals, at least for the church, include the full acceptance of gays and lesbians. Alison's writings attempt to neutralise that fear

---

1. Charles Baudelaire, last line of 'Au lecteur', from *Les Fleurs du mal*, cited by James Alison in *Broken Hearts & New Creations: Intimations of a Great Reversal* (London: Darton, Longman & Todd, 2010), 163.
2. *Broken Hearts & New Creations*; *Undergoing God, dispatches from the scene of a break-in* (New York: Continuum, 2006); and *The Joy of Being Wrong, Original Sin Through Easter Eyes* (New York: Crossroad Publishing Company, 1998).

by placing it in the context of a New Creation, the consummation of all things in Jesus Christ.[3] The biblical, theological and theoretical scholarship from which Alison's insights are drawn (conservative, yet challenging), are combined with a powerfully argued praxis that might actually lead to a significant breakthrough in understanding and to a Christian life practice that is satisfying to all parties in the debate, even though a final ruling might still be beyond us at this time.

The sweep of Alison's ideas

Before launching into a detailed discussion of those insights and praxis, it is incumbent upon us, as best we can, to set out the overarching views of James Alison for one very important reason: that it will enable us to appreciate the full extent of their reach into anthropology, biblical studies and theology.

James Alison's assessment of what is actually going on around us is at first unremarkable. There is nothing but a salutary reminder, for example, in his observation that the upheaval that we are undergoing today is bigger than any of us, part of something much larger than just our own ecclesial patch. But then comes a series of counter-intuitive optics that combine to produce a revolutionary *skopos* of the subversion that Christ has brought into our troubled world.

1. The invisible God is at work in the seesaw of life effecting change, that was first made visible in the birth, life, passion and resurrection of Jesus and continues through the Holy Spirit, the Spirit of Christ, into the present day. The changes we are experiencing are essentially about 'the collapse of all differences'[4] because difference presupposes

---

3. In *Broken Hearts & New Creations*, in a chapter entitled 'The priestly pattern of Creation and a fraudulent reading of St Paul', Alison establishes a strong link between the old and the new creation (209–29). In essence, whenever the High Priest walks from inside the Holy of Holies, through the veil, it was always the sign of the Creator of all things coming into Creation to bless and renew it (217). The High Priest then goes to the Altar of Sacrifice to make the offering of the lamb and pronounces the Name (of God). Alison draws on Phil 2:5–11, 3:1–17, Heb 5:5–10, Jn 1:14, Lk 9:32 to makes a convincing case for Christ coming to renew the creation, being in the form—the *temunah*—of God and being both the priest and the offering at the same time.
4. *Broken Hearts & New Creations*, 46. Here Alison means the breakdown of the

wrath against those who are different, such as those identifying as gay. And Alison sees this removal of the significance of difference as far more radical than that which is occurring at times in the world—driven as it is by a desire for value that is measured in capitalistic terms, as a disguised form of wrath.[5]

2. Human history is poised for a great reversal, through Christian revelation, for a great shaking up of what is apparently *right* and what is apparently *wrong*, 'as we get used to how falsified our *reason* has been by our violence, how dangerous our "goodness" is and how long and slow is the path by which we enter our right minds'.[6] This has a particular reference to the gay question but the reversal of violent (and therefore fake) goodness is far larger in its implications.

3. This 'Great Reversal'[7] is opening up for us 'a dynamic of human self-critical learning which he [God] was and is making available to us so that we can enter both painfully and joyfully into what is true and live accordingly…we find ourselves being given the offer of having our hearts, formed as they are in ways of being together that are too small narrow and violent, broken open by One who longs for us to have a bigger, richer heart',[8] a process of 'undergoing' which Alison elsewhere refers to as the 'New Creation';

4. We are called by that same One in Jesus Christ, to extricate ourselves from this naturalised 'state of hostility' emanating from a fake goodness which we carry around in ourselves, the legacy of all 'the ambivalences, loves and hatreds of our culture'.[9] The exemplar is Jesus, who loved 'those who were, without knowing it … enemies of God, locked into a failed mind and self-destroying patterns of desire, which is to say all of us…'.[10]

---

walls of division cited by St Paul (Gal 3:28–29), including the adversity between male and female.
5. *Broken Hearts & New Creations*, 47-48.
6. *Broken Hearts & New Creations*, xi. Alison draws on Matthew 12:7 and Mark 7:13. He might well have added Mark 3:28–30, given the fear, exposited below, that our presumed and defended goodness might turn out to be evil.
7. The phrase 'Great Reversal' captures Alison's notion of the overturning and expansion that is the defining characteristic of the New Creation. See *Broken Hearts & New Creations*, x, xiii and the illustration from Isaiah 66:1–2.
8. *Broken Hearts & New Creations*, xi.
9. *Broken Hearts & New Creations*, 171.
10. *Broken Hearts & New Creations*, 171.

5. All of us who are followers of the Book (Christians, Muslims, Jews) must learn that 'our access to the power and glory of God involves us in a very radical process of a re-learning about everything that is, so that we can discover what really is when no longer prisoner to our failed imaginations and to our violence which holds truth captive';[11]

6. The criterion of God here is one that is expressed in Christ as 'a forgiving human victim' rather than 'our typical victim-creating' idol that we are so ready to worship and align with. Monotheism does not mean a god like the other gods, only bigger and more powerful; rather this God is of a totally different ilk.[12] If forgiveness (the interiority and mark of this God), rather than being right or wrong (the interiority and mark of other gods) determines our existence, the fear of being wrong evaporates.[13]

A number of large-framed implications flow from these insights.

7. Given the forward momentum of this 'New Creation', Christian gays and lesbians are invited to resist the temptation to run away from dialogue with those who oppose them in the church. Hurtful and oppressive as that opposition has been, the invitation is to recognise themselves as part of the 'New Creation', a gift to the church that calls it into its true self.

8. Equally, those opposed to welcoming Christian gays and lesbians into the church need honestly to engage with the medical and scientific truth that being gay or lesbian is a non-pathological, regularly occurring, minority variant in a human condition that is neither determined by nor co-extensive with an intrinsic heterosexual humanity.[14] Here, as part of the change that is the New Creation, a 'faith-inspired anthropology of learning',[15] allows that we have permission to learn something new and to proceed to its formation. This learning combines a looking at 'where we come from' and 'where we are going'—in large terms, a recognition on the one hand of

---

11. *Broken Hearts & New Creations*, 271.
12. *Broken Hearts & New Creations*, 269.
13. *Broken Hearts & New Creations*, 275.
14. *Broken Hearts & New Creations*, xi, 273.
15. *Broken Hearts & New Creations*, 275.

monotheism and Creation and, on the other hand, of the Kingdom of God calling us forward.[16]

9. '[I]f any of us, Christians, Muslims or Jews, are able to make a pilgrimage together in which gays and lesbian people are to take part, fully ourselves, and fully in need of the same graces as everybody else, it will only be because we will have undergone an arduous process of learning in which we will all have been stripped of different sorts of idolatry . . . Our unity will no longer be that inspired by the fierce guardians of idolatrous righteousness. Our bonds will have become those of the broken-hearted.'[17]

10. This learning involves being able to 'question any type of ganging up of all against one, of all against some obvious wrongdoer and say: "Stand back! Might it not after all be the living image of God rather then a corrupting and seditious evildoer, that we are seeking to kill?"'[18]

On this basis then, we can move to the fear of being wrong about sexuality that hampers not merely the quagmired intransigence of church regulations but even the means of thinking about sexuality in terms of God's New Creation.

The existential terror of being wrong: love, truth, and the fear of God

Alison's picture of conservative and liberal Christians, and gays and lesbians (all of us together) invited to God's party, is not only a beautiful one but one to which we should aspire. When we can be relaxed about God wanting *them* at the party then 'we really will be able to get over our hidden fear that he can't really want *us*'.[19]

It had struck me quite independently of Alison, that it is the fear of being wrong that lies at the heart of the furious (at times histrionic) debates about sexuality that prevail. Clearly it is a fear that can beset both sides. Alison is quite candid about that.

---

16. *Broken Hearts & New Creations*, 269.
17. *Broken Hearts & New Creations*, 279.
18. *Broken Hearts & New Creations*, 272.
19. "Human Sexuality . . . or Ecclesial Discourse?" A presentation for the Sarum Consultation on Human Sexuality and the Churches, 9–10 February, 2004: <http://www.jamesalison.co.uk/texts/eng14.html>.

> Here we are talking not, I think, about a level-headed discussion concerning what is good, but a deep existential terror that I might be being sucked into the service of evil, part of that terror being that I would not even know that evil was what I had become. Such moments of fear have assailed me every now and then since that time, compounded in my case by very deep fears of being evil which seems to be common to gay youths from religious backgrounds.[20]

In another place Alison speaks of the 'fear of God' in a way that indicates that such a fear derives from a gnawing uncertainty about where it will all lead in terms of final consequences:

> Whether we like it or not, we are in new territory, and the one thing that is certain is that, whatever we do, there will be consequences. None of us knows what the consequences will be...[21]

Identifying fear, it seems, is the easy part: the fear of delusion, the fear that comes with not knowing what the final verdict of God will be. Defining the legitimacy of that fear, is quite another.

However, if the start and finish of all thinking about God is love, and if that same perfect love is able to cast out fear, perhaps it is right there in God's occupied zone of grace and love in this imperfect world, that the hermeneutic which leads to reconciliation can guide us—the hermeneutic of truth.[22] Alison again:

> And here I return to the fear of God. I consider that it is very dangerous to say, 'One of us is wrong, and since it is certainly not I, it must be you.' Instead of this, I would like to delineate a position which would allow us to seek the truth together and in good faith.[23]

---

20. *Broken Hearts & New Creations*, 2–3.
21. *Undergoing God*, 144.
22. *Broken Hearts & New Creations*, 248. Alison speaks here of Jesus as 'the living, active hermeneutical principle who is the Creator, contemporary with and prior to the texts of Scripture'.
23. *Good-faith learning and the fear of God* This text originally appeared in a collection of essays 'Opening Up: Speaking Out in the Church'. <http://www.jamesalison.co.uk/texts/eng17.html>.

The question then becomes, how do we honour others who believe differently from ourselves? More importantly, how do we go beyond the emotionally fraught atmosphere in which these issues are discussed, to a calmer more mature plane that deals with realities and truths rather than just opinions whose assumptions have never really been tested? For, claiming a revealed knowledge is no guarantee of anything, if it is not founded on reality.

Fear, revelation and reality

Alison discounts the possibility that we must stick with revelation as the only source capable of objectivity and he does so by exposing the Vatican Congregation's repeated formulation on homosexuality as a case in point, albeit an instance of revelation that Protestants, and perhaps Anglicans, might find more difficult to engage: 'The homosexual inclination, though not itself a sin, constitutes a tendency towards behaviour that is intrinsically evil and must therefore be considered objectively disordered.'[24] The simple fact is, Alison contends, that there are hardly any Catholic bishops in the English-speaking world, if any at all, who haven't been socialised since their youth into a 'significantly but discretely, gay culture.'[25] So, what we are seeing here is a flat contradiction between doctrine and practice, in effect, a deeply entrenched fissure between what is claimed and what is real, such that emotional and sexual honesty, authenticity in fact, are well nigh impossible at an ecclesial hierarchical level, and must be pretty much left (sadly) to the laity:

> the laity had to work through the issues of conscience and start to develop other ways of talking, including facing up to the demands of honesty and authenticity which the struggle to recover the link between the objective and the subjective brings to the fore . . .[26]

---

24. *Undergoing God*, 149. The citation is from the Congregation for the Doctrine of the Faith, *Letter to the Bishops of the Catholic Church on the Pastoral Care of Homosexual Persons* (1986), §3.
25. "Human Sexuality . . . or Ecclesial Discourse?"
26. *Undergoing God*, 165. The particular document that Alison here works from is *Humanae Vitae*. Nevertheless, the general observation holds, as is evident from the various surveys on lay attitudes to homosexuality, both within the church

The clergy and official Roman Catholic Church teaching is out of touch with reality in so far as they refuse to acknowledge the latest scientific findings on sexual orientation. But further, by adopting a posture of exclusion, they are set on a collision course with the very teaching of love, grace and truthfulness that they claim to uphold.

This whole scenario of unreality played out by the church (and not only the Catholic Church, but all traditions including Protestant and Eastern Orthodox) when they oppose the inclusion of gays and lesbians, or dismiss their orientation as deviant and reprobate, raises serious questions not only about what truth, reality and revelation actually are and how the three interface. But also it raises the problem of what then happens to doctrinal pronouncements when they *don't* align with these three.

If we can posit that all of human life is capable of being attuned to a reality upon which we can all agree; if we can reasonably argue that at the heart of moral reality, goodness (grace) and love are to be found; and if we can go further and propose that the identification of the real with the good is made known to us by the fact that it is through the exercise of virtues (like courage and integrity) that we come closer to reality, then is it not also true that what is at issue here is the possibility that one's life might be lived in illusion, that one might fail to be properly oriented towards the real with the pain that this state of mind entails? And this would lie precisely in that lack of accord with reality, goodness and love and a deficit of courage and integrity-in-relation. And if that may be the case, then our moral perception or vision is necessarily distorted, and deep responsiveness to the reality of other people (never mind gays) is impossible.[27]

Such probing reflection is in fact a response to the God of the Old and New Testament who invites us to come 'and reason together'.[28] A God who, in Jewish sacred text, opens things up for exploration and negotiation in the guise of *midrash*, who in the very way in which

---

and in society at large.

27. I am indebted here to Sarah Bachelard's lengthy discussion of 'moral transcendence' in dialogue with the ideas of the philosophers Raimond Gaita, and Iris Murdoch, in her *Resurrection and Moral Imagination* (Farnham, Eng: Ashgate, 2014); in particular, see 4, 11, 13–14, 31, 70 93–103, 119–121.
28. 'Come now, let us argue it out, says the Lord: though your sins are like scarlet, they shall be like snow; though they are red like crimson, they shall become like wool' (Is 1:18).

the canon of Christian sacred text has been framed (by constructive debate and scholarly discussion), provokes us to hard questioning, encourages us to examine our assumptions, causes us to test our conclusions and so to be honest and brave enough to admit any inconsistencies of argument that might be exposed through such a rigorous process—and this on the basis of a prior relationship established by invitation.

Being close to God, far from a comfortable feeling of certitude,[29] is more often like the life of a prophet filled with discomfort, anguish and an agonised wrestling with truth.[30] This is the painful companion of the joy of the 'Great Reversal'.[31] Indeed, the mark of true faith is the conviction that God calls people to a confession arising from being addressed and a vocation of self-criticism[32] from which revelation arises.[33] To this, I turn.

---

29. The cultural Jewish writer Lesley Hazelton was writing a biography of Muhammad *The First Muslim* when she was struck by something: the night he received the revelation of the Koran, according to early accounts, his first reaction was doubt, awe, even fear. This experience became the bedrock of his belief. Hazelton calls for a new appreciation of doubt and questioning as the foundation of faith—and an end to destructive fundamentalism of all kinds. See <http://www.ted.com/talks/lesley_hazleton>.
30. Sarah Bachelard in *Experiencing God in a Time of Crisis* (Miami, FL: Convivium Press, 2012), 39.
31. *Broken Hearts & New Creations*, xi.
32. *Experiencing God in a Time of Crisis*, 21–22. Such self-criticism is so often missing in ideological and dogmatic and doctrinal discourse, where dialogue and discussion are closed down, an intransigence often marked by an intellectualism unchallenged by experience. Bachelard in *Resurrection and the Moral Imagination*, 35–39, contends (my paraphrase) that witness and confession arise out of an experience that is anchored in reality and therefore in truth.
33. This 'revelation' is understood in a very specialised sense. Bachelard speaks of: 'What might open up in our moral lives, as individuals and communities, if we were to hold ourselves accountable for deepening our perception of what is before us, being transformed through our relationship to the living Christ so as to be capable of being present to and revealing reality more truthfully? This may be an experience of acute moral vulnerability, since the reality of God's life tends to shake up the false security of our lives and the concepts through which we understand them. Yet this may turn out to be the deepest contribution of an ethic of resurrection to the life of the world.' *Resurrection and the Moral Imagination*, 120–21.

Negotiating the fear of being wrong within ourselves and with one another in the light of truth

What is called for, then, is something far more challenging than a straight ecclesial or biblical or intellectual discussion. Alison models what this looks like, sounds like: admonishing himself to undo his own paranoia, his fear of his own fundamentalism, his own dictatorial tendencies, all of which, he admits, is terribly easy to project onto the Vatican. This is such good advice—for all gays and lesbians, and those who speak on their behalf (irrespective of their stance on the nature and authority of scripture and revelation) to prevent the projection of our sense of vulnerability onto others or at least expose it to view, as Alison does.

Alison's admonition that we stay close to those with whom we disagree is a timely one, when so many are either closing themselves off or shutting conversations down. For if such sound counsel is ignored, we will find ourselves, Alison notes, condemned to something unimaginably horrible: the mutually incorrigible umbrage of mirror-image sects.[34] In consequence, there is a very serious obligation on *all of us* to make it easier not more difficult for those we consider to have got it wrong.

> ...this means that a considerable part of the theological effort which I think is called for is the courtesy of constructing bridges for the benefit of others, being vulnerable on their turf, exercising magnanimity towards foes. It is for this reason that I think that the patient work is not engaging in debates in the here and now, since the agonistic structure of such things almost invariably seduces us into the need to win, but slowly trying to construct ways of talking into which people will be able to relax when they tire of the current fights.[35]

A footnote to an introduction to a Bible Study on Jude as part of the Resources for the Lambeth Conference of the Anglican Communion underlines the urgency of this approach: 'Sadly, much of the attention and anger is over beliefs and policies concerning homosexuals. The root problem of biblical interpretation and authority is less commonly

---

34. "Human Sexuality . . . or Ecclesial Discourse?"
35. "Human Sexuality . . . or Ecclesial Discourse?"

discussed. Yet it is through discussion of these matters that resolution will finally occur.'[36] That reflection goes to the heart of the matter. And here the hermeneutic suggested by Alison is most helpful. He establishes strong links between how we might negotiate truth, deal with fear and understand the so-called 'wrath of God'.

For example, Alison's terminology for the process of 'overcoming fear and undergoing God' is compelling: he calls it 'navigating wrath'. For the fear of wrath, which arises from the double-edged images of the Book of Revelation, can only be understood in the light of God's final revelation in the risen Christ. Says Alison:

> Jesus reveals that there is no wrath in God, but the effect and the shape of his coming opens up the possibilities of wrath for those who don't receive him, in ways which could not be imagined. The workings of 'wrath' become a measurable, detectable anthropological reality as the innocent lamb exposes to us our own responsibility for what we, deceived by the hallucinations of our own mob behaviour, thought of as the anger of a divinity.[37]

The upheavals in our time, the collapse of differences,[38] the shaking up of what we think is right and wrong, the breaking open of narrow channels, the serious calling into question of culture and ecclesial culture in particular (both interfaith and Christian faith) are, undoubtedly as Alison's theology sees them, either to be eschewed in fear or embraced in the confidence that love endows. If God is doing something new among us, and beyond us, and these are the long-foretold birth-pangs of a new creation, then the reconciliation of all things and our role in it, is indeed the 'arduous process of learning'

---

36. Compare <htpp://www.religioustolerance.org/hom_ang.html>—the original reference, alas, is not to be found; however, this is very close to the original text—it reads: 'Sadly, much of the attention and anger is over beliefs and policies concerning homosexuals. The root problem of biblical interpretation and authority is less commonly discussed. Yet it is through discussion of these matters that resolution will finally occur.'
37. Alison, 'Wrath and the gay question: on not being afraid, and its ecclesial shape' at <www.jamesalison.co.uk/texts/eng32.html>. Last accessed May 2015.
38. I think here, apart from the Galatian reference previously discussed (see above), Alison underlines the fact that it is the denial of our 'sameness' under the guise of 'difference' that causes so much grief.

(dare I say it, also unlearning!). Part of the pain of this 'Great Reversal' will be humbly recognising one another as 'friends of God' in the kingdom of grace that is coming and has come among us.[39]

Like Peter, we may feel that what we have been asked to 'consume' is unclean but the call to reconciliation is unmistakable.[40] Consider too how traumatizing Peter's visit under Cornelius' roof would have been until the gift of the Spirit was given to those hitherto considered outside the pale of God's kindness.[41] Just imagine how different the Christian church would be today if Peter had disobeyed the call in his day, and the church had not resolved its differences about what was permissible and non-permissible in terms of Jewish practice, and who was 'in' and who was 'out'. Yet, stubbornly, the stumbling block of the fear of being wrong remains. Alison defines it with clinical precision:

> [There are] [t]hose [who are] moved by the *fear of God* fear[ful] lest our own irresponsibility, our own hardness of heart and defect of vision perhaps [might] carry . . . us down a route that is too easy, one that is ever more free of voices which question and challenge us . . .[42]

This insight raises more questions. How much of this so-called 'fear of God' is of our own making? Is the consensus that we reach only to be achieved by quashing the voices that would challenge us? When is the process of questioning and challenging just a case of stubborn obstructionism and hardness of heart? Is it perhaps that what we really fear is the new freedom that God offers us? And finally, how will we know, *can* we know, that it is Jesus calling the church to a

---

39. See Janet Gaden, '"Friends of God and Prophets", in *AIDS: The Church as Enemy and Friend*, edited by AH Cadwallader (Blackburn: CollinsDove, 1992), 137–45.
40. I like Eugene Peterson's paraphrase in *The Message*: 'He saw the skies open up. Something that looked like a huge blanket lowered by ropes at its four corners settled on the ground. Every kind of animal and reptile and bird you could think of was on it. Then a voice came: "Go to it, Peter—kill and eat." Peter said, "Oh, no, Lord. I've never so much as tasted food that was not kosher." The voice came a second time: "If God says it's okay, it's okay. This happened three times, and then the blanket was pulled back up into the skies.' Acts 10: 9–16.
41. Acts 10:28 (*NRSV*) actually has St Peter saying: 'You yourselves know that it is unlawful for a Jew to associate with or to visit a Gentile; but *God has shown me that I should not call anyone profane or unclean.*' (My emphasis).
42. *Undergoing God*, 141.

radical revisionist direction, and not a perilous falling into heresy and perdition?

These questions are not lightly to be dismissed.

Jesus the great revisionist subverts traditional notions of sin and judgment

Alison's hermeneutic is instructive. Jesus is seen as the great revisionist radically redefining our notions of sin and judgment. Nowhere is this more dramatically portrayed than in the Johannine story or meditation on the healing of the man born blind.[43] In John 9 we are treated to a profound insight into what sin actually is and how judgment will, and must, be enacted. The story powerfully calls into question our assumptions about original sin, our understanding of purity and impurity. Alison sums it up this way:

> In this story then we watch a revolution in the understanding of sin, a revolution that takes place around the person of Jesus but is actually worked out in the life of someone else. The structure of the story is the same as it is to be found time and time again in John: that of an expulsion, or proto-lynching, one of the many that lead up to the definitive expulsion of the crucifixion, which is also the definitive remedy for all human order based on expulsion.[44]

Sin thus is no longer seen as some kind of defect (as it is presented at the beginning of the story) but rather it *is* the act of expulsion itself. That is the real blindness, one not only 'present in those who exclude, but actually grows and intensifies during the act of exclusion'. The final comment, 'For judgment I came into the world, that those who do not see may see, and that those who see may become blind', is in fact Jesus' assessment of the whole story.[45]

Jesus' revisionism, I think, has profound implications for how the church currently practises the exclusion of gays and lesbians from its community on the basis of the perception of defect and sinfulness.

---

43. I lean heavily here on Alison's account in his *The Joy of Being Wrong, Original Sin Through Easter Eyes* (New York: Crossroad Publishing Company, 1998), 120–25.
44. *The Joy of Being Wrong*, 121.
45. *The Joy of Being Wrong*, 121.

That very act of exclusion, on such a reading from John 9, is itself the sin and the defect.

If it is now scientifically established that the predisposition for same-sex attraction and love is a given for a small percentage of the population, just as left-handedness is, what are we trying to prove by hounding and condemning those who have been handed this genetic lottery, even if it is also demonstrable that *some* choose their sexual expression? By attributing their state to some original sin, are we actually condemning ourselves? For if the sin of the world is understood in this story as the work of 'your father the devil' who 'was a murderer from the beginning' (Jn 8:44),[46] what we see here is a complete recasting of our notion of real sin as to be found *not* in the breaking of the law so much (which is forgiven and healed) but in the mechanism of expulsion.

Just as Jesus here 'subverts the notion of judgment from within, so also the notion of sin is subverted from within'. He doesn't abolish the concept of sin or simply define it much more strongly than before',[47] he actually blasts apart our whole understanding of the way God judges in general. Alison summarises it this way:

> ... when Jesus speaks, at the end, about judgment it is clear that he is not concerned with a particular local incident, but about a discernment relating to the whole world (*kosmos*). Here we have a highly subtle teaching about the whole world being blind from birth, from the beginning, and about Jesus, the light of the world coming to bring sight to the world, being rejected precisely by those who, though blind, claimed to be able to see. All humans are blind, but where this blindness is compounded by active participation in the mechanisms of exclusion pretending to sight, this blindness is culpable.[48]

When we obsess about how gays and lesbians are 'defective', when we actively and cruelly exclude gay and lesbian couples who are in faithful

---

46. This text is cited by Alison with the comment that this is part of the proto-lynching that immediately precedes the story of the man blind from birth (*The Joy of Being Wrong*, 122n10).
47. *The Joy of Being Wrong*, 122.
48. *The Joy of Being Wrong*, 123.

relationships from Christian community, from active participation in the Eucharist, we might in reality be condemning and excluding ourselves: 'Being wrong can be forgiven: it is insisting on being right that confirms our being bound in original murderous sin.'[49]

How the elaborate conjuring trick to keep the delusion of difference alive sustains the fear

In probably the most insightful chapter of all, entitled 'Wrath and the gay question: on not being afraid, and its ecclesial shape',[50] Alison dissects the nature of fear in the guise of the 'wrath of God' and how this plays out in the social sphere, in literature and in Biblical hermeneutics. Alison considers that understanding this may help us find ways forward in the current debate that is so enmeshed with issues of 'living with difference' or 'tolerance and diversity'.

The main question to be addressed here is, how do straight, let alone gay and lesbian Christians, come to terms with the notion of God's anger that, at face value, is intrinsically intolerant of 'difference'?

First, through the portrayal of Shylock the Jew in Shakespeare's *Merchant of Venice*, Alison establishes the premise that it's not about difference so much as 'sameness'. Effectively, what Shakespeare puts in the mouth of Shylock is the simple mantra that 'I am the same as you, exactly the same as you', and is instantly and constantly ignored by all the other characters for whom his difference is very important.[51] And this is the reality: every single attribute which they despise in Shylock, 'is a dominant feature of their own lives'. And the other reality is that their insistence on 'difference' is part of an elaborate conjuring trick to keep the delusion of difference alive.[52]

Second, Alison exposes fundamentalism of all kinds, be it Christian, Jewish, Muslim, Hindu, Marxist or secularist for what it is: in the way that it allows, through partial self-selection, to see themselves as secret 'insiders', 'with a direct line in to What's Really Going On'.[53] While we might have predicted that, not so obvious

---

49. *The Joy of Being Wrong*, 125.
50. *Broken Hearts & New Creations*, 34–53.
51. *Broken Hearts & New Creations*, 36.
52. *Broken Hearts & New Creations*, 37.
53. *Broken Hearts & New Creations*, 38.

is the reflection that for the fundamentalist the violence is always associated with God: '. . . directly or through those charged with interpreting 'His' (and it usually is *His*) message. In fact without the violence there would be no sign of God's activity in the world, which effectively means there would be no God.'[54] Alison's irony is not lost on us. It alerts us to something insidious and deeply entrenched in the human psyche that projects its fear and violence onto a god that it can appropriate. For God to be in the world, according to this line of argument, he must be a god who destroys.[55]

The wrath of the Lamb which brings peace and a critical choice in the midst of our fears

Alison's attempt to 'rescue the notion of wrath' may be seen by some as molding the word 'wrath' to his own specifications. For Alison the 'wrath of the lamb' is the window through which we see what that wrath actually is:

> I love the image of the 'wrath of the lamb'. There is the lamb, permanently and forever standing alive, as one slain on the altar in heaven, his blood given to us as we accept this purely peaceful self-giving and allow ourselves to be moved out of the whole 'old creation' dominated by wrath . . . [He] offers people a choice, one which most of us do not want to make: follow the lamb, and so become liable to be treated as the lamb was treated. Or, resist what the lamb has revealed and so be involved in ever increasing wrath without the means to handle it.[56]

The hermeneutic Alison employs is difficult to gainsay—for his focus is on the centrality of Christ and the work of redemption as part of the New Creation. He laments the schism that divides the enlightened and the fundamentalist whom he describes as 'enemy

---

54. *Broken Hearts & New Creations*, 38.
55. The notion that a god able to be appropriated can only be one who destroys is common to Hölderlin, Nietzsche and Girard. See G Poettker in his unpublished paper, 'Beyond Nietzsche's War Rhetoric: Ascesis, Sacrifice, and the Recovery of Health', CoV&R Meeting in Freising, Germany, July 23, 2014, 8.
56. *Broken Hearts & New Creations*, 44.

twins' and claims that what he is recovering in fact is 'a sense of the anthropological effect in our midst of the covenant of peace', one that enables us not to be afraid.[57]

To establish this 'anthropological effect', Alison proceeds to resolve the apparent contradictions in Jesus' own statements: on the one hand Jesus speaks of peace (Jn 14:27); on the other hand he speaks of the sword that will divide families (Matt 10:34; Lk 12:51), and the book of Revelation seems to add weight to those words by its references to 'the wrath of the Lamb' (Rev 6:15-17). What Alison seeks to do is *not* explain away 'wrath' but rather set it in its total context to show that (1) there is no violence in Christ, and (2) yet, the result of Jesus' coming, paradoxically it seems, includes violence.[58]

Often the Old Testament is cited as the testament of a fearful and angry God. Alison's demythologises this notion by unpacking Achan's ritual execution in Joshua 7 to show that behind the 'liturgical mechanism of the lottery' and the Lord turning from his burning anger (Josh 7:26) lies a murder and the 'fear and mutual recrimination which had riven the people.'[59] Alison's exegesis is worth noting:

> From their perspective, it feels as though 'peace had been given them'. This is, in fact, in the way the world gives, the peace which comes from unanimity in righteous hatred of an evil doer. But it is misperceived by the participants as peace flowing from the divinity thanks to the right sacrifice having been offered.[60]

The cover-up is disconcerting to say the least, for the reality is that the original murder of a victim, which most likely involved the participants being splattered with blood, is then reproduced liturgically, 'assuaging ... the wrath ... remembered and made newly present'.[61]

The issue is finally resolved when we compare and contrast Jesus' message with that of John the Baptist's. John was clearly expecting the coming of Jesus to produce wrath (Matt 3:7), and he expects a

---

57. *Broken Hearts & New Creations*, 39.
58. *Broken Hearts & New Creations*, 40.
59. *Broken Hearts & New Creations*, 40.
60. *Broken Hearts & New Creations*, 40.
61. *Broken Hearts & New Creations*, 41.

baptism with the Holy Spirit and with fire (Matt 3:11). So when Jesus actually comes on the scene, he doesn't act in the way that John thinks that he is going to. And this provokes the question from John with time to think in prison, 'Are you he who is to come, or shall we look for another?' (Matt 11:3).

Once again Alison's exegesis is compelling: he draws attention to the fact that Jesus, while appearing to fit into the ancient world's views about sacrifice and wrath, is in fact doing the reverse. The cup that he drinks to the dregs *is* a wrath but one not generated by God, but rather the humans into whose lynch-mob circle of anger Jesus allows himself to be taken. For there is no wrath in what Jesus is doing, and there is no wrath in the Father.[62] The reality into which Jesus allows himself to be dragged is an enormous self-deception—that is to say, the attribution of anger to God, indeed the transformation of the sacred into wickedness and with it the 'world of the sacred totter[ing] and fall[ing]'[63] because it has been de-sacralised.[64] It follows that because we can no longer play at this kind of deception, because the *modus operandi* is exposed by Jesus in his death, all the sacred structures which hold groups together start to collapse. And because desire[65] has been unleashed, the sacred bonds of families and groups have been weakened and 'All, in fact, will be afloat on a sea of wrath',[66] because there is nowhere to hide and nowhere to direct their own wrath away from themselves.

The relevance of Alison's exegesis of wrath for the gay and lesbian debate

In the gay and lesbian controversy, those who are by many in the church perceived to be under God's wrath and judgement suddenly find themselves relieved of this burden. Those who judge gays and lesbians misjudge God's character because there is no wrath, no anger

---

62. *Broken Hearts & New Creations*, 43.
63. *Broken Hearts & New Creations*, 43.
64. A Girardian term akin to how we use the terms 'demythologise' and 'deconstruct'.
65. Alison's take on 'desire' is very much in the Girardian vein: perceived in 'mimetic' terms as potentially rivalrous, but when yoked to the love, the peace and the humility of the forgiving Christ, frees us from the necessity of such rivalry.
66. *Broken Hearts & New Creations*, 44.

in God and in his Christ. They not only find themselves exposed, but render themselves susceptible to the very anger (their own) and the mob mentality that goes with it, which withers the human spirit and closes the heart of compassion.

St Paul takes this further; the consequences of this bloody-mindedness are brutally brought home to us by this former 'agent of wrath'.[67] Alison argues that it is St Paul who effectively exposes the system of goodness based on purity and difference. The Law is revealed to be a divisive and destructive mechanism—a mechanism that enables you to know who's 'in' and who's 'out'—a false goodness opposed to the goodness given by the Holy Spirit 'without any of the comforting crutches of sacred separations'.[68]

Who better to have seen through it than Paul, the 'apostle of the new creation…who realises that systems of goodness are all the fruit of, and agents of, wrath, and that only the Crucified One can get us out of wrath, and only the Spirit which he gives can take us into the New Creation.'[69]

Alison's overall case, in summary form, goes something like this:

1. There is no wrath in God or in Christ.

2. If there is a wrath, it is in the world and if we stay in that world's mindset, that old creation, we do so at our own peril.

3. When we focus on what divides rather than on what brings people together, we build again the walls broken down by Christ.

4. When we judge others and wish them to come under the wrath of God, we become complicit in the destructive system of separating goodness with agents of wrath.[70]

5. Without Christ's intervention to save us from our anger, and the giving of the Holy Spirit, we are left stranded in the old creation of our own making.

6. And finally therefore, the reasons for excluding gays and lesbians from the grace of God and the New Creation are totally invalid.

---

67. *Broken Hearts & New Creations*, 45.
68. *Broken Hearts & New Creations*, 46.
69. *Broken Hearts & New Creations*, 46.
70. See *Broken Hearts & New Creations*, 45 where Alison notes that 'The more zealous you are, the clearer will be your sense of the boundaries of your group and, of course, the narrower and more incorrigible your righteousness will become.'

Dishonesty driven by fear has only one solution: the courage to be and to change

The question is this: will we open our hearts and minds to those like Alison who say to us:

> I am interested in becoming a son and heir to the whole of Creation through the arduous discovery of my likeness with my sisters and brothers. I understand how it is one of the delusions of wrath that it is able to point to the growing visibility and public acceptability of gay people and their lives and relationships, and see this as an attack on the 'family' and the 'divinely given order of society'. But it's a delusion of wrath, like that of the Venetians against Shylock...'[71]

Will we listen to the plea that asks us to be honest about our own enmeshment in the brutal capitalist *status quo*, to be open about the fact that we are not only subverted by that world but are complicit with its destructive desires? Will we admit that, in our arduous search for holiness, of desire and of relationships, including family relationships,[72] we are all in this together, rather than allowing ourselves to be set up by all this to fight rather than 'help each other out of the hole'? Or will we have to continue to wear the stinging criticisms of those outsiders who see things more clearly than we see ourselves?

> The weightiest criticisms of Christian speech and practice amount to this: that Christian language actually fails to transform the world's meaning because it neglects or trivialises or evades aspects of the human. It is notoriously awkward about sexuality; it risks being unserious about death when it speaks too glibly and confidently about eternal life; it can disguise the abiding reality of unhealed and meaningless suffering. So it is that some of those most serious about the renewal of a moral discourse reject formal Christian commitment as something that would weaken or corrupt their imagination.[73]

---

71. *Broken Hearts & New Creations*, 47.
72. *Broken Hearts & New Creations*, 47.
73. Rowan Williams, *On Christian Theology* (Oxford: Blackwell, 2000), 40.

To consider that lack of honesty (driven by fear) might be one of the principal problems facing the Church today[74] is a sobering thought. It may spur us on to become more attuned to what God is actually doing among us as part of the New Creation, in all of its grace and truth, is revealed to us in the forgiving, risen Christ. The Gospel of this New Creation speaks of an *inclusion* that goes much further than any of us have ever dared believe and is much bigger than any one of us and all of our fears.[75]

A Reflective Postlude

After my conversion, certain brands of evangelicalism taught me to despise all of my catholic past—*they*, the *Catholics*, were pagans. I was taught to frown on those who were divorced and had remarried, to consider women's ordination as 'unscriptural', to pity gays and lesbians, even though *reality* and *experience* were teaching me something quite different: that the Catholic tradition (Benedictine, Franciscan, Ignatian to mention just three) offered a spiritual legacy by which to enrich my faith; that second marriages actually did work out quite well; that female priests often outshone male priests—not to mention how well women serve the church on the mission field in administration, preaching, teaching and healing; that the young gay man with *the vibrant faith who wanted to be honest* but was told, to his great sadness, that he had no place in Christian community (because no amount of Bible memory work or 'exorcisms' could 'cure' him), might today be honoured for his openness and embraced and accepted in the family of God as he is.

---

74. In *Undergoing God*, 179, Alison writes, '. . . one of the principal problems we have in the Church . . . is a lack of honesty . . . honesty is too important a matter to be allowed to be cheapened by its use as a weapon, as a means of comparison against some other group, or as a form of accusation against others . . . [it concerns] one of the most pivotal realities of the Church, which is the reality of witness.'
75. This inclusivity is especially seen in Matt 8:5–13//Lk 7:1–10 and Matt 15:21–28// Mk 7:24–30. See further Alan Cadwallader, 'Surprised by faith: a Centurion and a Canaanite query the limits of Jesus and the disciples', in *Pieces of Ease and Grace*, edited by AH Cadwallader (Adelaide: ATF Press, 2013), 85–100 and *Beyond the Word of a Woman: Recovering the Bodies of the Syrophoenician Women* (Adelaide: ATF Press, 2008).

And as we endure the heat of the struggle together, let us also be, firstly, encouraged by the words of Blaise Pascal 'Hard as it may struggle, violence cannot weaken truth, and its efforts only make truth stand out more clearly'.[76] And, secondly, let us embrace Girard's admonition that we 'remain at the heart of violence' with those who offend us.[77]

---

76. 'C'est une étrange et longue guerre que celle où la violence essaie d'opprimer la vérité . . . et ne servent qu'à la relever davantage', the epigraph in René Girard, *Achever Clausewitz* (Paris: Carnets Nord, 2007).
77. Cited by Poettcker, 'Beyond Nietzsche's War Rhetoric', 9.

Chapter Ten
How Do We Get It? Pray for It!
Liturgical Resources for a Long Journey

Elizabeth J Smith

From protest to prayer

I think I first said it on a march from downtown Perth to the State Parliament building, in protest against Aboriginal deaths in custody. The call-and-response chants of protest marchers are fairly predictable. What do we want? Justice! When do we want it? Now! And sometimes someone would add: How do we get it? Fight for it! Suddenly, in the quiet of the pause a beat after 'Fight for it!' this clergy-shirted Anglican found herself adding, loudly, 'Pray for it!' This small act of verbal deviance brought amusedly tolerant smiles to the faces of my fellow marchers, and sparked introductions to the Quakers, Uniting Church, Catholic and other religiously-motivated people in the crowd. I now routinely use the same mildly attention-seeking phrase when demonstrating in support of refugees, against budget cuts to schools or in favour of 'marriage equality'. And what I say at a protest march, I need to be willing to do.

I am not at all sure that 'marriage equality' is a big enough goal for Christians who want to be advocates for the full recognition of lesbian, gay, bisexual, transgendered and intersex people (LGBTI) in the church, as in society. But it is the language being used by the groups that are out there making the most noise, attracting the heat of the debate, organising the public occasions when anyone can stand up and be counted for something positive that is desired by many LGBTI people, and stand against fear, hatred and the marginalisation of some of our fellow human beings. So I am prepared to pray for 'marriage equality', but that is not all I want to pray for.

I want us to pray for the protection—physical, emotional and spiritual—of our friends and neighbours and work colleagues who are LGBTI or whose beloved family members don't fit the straight suburban stereotype. No one should run the risk of verbal abuse, a physical bashing, unfunny homophobic humour or a moralising lecture about what constitutes a proper relationship when introducing ourselves or the people we care about.

I want us to pray for the fruitful solitude of all people who are not in relationships of sexual intimacy. As someone who has spent most of her adult life single, and happily so, I want to pray for respite from the cultural and consumer-driven assumptions that everyone, always and everywhere, wants to be and, really, *ought* to be part of a couple. Celibacy ought not to be compulsory for anyone, because it is a gift and a vocation as well as a discipline that may be embraced for a time. But coupledom and marriage ought not to be compulsory, either.

I want us to pray for the church to be enriched by and able to celebrate the spiritual and practical gifts of its LGBTI members. Many LGBTI Christians already serve God generously in the church, providing everything from pastoral care and ordained leadership to teaching, healing and evangelistic ministries and financial support. But while a congregation might proudly advertise the contributions of 'our young families', 'our seniors' or 'our men's group', the presence and service of LGBTI members is seldom acknowledged, let alone celebrated.

I want us to pray for the Good News to be offered to LGBTI people with no strings attached, or at least with no more strings than for anyone else who is found by the love of Jesus Christ and given grace to live abundantly, with new freedoms to enjoy and new sacrifices to make. There are many people, both gay and straight, whose closest relationships need a radical Gospel overhaul. While sexual behaviour will often be called into question through conversion to Christ, the church has a lot of work to do to remove the well-founded perception that sexuality in general and homosexuality in particular, are almost the only things under the ethical spotlight. Gossip, greed and bitter unforgiveness are just as toxic to spiritual health, and far more widespread.

I want us to pray for church leaders to find the courage to be advocates for LGBTI people both inside and outside the churches. A very few have spoken up, and the torrent of criticism that follows is testimony to how afraid so many people still are of the mere presence of LGBTI people, let alone their public affirmation or their theological validation. It does take spiritual courage to speak up, knowing you will trigger the responses of the mad, the bad and the hate-filled in church and society. So I also want us to pray for the loving and affirming letter-writers to be even more active than the attackers.

And yes, I do want us to pray for the day when two men who love each other, two women who love each other can stand together in the presence of God and of their Christian community and declare that they are making a life-long commitment to mutual love and faithfulness. I want to pray for the day when same-sex couples will be seen with opposite-sex couples at the heart of the church, bearing witness to the risky and joyful business of sharing their goods and their home, of becoming more fruitful in prayer and service together than they could be alone. I want to recognise afresh the body of Christ in the midst of the eucharistic assembly, as same-sex couples promise to each other the holy hospitality of each other's bodies and each other's lives.

And there are prayers we will need to pray that are less hopeful, though just as important. What shall we pray at the funeral of a teenager or young adult who has taken her or his own life in despair at homophobic bullying at school, or in the fear of being rejected by family and friends for a sexual identity that cannot be resisted but seemingly cannot be celebrated either? What shall we pray at the bedside of the victim of a bashing, or on the day after another synod debate is lost, or as we scrub the homophobic graffiti off the church fence or the rectory after our parish comes out in support of its LGBTI members? What shall we pray as we write to members of parliament, trying to differentiate our Christian stance from that of others, even in our own denominations, and asking for the laws to be changed to provide public recognition and protection for same-sex couples?

Blessing in all directions

At one 'marriage equality' rally, I carried a small sign that read 'free blessings' and a handful of flyers which I gave to all and sundry. I had a few knockbacks from people who said that they were not religious, but among the demonstrators and in the curious audience along the city streets where we walked most people were happy to receive a blessing or three. Two were 'take it away and pray it yourself' blessings, though one was a form of words that I prayed then and there for anyone who asked for it. It was quite a theological and linguistic challenge to decide how each blessing might be phrased.

One is a blessing for a couple. People expect a priest to offer blessings. Even though Anglican clergy are not yet authorised to offer formal, liturgical blessings of same-sex couples, some would argue that the priest as a person of blessing can and should be blessing people all the time. I hesitated about using the conventional Trinitarian formula, for all the usual reasons about fossilising the originally powerful metaphors of Father and Son, re-inscribing patriarchal family patterns in a postmodern world and imposing overtly male God-language on women, particularly, who are finding holiness in each other's hearts and bodies rather than in relationships of submission to male authority. For those of Catholic or Orthodox background the sign of the cross is a key physical indicator of a blessing, so I included the sign of the cross both in the text I handed out and also in my performance of this blessing for anyone who asked me to pray it for them. I headed it 'a blessing for a couple in God's name'.

> ✠ The blessing of the living God be upon you with constant faithfulness as you care for each other.
> ✠ The blessing of the Lord Jesus be upon you with hospitality and generosity in your home.
> ✠ The blessing of the Holy Spirit be upon you with courage to make a difference in the world.
> ✠ The blessing of the holy and glorious Trinity be upon you now and for ever. Amen.

The second was a mutual blessing for a couple to pray for each other. Christians have always blessed each other both formally and informally. A parent who 'kisses it better' when a child scrapes a knee, anyone who says 'bless you!' when a friend or stranger lends a hand, and even the 'bless you!' response to a sneeze is a form of blessing. This time, in deference to conventional formulae and to underline the solidly Christian intention of the blessing, I used 'Father, Son and Holy Spirit' as well as the sign of the cross. I headed it, 'words for a couple to bless each other. Each may make the sign of the cross on the other's forehead.'

> I bless you with my love and trust.
> I bless you with my friendship and forgiveness
> And I pray for the God of everlasting love to live with us and to make us a blessing for others,
> ✠in the name of the Father, and of the Son, and of the Holy Spirit. Amen.

The third blessing was formulated in response to Jesus' injunction to his disciples in Luke 6:27–28 to 'bless those who curse you, and pray for those who abuse you'. The focus here is not on the Trinitarian formula but on the name of Jesus Christ, which brackets the simple text. I wanted to promote the idea of LGBTI people as active agents of Christlike blessing in the world, not merely passive supplicants waiting for some ecclesiastical authority to deign to dignify their faithful relationships with a formal blessing. I cited the Luke passage at the head of this blessing, offering it as 'a blessing for LGBTI people to pray for all who still cannot see God's love in faithful same-sex couples, and to pray for all whose words and actions stir up hurt and hate'.

> We bless you in the name of Jesus Christ, and in the power of the Holy Spirit.
> ✠God bless you with eyes to see our love as a gift from God.
> ✠God bless you with ears to hear of holiness in the stories of our lives.
> ✠God bless you with a heart to work with us as partners to set all people free from hatred and fear, through Jesus Christ our Lord. Amen.

Good Friday grieving for justice

Much of the advocacy for the legal recognition of same-sex couples is based on the idea of equal rights. The phrase 'marriage equality' points in this direction. It is an easy plea to make in a society that has, over the last century or so, made real if slow and sometimes grudging steps towards recognising the rights of women, indigenous peoples, people with disabilities, racial and linguistic minorities and so on.

Sometimes Christian leaders criticise the focus on 'rights' for LGBTI people as too secular and insufficiently biblical and theological. The idea of 'justice' is more congenial to a theological approach, hallowed by the biblical prophets' constant calls to the community to treat fairly its widows, orphans, outsiders and most vulnerable people. With their key intimate relationships unrecognised and unsupported by the law and by the Church, same-sex couples may be seen to share in the kind of marginalisation and vulnerability that calls for prophetic advocacy and care from the followers of Jesus Christ.

Yet in order to maintain a stance against advocacy for LGBTI people under the heading of 'justice', a further complaint is sometimes levelled: that there are so many other people who suffer much greater injustices in Australia and round the world than LBGTI people do, and that Christians ought to put those people's needs first. Only when all the poor have been fed and housed, only when all the refugees have been welcomed and only when the gap of disadvantage has finally been closed between the First Peoples and the rest of us, only then will it be time to deal with the justice needs of LGBTI people in first-world Australia. This complaint is a pretext for not attending to the real difficulties faced by many LGBTI people even in affluent, first-world Australia. It also perpetuates an either-or rather than a both-and approach to matters of justice, which is not supported by the Christian narrative of the death of Jesus Christ for all the sins of the world, without ranking or distinction. And it fails to recognise the fact that many LGBTI Christians are active leaders in a wide variety of social justice advocacy and service roles. Recognising one's own marginalisation can have a profoundly conscientising effect on one's commitment to working for others whose needs are even more urgent.

The last half-century's renewal of the great Good Friday liturgies of word and prayer and the proclamation of the Cross has been a blessing to the churches. It has, however, been accompanied by the decline or loss of other and more varied Good Friday forms of worship. The Three Hour service with half a dozen sermons or meditations may never undergo a great renaissance. The Stations of the Cross in their traditional form or in ecumenical adaptations are known to some. New models for Good Friday prayer are being developed in the context of 'Fresh Expressions' of church. A small

Fresh Expression with which I am associated is the Community of the Beatitudes. It was conceived as a nourishing form of Christian community for people active in social justice movements and in community service workplaces: 'Blessed are those who are hungry and thirsty for justice, for they will be satisfied' (Matt 5:6).

On Good Friday 2010, six or seven of us experimented with Good Friday prayers in a city park, sitting on the ground around a wooden cross and praying through half a dozen different themes for prayer for justice and compassion. Prayer for LGBTI people was the fourth of the six themes. Other themes were vulnerable children, Australia's First Peoples, people with mental illnesses, women victims of violence and the suffering earth. Thus the cry for justice for some was situated in the context of justice for all. The suffering of all was placed in the suffering of Jesus Christ himself, the redeemer of the world. Each theme was paired with a reading from one of the gospel Passion narratives. The structure and text of the bidding and prayer included lament and question and moved to petition. The prayer for LGBTI people is given here together with the prayer for the First Peoples, to demonstrate how the themes of suffering and justice are placed alongside each other and in dialogue with the Crucified One. The Bible reading, preceding the prayer for the First Peoples, was John 19:16–23, the account of Pilate authorising the inscription for Jesus' cross.

> On this dark day, in the shadows of history, of the political margins, of cultural dispossession, are the First Peoples of this land.
>
> When Imperial power hunted you down, Lord Jesus, you died a member of a race invaded, dislocated, subjugated, cut out of your inheritance by a military power.
>
> There were three languages, none of them your mother tongue, written on your cross, satirically announcing your identity, Jesus of Nazareth, King of the Jews.
>
> Does your heart break today for the silenced tongues of this land, words, ideas and rituals that died with the last speakers of a hundred languages?

Your mother watched you die,
her firstborn stolen from her
by an alien government
concerned only for its own security
in a land whose laws it neither knew nor honoured.

Does your heart break today
for the shattered families of the First Peoples,
for the tears of the children who thought themselves abandoned,
the parents who knew themselves bereft,
the communities aching with inconsolable grief?

You died in custody,
brutally handled by police
humiliated, stripped,
thirsty, bruised and bleeding.

Does your heart break today
for all the prisoners
battered in mind and body by a self-righteous state?

Christ of all the broken-hearted peoples,
give powerful speech to those who have been silenced,
treasure the tears of those who have been bereaved,
and set the prisoners free
for life with dignity and hope.

Now the prayer for LGBTI people, which was associated with John 19:25–27, where the crucified Jesus redefines family relationships, entrusting his mother to his dear friend and his friend to his mother.

On this dark day,
in the shadows of rejection,
haunted by difference,
yearning to belong and to be recognised,
are the same-sex attracted people,
gay, lesbian, bisexual,
the transgendered and the intersex,
the queer and questioning people.

> Lord Jesus, in the record of your life and death
> you had no wife, no children of your body.
>
> You challenged the meaning of "family" in your day,
> rejecting birth and blood and conventional father's household
> and naming as your own kin
> all who hear your word and do it.
>
> When you were dying, one dear disciple watched.
> You named him a son to your mother.
>
> Will you name as your own beloved ones today,
> so that they can hear it and believe it,
> our sisters, our brothers, our children,
> ourselves,
> whose holy desires are shunned by society and church
> and who are asked to hide their deepest intimacy?
>
> Will you name as your own treasured family today,
> so that the world can hear it and believe it,
> our neighbours, our colleagues, our friends,
> ourselves,
> whose loves do not fit the patterns we have inherited,
> and whose loyalties are rejected by other people's fear?
>
> Lord Jesus, today,
> as you redefine your family from your cross,
> shake and soften the rigid righteousness of your Church
> until we learn to embrace all your friends with gentleness.
> Protect all those you love from the violence of hateful speech
> and physical aggression.
> Teach your Body how to honour its gay and lesbian members,
> some joyful in singleness,
> some blessed and blessing in couples,
> all graced and growing, hearing your call.

As a direct result of their sexual identity, suffering is real for many LGBTI people. The tragedy of teenagers' and young adults' self-harm and suicide is testimony to the emotional and spiritual cost of recognising in oneself an identity which cannot be denied yet which is exceedingly risky to express and likely to precipitate shock, disapproval and even condemnation. The church's official pronouncements currently give no comfort to LGBTI people, while giving considerable encouragement to those who speak and act against them. Putting this hostility and violence in the context of the suffering and death of Jesus Christ, as well as in the context of the suffering of others, is an important move in the journey of prayer.

Good Friday is not the only day when this juxtaposition can be made. An every-Friday prayer focus could be offered in Lent or at other times. Memorial prayers for those who have died as victims of violence could be the focus of occasional non-eucharistic liturgy, perhaps in rapid response to a particular local, national or international tragedy. While media attention is often focussed on particular victims, such as those killed when Malaysian Airlines flight 17 was shot down in July 2014, or those killed in an earthquake, tsunami or typhoon, one grief often triggers in people the memory or the realisation of other griefs. The sorrows of LGBTI people and those who love them are part of the constant background to the sharp pain of other headline-grabbing tragedies. The cross of Jesus Christ has always been the safe place for people to bring all our griefs and sorrows, and it is also the safe place for LGBTI people and the people who love them to come with our laments, our questions and our prayers.

Advent yearning for change

If we spend much of our time in progressive circles and as little time as possible listening to talkback radio, it is easy to forget how widespread are ignorance about and fear of LGBTI people in the Christian community and the wider community. A synod debate, while generally courteous and measured, can remind us of the diversity of opinion and attitude and the ongoing need for change. In the synod of the Diocese of Perth in 2012, many people spoke both for and against a motion recognising diversity of sexual identities and calling for government to legislate for civil unions for same-sex couples. In the wake of that synod debate, a parish whose clergy and people were supportive of LGBTI people in the church and the community offered to host an event declaring that support, and inviting all and sundry to attend. In early Advent, a carol service on a 'Changing Attitude' theme seemed appropriate.

The service was preceded by colourful cocktails in the parish hall, and the church was resplendent with rainbow candles in front of the altar. The organist struck up rousing accompaniments to the congregational singing of Advent carols from *Together in Song*[1] and other sources. Congregation members were recruited to read from the Bible and lead the prayers. There was some confusion and distress. A few parishioners had come expecting Christmas carols. Someone critiqued an imbalance between female and male voices in the readings and prayers, an unintended consequence of a bias towards lay rather than ordained voices, and a trigger for more reflections on what it means for worship to be 'inclusive'. Not all the carols were well known. Some had to be introduced before they could be sung, perhaps hindering the meditative flow of the service. Generally, though, the prayer was heartfelt and the gathering was an important declaration of solidarity with and hope for the gay and lesbian people who are part of so many churches, families, workplaces and friendship networks.

Advent is a good season to express longing, yearning and hope for God's future to break into a difficult present. While some Advent carols look forward to Christmas, others look to Christ's coming again in glory. In the prayers below, the words occasionally echo the texts of the carols. Hymn numbers refer to *Together in Song*. Silences and Bible readings were included with the songs.

> *Lo! he comes with clouds descending (272)*
> *Pull back the veil on the dawn of creation (326)*

Let us pray for a sense of urgency in the life and mission of this Diocese.

> Lord Jesus, come!
> Come and bring and end to the rejection suffered
> by lesbian, gay and bisexual Christians.
> Come and confirm the gifts of your Spirit in them,
> given for the building up of the Church.
> Come and change hearts and minds
> so that everyone may recognise your redeeming love
> in the lives of all your friends without distinction,

---

1. *Together in Song: Australian Hymn Book II* (East Melbourne: HarperCollinsReligious, 1999).

straight and gay and lesbian, single and partnered.
Lord Jesus, come!

When he comes back (280)

Let us pray for true hospitality to shine in the churches of this Diocese.

Lord Jesus, come!
Come and teach all the members of your Church to see your face
in the faces of the hungry, the stranger, the sad.
Come and rekindle the welcoming light in our communities,
inviting the excluded and the vulnerable to come in
and share your feast.
Come and begin the dance of your homecoming,
where all Christians, whatever our sexual identity,
will be glad to embrace each other as your chosen ones.
Lord Jesus, come!

The voice of God goes out to all the world (282)

Let us pray for the gentleness of Christ to be found in all our relationships.

Lord Jesus, come!
Come with power and with justice to walk your way,
binding up the wounds of rejection, lighting the lamp of hope.
Come with comfort and kindness
to gay and lesbian people and to those who love them.
Come and pour out your Spirit
with grace to tell the stories of faithful love,
until those still held in prisons of fear can be set free.
Lord Jesus, come!

O bless the God of Israel (284)

Let us pray for the prophets who challenge us to change.

Lord Jesus, come!

Come and inspire your Church with courage to speak up
against hatred and violence directed at lesbian and gay people.
Come with words of truth to speak at the right moment,

and endurance to keep going through difficult times.
Come with a powerful and persuasive vision
of a humanity where diversity is received as a blessing
and love is the gift that holds us all together.
Lord Jesus, come!

Lord, make us turn to you (42)

Let us pray for people despairing or discouraged by the slow pace of change.

Lord Jesus, come!
Come and sustain us when our hearts are heavy
and our work for change is slow to bear fruit.
Come and refresh us with each other's company,
with prayer and song and story-telling along the way.
Come with new allies in support of gay and lesbian Christians,
with fresh ideas and strong teamwork,
with surprises of grace that renew our hope.
Lord Jesus, come!

The angel Gabriel from heaven came (302)

Let us pray for the work of the Incarnation to go forward.

Lord Jesus, come!
Come with the joy of your virgin Mother, Mary,
and make us eager to bear your love for the world.
Come with the strength and glory of your holy angels,
conquer our fears and inspire us to action.
Come with the Holy Spirit to overshadow us
and make us fruitful messengers of abundant life,
whatever our sexual history or our sexual identity.
Lord Jesus, come!

A wife so long childless[2]

---

2. 'A wife so long childless' is a hymn text telling the story of the Visitation.

The Lord's Prayer

Joy to the world (273)

The living God bless you with love and longing in a world still hungry for justice and peace.

The Lord Jesus bless you with courage and creativity in a church still struggling to trust his boundless generosity. The Holy Spirit bless you with a clear mind and wise words in the conversations still needed as we work for change. And the blessing of the holy and glorious Trinity be among you and remain with you always. **Amen.**

The Advent theme of Christ's coming again to judge the world could receive more attention in the prayer of Christians who are advocates for justice and peace. While much of the apocalyptic imagery of the Bible is foreign and off-putting to many thoughtful twenty-first century Christians, it sprang from the spiritual imagination of people not unlike ourselves who were passionate about the truth, who were suffering in its absence, and who were convinced that only the appearing and direct intervention of Jesus Christ himself could resolve the dilemmas of their time and restore harmony to the universe. Proclaiming that Christ will come again is not necessarily a denunciation of those who are seen as causing problems for the faithful here and now. Rage against injustice and yearning for compassion and healing need to be expressed, even when the desire for revenge and retribution needs to be held in check. Advent is a natural setting for that expression. The ancient cry of '*maranatha,* come, Lord Jesus', needs to be restored to the Church's liturgical vocabulary for use in times of stress, of justice denied or delayed, and of longing for love to triumph once and for all. The hostility faced by LGBTI people inside and outside the churches indicates that we are living in just such a time.

A song for a couple

Elizabeth J Smith, *Songs for Saints and Sinners* (Bentleigh: BEAUT Publications, 2008), 2.

Twenty years ago, at Good Shepherd Church in Berkeley, California, I was part of a congregation which celebrated, with its bishop's permission, a eucharist in which we gave thanks for the abiding relationship of two of its members. We thanked God for Barbara and Kathleen and for the blessings which they brought to the church through their love for each other and their ministry among us. A great deal of theological, pastoral and liturgical reflection preceded the celebration. It was not adapted from or modelled on the marriage service. It was not a rite of passage, designed to mark a transition from singleness to coupledom or from casual to committed relationship status. It was a celebration of something precious that already existed and that we wanted to recognise. 'Blessing' in this service was not something that the couple sought *from* the church. Rather, it was something that the couple brought, and were honoured for bringing, *to* the church. One of the most moving acts of the liturgy came at the offertory when, as we watched, the couple dressed the altar of the church for the celebration of communion with the finest table linen and vessels from their own home. The connection between the intimate domestic community of Christians and the intimate ecclesial community of Christians was made very clearly. I wrote a hymn text for Kathleen and Barbara, which we sang at the celebration.

> Loving God, you called these two, made them yours, and made them one, set them in our midst to do more of what the saints have done, living out for all to see intimate community.
>
> Holy God, our sisters bring gifts from you to share with all. So we praise you, honouring your grace in this couple's call. Joyfully we recognise fruitful, faithful Christian lives.
>
> God of hope, let justice shine in your church and world to day. Let these lovers be a sign that your Good News finds a way through our dark times, that you bless all who seek your holiness.
>
> God of mercy, hear our prayer; pour your blessing on these two. Patience, pleasure, trust and care dwell with them their

whole lives through. As they flourish, so may we grow in love and unity.[3]

The text asks God to bless the couple, just as many hymns and songs ask for God's blessing on the singers. The first and second stanzas declare the community's confidence that the two in their midst are indeed called by God to be together. The third stanza prays for justice to shine out in dark times, and the fourth prays for the whole community to grow together along with the couple. Hymns to be sung at the celebration of a marriage need to avoid descending into sentimentality or the idolatry of romantic love, and the same is true for singing when celebrating the blessing offered to or brought by same-sex couples. Good theology does not necessarily produce good poetry, but bad theology should never be dignified with good poetry. In this text, the poetry is not particularly memorable but the theology should stand up to scrutiny.

Normalising common prayer with and for LGBTI people

There are many welcoming and affirming Christian communities where there is a strong consensus in favour of active hospitality towards LGBTI people. Some people in those communities will still have reservations about 'equal marriage'. But all those who are supportive, whether extravagantly or tentatively, need opportunities to pray on ordinary as well as extraordinary occasions. It is important simply to use the words 'gay', 'lesbian', 'bisexual', 'transgender', 'intersex', 'same-sex' and 'homosexual' as part of our common liturgical discourse. If this vocabulary is only heard in the context of homiletical rhetoric, synod resolutions or protest marches, it will continue to be uncomfortable at best or taboo at worst for most worshippers to hear, let alone to say.

So, for example, in the Sunday intercessions, a prayer leader might pray 'for our local schools, for the gay and lesbian teenagers among the students, and for the teachers, parents and chaplains who support them. Lord Jesus, give them confidence that you are always with

---

3. Words © Elizabeth J Smith 1994, suggested music RATISBON, INWARD LIGHT, BREAD OF HEAVEN.

them, protect them from bullies, and guide them to the strong and healthy relationships that will bless them and those around them'.

A heterosexual Christian couple, marrying, might include in the service booklet for their wedding day a prayer 'for our friends, family members and co-workers who are gay, lesbian and bisexual, and who are not yet free to celebrate their lifelong commitment in the community or in the church. God of love, bring us to the day when the people in every home will share equally in the blessing you offer to the friends of your Son, Jesus Christ'.

A prayer for those in authority might ask 'for courage and compassion among our political leaders, so that care may be offered in this land to all who are on the edges: for Aboriginal and Torres Strait Islander peoples, for refugees and asylum seekers, for homosexual people whose relationships cannot be publicly recognised and who face discrimination and hostility, and for young unemployed people with little hope of finding work. God of justice, give strong hearts to our leaders as they guide us towards life-giving change'.

Intercessions for the life of the church might give God thanks 'for the gifts that you are offering to your church through our members who are lesbian, gay, bisexual and transgendered, single and with partners. Come, Holy Spirit, and make us always more ready to take pleasure in the diversity of faces, voices, bodies, relationships and spiritual wisdom that is your gift to us'.

Because many gay and lesbian households include children, prayers for Fathers' Day and Mothers' Day could puncture the bubble of the mythical suburban family. We could pray for 'all the men [women] who are called dad [mum] by their children, as part of married couples, as single parents, in same-sex couples, as foster parents, step parents or adoptive parents. Fill every family, whatever its shape or size, with the expanding love that Jesus gives to everyone who needs it'.

And we will pray for those with whom we find ourselves travelling, towards the distant goals that seem so far away, towards the new heaven and the new earth where every tear will be wiped away, towards the resurrection where they neither marry nor are given in marriage. We are still called to fight for what we long for, agitate for it, lobby for it, donate for it, and make sacrifices for it. We are not alone in longing for it, although we may be alone among activists in praying for it.

So we will pray for the companions with whom we march against war and poverty, for justice and compassion. 'Lord Jesus, we thank you for those who do not know you, yet who care for others gladly, showing kindness, taking risks, providing leadership. Show your face to all who are working towards the full recognition of gay, lesbian and bisexual people in the world and in the church. Pour out your blessing until all who mourn are comforted, until all who are hungry and thirsty for justice are satisfied, until all the pure in heart see God.'

Contributors

Sarah Bachelard is a theologian, speaker and retreat leader. She is the founder and director of Benedictus Contemplative Church, an honorary research fellow at the Australian Catholic University, and a facilitator with the Center for Courage and Renewal. Sarah is the author of *Experiencing God in a Time of Crisis* and *Resurrection and Moral Imagination*.

Nikolai Blaskow is an Anglican priest, Chaplain and Head of Religious and Values Education at Radford Grammar School, in Canberra. He is the Chair of the Editorial Board of *Dialogue Australasia Network,* a Journal that resources teachers in schools and has completed a screenplay entitled *Once Upon A War.* He is currently researching a study of Friedrich Nietzsche and René Girard.

Gary D Bouma AM is the UNESCO Chair in Intercultural and Interreligious Relations—Asia Pacific, Emeritus Professor of Sociology and Director of the Global Terrorism Research Centre at Monash University. He is an Associate Priest in the Anglican Parish of St John's East Malvern. He is President of the Australian Association for the Study of Religions. He was invested as a Member of the Order of Australia (AM) for services to Sociology, to interreligious relations and to the Anglican Church of Australia.

Alan Cadwallader is a researcher and Anglican priest, combining interests in archaeology, Scripture and contemporary issues. His most recent book is *Fragments of Colossae* (ATF Press, 2015), and he is currently working on the politics involved in the translation of the Revised Version. He is Senior Lecturer in Biblical Studies at the Canberra campus of the Australian Catholic University.

Stephen Pickard is Executive Director, The Australian Centre for Christianity and Culture, and Professor of Theology, Charles Sturt

University, Canberra, Australia. He is also an Assistant Bishop in the Anglican Diocese of Canberra and Goulburn. He is the author of a number of books including: *Seeking the Church: An Introduction to Ecclesiology* (SCM, 2012) and *In-Between God: Theology, Community and Discipleship* (ATF, 2011).

Duncan Reid is an Anglican priest in Melbourne who teaches at Camberwell Girls Grammar School and is an Honorary Research Associate of the MCD University of Divinity. He holds a doctorate in theology from the University of Tübingen and a master of education from Flinders University. He has previously published on trinitarian and ecological theology as well as educational matters, and his former roles include Head of the School of Theology at Flinders University Adelaide, and Dean of United Faculty of Theology Melbourne.

Peter Sherlock is Vice-Chancellor of the University of Divinity and a Lay Canon of St Paul's Cathedral, Melbourne.

Elizabeth Smith The Revd Dr Elizabeth Smith is Mission Priest based in Kalgoorlie, in the far east of the Diocese of Perth. She is a member of the Liturgy Commission of the Anglican Church of Australia, a writer of widely-sung hymn texts, and a producer of liturgical texts for both national and local use.

Cathy Thomson has been an Anglican priest for twenty years and is currently Director of Formation and Lecturer in Systematic Theology at St Francis' Theological College, Brisbane which is affiliated with Charles Sturt University. Through her teaching and through membership of various committees in diocesan, national and international contexts, she has developed an interest in Anglican ecclesiology. Cathy is currently chair of the National Council of Churches Faith and Unity Commission.

Phillip Tolliday is an Anglican priest who teaches Systematic Theology for Charles Sturt University. He is located in Adelaide and his interests include reconciliation and hermeneutics. Phillip has an ongoing collaboration with the Jena Center for Reconciliation Studies at the Friedrich Schiller University in Jena, Germany, and is presently engaged in editing a volume of essays on reconciliation from an interdisciplinary perspective in an Asian context.

Bibliography

Aland, K and B, *The Text of the New Testament*. Grand Rapids: Eerdmans, 1987.

Alexander, M and J Preston, *We Were Baptized Too: Claiming God's Grace for Lesbians and Gays*. Louisville, KY: Westminster John Knox, 1996.

Alison, J, *The Joy of Being Wrong, Original Sin Through Easter Eyes*. New York: Crossroad Publishing Company, 1998.

— *Faith Beyond Resentment: Fragments Catholic and Gay*. New York: Crossroad, 2001.

— *Human Sexuality... or Ecclesial Discourse?* A presentation for the Sarum Consultation on Human Sexuality and the Churches, 9–10 February 2004. <http://www.jamesalison.co.uk/texts/eng14.html>

—'Good-faith learning and the fear of God', in *Opening Up: Speaking Out in the Church*. Edited by P Stanford and J Filochowski; London: Darton, Longman & Todd, 2005), 66–80. <http://www.jamesalison.co.uk/texts/eng17.html>

— *Wrath and the Gay Question* (2006). <http://www.jamesalison.co.uk/texts/eng32.html>

—*Broken Hearts & New Creations, Intimations of a Great Reversal*. London: Darton, Longman & Todd, 2010.

—*Undergoing God, dispatches from the scene of a break-in*. New York: Continuum, 2006.

Armstrong, PW, *The English Parson Naturalist A Companionship between Science and Religion*. Herefordshire: Gracewing, 2000.

Atherton, J, *Christianity and the Market: Christian Social Thought for our Times*. London: SPCK, 1992.

Australian Bureau of Statistics, *3310.0 - Marriages and Divorces, Australia, 2011.* Canberra: Australian Bureau of Statistics, 2012.

Avis, P, *Ecumenical Theology and the Elusiveness of Doctrine.* London: SPCK, 1986.

—*Authority, Leadership and Conflict in the Church.* London: Mowbray, 1992.

Babie, P and N Rochow (editors), *Freedom of Religion under Bills of Rights* Adelaide: University of Adelaide Press, 2012.

Bachelard, S, *Experiencing God in a Time of Crisis.* Miami, FL: Convivium Press, 2012.

—*Resurrection and Moral Imagination.* Farnham, Eng: Ashgate Publishing Company, 2014.

Bagnall, RS, *Everyday Writing in the Graeco-Roman East.* Berkeley, CA: University of California Press, 2012.

Baile, D, *Eros and the Jews: from Biblical Israel to Contemporary America.* New York: BasicBooks, 1992.

Barclay, JDG, *Jews in the Mediterranean Diaspora: From Alexander to Trajan (323 BCE - 117 CE).* Edinburgh: T & T Clark, 1996.

Barnett, P, 'God, Creation and Sexuality in First Corinthians: A Response to *Alan Cadwallader*', in *Sexegesis: An Evangelical Response to Five Uneasy Pieces on Homosexuality.* Edited by M Bird and G Preece; Sydney South: Anglican Press Australia, 2012, 105–16.

Bates, S, *A Church at War: Anglicans and Homosexuality.* London: Tauris, 2004.

Bayer, O, 'Hermeneutical Theology', in *Philosophical Hermeneutics and Biblical Exegesis.* Edited by P Pokorný and J Roskovec; Tübingen: Mohr Siebeck, 2002, 103–20.

Berdyaev, N, *The Destiny of Man.* New York: Harper, 1960.

— *Christian Existentialism: A Berdyaev Anthology.* Edited by DA Lowrie; London: George Unwin & Allen, 1965.

Best, G, *Bishop Westcott and the Miners.* Cambridge: Cambridge University Press, 1966.

Bieżunka-Małowist, I, 'La traite des esclaves dans l'Égypte', in *Archaeologia Polona* 14 (1973): 147–53.

Bingham, J, 'Archbishop urges Christians to "repent" over "wicked" attitude to homosexuality' *The Age*, 29/8/2013. < http://www.

theage.com.au/world/christians-should-repent-over-treatment-of-gays-archbishop-of-canterbury-20130829-2ss28.html>

Bird, M and G Preece, (editors), *Sexegesis: An Evangelical Response to Five Uneasy Pieces on Homosexuality*. Sydney South: Anglican Press Australia, 2012.

Bita, N, 'Marriage equality wins support of two out of three', *The Australian*, 16 July, 2014. <http://www.theaustralian.com.au/50th-birthday-news/marriage-equality-wins-support-of-two-out-of-three/story-fnmx97ei-1226990227810>

Bonhoeffer, D, *Life Together*. London: SCM, 1954.

—*Letters and Papers from Prison*. Edited by E Bethge; London: SCM Press, 3rd Ed, 1967.

Boer, R, *Political Myth: On the Use and Abuse of Biblical Themes*. Durham, NC / London: Duke University Press, 2009.

Bouma, G, 'Religious Resurgence, Conflict and The Transformation of Boundaries', in *Religion, Globalization and Culture*. Edited by Peter Beyer and Lori Beaman; Leiden: Brill, 2007, 187–202.

—*Being Faithful in Diversity: Religions and Social Policy in MultiFaith Societies*. Adelaide: ATF Press, 2011.

—'Diversity of religions and freedom of religion and belief', in *The Routledge International Handbook of Education, Religion and Values*. Edited by J Arthur and T Lovat; London: Routledge, 2013, 55–61.

Bouma, G, D Cahill, H Dellal, and A Zwartz, *Freedom of Religion and Belief in 21st Century Australia*. Sydney: Australian Human Rights Commission, 2011.

Bourdieu, P, 'Thinking about Limits', in *Theory, Culture, Society* 9.1 (1992): 37–49.

Brittain, CC and A McKinnon, 'Homosexuality and the Construction of "Anglican Orthodoxy": The Symbolic Politics of the Anglican Communion', in *Sociology of Religion* 72.3 (2011): 351–73.

Brown, P, *The Body and Society: Men, Women, and Sexual Renunciation in Early Christianity*. New York: Columbia University Press, 1988.

Burgon, JW, *The Last Twelve Verses of the Gospel according to S. Mark vindicated against recent critical objectors . . .* Oxford/London: J Parker, 1871.

— *The Revision Revised*. London: John Murray, 1883.

Cadwallader, AH, 'Male Diagnosis of the Female Pen in the late Victorian Britain: Private Assessments of *Supernatural Religion*', in *Journal of Anglican Studies* 5 (2007): 67–86.

— *Beyond the Word of a Woman: Recovering the Bodies of the Syrophoenician Women*. Adelaide: ATF Press, 2008.

— 'Refuting an Axiom of Scholarship on Colossae; fresh insights from new and old inscriptions', in *Colossae in Space and Time: Linking to an Ancient City*. Edited by AH Cadwallader and M Trainor; Göttingen: Vandenhoeck & Ruprecht, 2011, 151–79.

— 'Keeping Lists or Embracing Freedom', in *Five Uneasy Pieces*. Edited by NMcI Wright; Adelaide: ATF Press, 2011, 41–58.

— 'Star-cross'd lovers: John Henry Newman and the Revision of the Bible', in *Australian eJournal of Theology* 19.3 (2012): 229–43.

— (editor), *Pieces of Ease and Grace*. Adelaide: ATF Press, 2013.

— 'Surprised by faith: a Centurion and a Canaanite query the limits of Jesus and the disciples', in *Pieces of Ease and Grace*. Edited by AH Cadwallader; Adelaide: ATF Press, 2013), 85–100.

— 'History as bulwark, bridge and bulldozer: *Dei Verbum* and ecumenical, biblical endeavour', in *God's Word and the Church's Council: Vatican II and Divine Revelation*. Edited by C Monaghan and M O'Brien; Adelaide: ATF Press, 2014, 207–24.

— *The Politics of the Revised Version*. Sheffield: Sheffield Phoenix, forthcoming.

Carpenter, SC, *Church and People, 1789–1889: A History of the Church of England from William Wilberforce to 'Lux Mundi'*. London: SPCK, 1933.

Carr, EH, *The Making of History*. Harmondsworth: Penguin, 1987.

Cecil, G, *Life of Robert, Marquis of Salisbury*. London: Hodder & Stoughton, 4 vols, 1932.

Chamberlain, L, *Motherland: A Philosophical History of Russia*. New York: Overlook/Rookery, 2004.

Charry, ET (editor), 'Same-Sex Relationships and the Nature of Marriage: A Theological Colloquy', in *Anglican Theological Review* 93:1 (Winter 2011).

Clayton, J, *Bishop Westcott*. London / Oxford: AR Mowbray, 1906.

Collins, RF, 'A Significant Decade: The Trajectory of the Hellenistic Epistolary Thanksgiving', in *Paul and the Ancient Letter Form*. Edited by SE Porter and SA Adams; Leiden: Brill, 2010, 159–84.

Congar, JJ, 'Proceedings of the American Psychological Association', in *American Psychologist* 30 (1975): 620–51.

Cooper-Clarke, D, 'An Evangelical Perspective on the Morality of Homosexual Behaviour', <www.bioethicscolloquium.com.au>

Cotter, W, 'Women's Authority Roles in Paul's Churches: Countercultural or Conventional', in *Novum Testamentum* 36.4 (1994): 350–72.

Cox, L, 'Poll shows growing support for same-sex marriage', *Sydney Morning Herald*, July 15, 2014. <http://www.smh.com.au/federal-politics/political-news/poll-shows-growing-support-for-samesex-marriage-20140714-3bxaj.html>

Crafton, BC, *Let Us Bless the Lord, Year One: Advent through Holy Week*. Harrisburg, PA: Morehouse, 2004.

Critchley, S, *The Ethics of Deconstruction: Derrida and Levinas*, Oxford: Blackwell, 1992.

Crouch, S, 'The Australian Study of Child Health in Same-Sex Families (ACHESS) Interim report' at <http://mccaugheycentre.unimelb.edu.au/__data/assets/pdf_file/0008/786806/simon_report_.pdf>

Croucher, R, 'Homosexuality: Rowland Croucher's Views', *John Mark Ministries*, 22 July 1997. <http://www.jmm.org.au/articles/599.htm>

Daffern, M, 'Review of Pieces of Ease and Grace', in *Journal of Theological Studies* (NS) 66 (2015): 277–79.

Darwin, C, *On the Origin of Species*. London: John Murray, 1859.

Derrida, J, *The Gift of Death*. Translated by D Wills; Chicago: University of Chicago Press, 1995.

Dessaix, Robert, *(and so forth)*. Sydney: Macmillan, 1998.

Doe, N, *Canon Law in the Anglican Communion*, Oxford: Clarendon Press, 1998.

Doering, L, *Ancient Jewish Letters and the Beginnings of Jewish Epistolography*. Tübingen: Mohr Siebeck, 2012.

Driver, J, *A Polity of Persuasion: Gift and Grief of Anglicanism*. Eugene, OR: Cascade, 2014.

Edwards, D, *Jesus the Wisdom of God: An Ecological Theology*. Maryknoll: Orbis, 1995.

Evans, Carolyn. *Legal Aspects of the Protection of Religious Freedom in Australia*. Melbourne University Law School, 2009. <https://www.google.com.au/webhp?sourceid=chrome-instant&rlz=

1C1CHMO_enAU550AU552&ion=1&espv=2&ie=UTF-8#q=religion+in+the+australian+courts>

Farrar, FW, *Chapters on Language*. London: Longmans, Green & Co, 1865.

Farrer, A, *The Freedom of the Will: The Gifford Lectures in the University of Edinburgh 1957*. London: A & C Black, 1958.

Frame, T, *Anglicans in Australia*. Kensington, NSW, UNSW Press, 2007.

Frey, J-B, *Corpus Inscriptionum Judaicarum*. Rome: 2 vols, 1936, 1952.

Gaden, J, '"Friends of God and Prophets"', in *AIDS: The Church as Enemy and Friend*. Edited by AH Cadwallader; Blackburn: CollinsDove, 1992, 137–45.

Gagnon, RJA, *The Bible and Homosexual Practice: Texts and Hermeneutics*. Nashville: Abingdon, 2002.

Garrett, G, 'Open Heaven/Closed Hearts: Theological Reflections on Ecumenical Relations', in *Faith and Freedom: Christian Ethics in a Pluralist Culture*. Edited by D Neville and P Matthews; Hindmarsh: ATF Press, 2003, 63–80.

Giddens, A, *The Consequences of Modernity*. Cambridge: Polity Press, 1990.

Giles, K, *Patterns of Ministry among the First Christians*. North Blackburn, Vic: Collins Dove, 1989.

— *The Trinity and Subordinationism: The Doctrine of God and the Contemporary Gender Debate*. Downers Grove, ILL: IVP, 2002.

— *Better Together: Equality in Christ*. Brunswick East, Vic: Acorn Press, 2010.

— 'Paul's Condemnation of Porneia: Sexual Immorality in 1 Corinthians 6:9–10', in *Ethos: Centre for Christianity and Society* blog, at <www.ethos.org.au/Online-Articles/Blog>

Giordiano, C and I Kahn, *The Jews in Pompeii, Herculaneum, Stabiae and in the Cities of Campania Felix*. Rome: Bardi, 3rd ed., 2001.

Girard, R, *Achever Clausewitz: Quand la violence menace la planète*. Paris: Carnets Nord, 2007

—*Battling to the End: Conversations with Benoît Chantre*. Translated by M Baker; East Lansing: Michigan State University Press, 2010.

Goldsworthy, K, 'The "almost" Fully Ordained meat Pie' (2006) at <http://www.perth.anglican.org/download/Spirituality_Theology/The%20almost%20fully%20ordained%20meat%20pie.pdf>

Gotta, G, RJ Green, E Rothblum, S Solomon, K Balsam, and P Schwartz, 'Heterosexual, lesbian and gay male relationships: A comparison of couples in 1975 and 2000', in *Family Process*, 50 (2011): 333–76.

Grabbe, LL, *Judaic Religion in the Second Temple Period: Belief and Practice from the Exile to Yavneh*. London: Routledge, 2000.

Grayling, AC, *Friendship*. New Haven and London: Yale, 2013.

Griffin, GM, 'Christian Attitudes to Sexuality: An Historical Romp', in *Ministry, Society and Theology* 7.2 (1993): 5–21.

Gunderson, J, 'Inscribing Pompeii: a Re-evaluation of the Jewish Epigraphic Data'. Unpublished MA thesis, University of Kansas, 2013.

Gwatkin, HM, *Studies of Arianism*. Cambridge: Deighton, Bell & Co, 1882.

Habel, N, 'Geophany: The Earth Story in Genesis 1', in *The Earth Story in Genesis: The Earth Bible, 2*. Edited by N Habel and S Wurst; Sheffield: Sheffield Academic Press, 2000, 34–48.

Hanks, TD, 'Tom Hanks Paper on Loader, SBL 2013', available from *Other Sheep: Multicultural Ministries with Sexual Minorities* <http://www.fundotrasovejas.org.ar/ingles/resenas/Loader%20Romans%202010.pdf>

Harding, J, 'Opposite sex marriage a biblical ideal?', in *Pieces of Ease and Grace*. Edited by AH Cadwallader; Adelaide: ATF Press, 2013, 35–52.

Hauerwas, S, 'Sex in Public: How Adventurous Christians Are Doing It', in *The Hauerwas Reader*. Edited by John Berkman and Michael Cartwright; Durham, NC: Duke University Press, 2001, 481–504.

—"The Radical Hope in the Annunciation: Why Both Single and Married Christians Welcome Children', in *The Hauerwas Reader*. Edited by John Berkman and Michael Cartwright; Durham, NC: Duke University Press, 2001, 505–518.

Hazelton, L, *The First Muslim: The Story of Mohammad*. New York: Riverhead, 2013.

Hearon, HE, '1 Corinthians', in *The Queer Bible Commentary*. Edited by D Guest, RE Goss, M West and T Bohache; London; SCM, 2006, 606–23.

Heidegger, M, *Being and Time*. Translated by Joan Stambaugh; Albany: SUNY Press, Rev. Ed., 2010.

Hellerman, J, *The Ancient Church as Family*. Minneapolis: Fortress Press, 2001.

Hengel, M, *Judaism and Hellenism*. Translated by J Bowden; London: SCM, 1974.

Hill, W, 'Simplicity of God', in *New Catholic Encyclopedia of Theology*. Edited by State Catholic University of America; Washington: McGraw-Hill, 1967, Volume 13, 230.

Hooker, R, *Of the Laws of Ecclesiastical Polity*. Everyman Edition; London: Dent, 1907 [1593].

Horbury, W, and D Noy, *Jewish Inscriptions of Graeco-Roman Egypt*. Cambridge: Cambridge University Press, 1992.

Hort, AF, *Life and Letters of Fenton John Anthony Hort*. London: Macmillan, 2 vols, 1896.

Hughes, P and L Fraser, *Life, Ethics and Faith: Facts and Figures*. Melbourne: CRA, 2014.

Inter-Anglican Theology and Doctrine Commission, 'Summary Argument for the IATDC's "Communion Study"' (2006) <http://www.anglicancommunion.org/ministry/theological/iatdc/docs/2006study.cfm>

Ivarsson, F, 'Vice Lists and Deviant Masculinity: The Rhetorical Function of 1 Corinthians 5:10–11 and 6:9–10', in *Mapping Gender in Ancient Religious Discourses*. Edited by T Penner and C Vander Stichele; Leiden: Brill, 2007, 163–84.

Jensen, M, *Sydney Anglicanism: An Apology*. Eugene, OR: Wipf & Stock, 2012.

Jewel, J, 'Apologia Ecclesiae Anglicanae: An Apology of the Church of England and Defence of the Apology', in *The Works of John Jewel*. Edited by J Ayre; 4 volumes; Cambridge: The Parker Society/Cambridge University Press, 1848, volume 3.

Jones, G, 'Thy Grace Shall Always Prevent...', in *Gays and the Future of Anglicanism* (edited by A Linzey and R Kirker; Hants, UK: John Hunt Publishing, 2005), 116–37.

Jones, T, *Sexual Politics in the Church of England, 1857–1957*. Oxford: Oxford University Press, 2013.

Jordan, M (editor), *Authorizing Marriage: Canon, tradition, and critique in the blessing of same-sex unions*. Princeton: Princeton University Press, 2006.

Jüngel, E, *God's being is in becoming: the trinitarian being of God in the theology of Karl Barth*. Grand Rapids: W B Eerdmans, 2001.

Kaye, B, *Conflict and the Practice of Christian Faith: The Anglican Experiment*. Cambridge: Lutterworth, 2011.

von Kellenbach, K, *The Mark of Cain: Guilt and Denial in the Post-War Lives of Nazi Perpetrators*. Oxford: Oxford University Press, 2013.

King, FJ, 'Review of *Five Uneasy Pieces*', in *Colloquium* 46.1 (2014): 132-34.

Kirker, R, 'Afterword: Why Gays Refused to be Unchurched'in *Gays and the Future of Anglicanism* (edited by A Linzey and R Kirker; Hants, UK: John Hunt Publishing, 2005), 329-34.

Knowles, GB and F Westcott, *The Floral Cabinet and Magazine of Exotic Botany*. London: William Smith, 3 Vols, 1837-40.

Krautbauer, A, S Llewellyn and B Wassell, 'A Gift of One Eunuch and Four Slave Boys: *P.Cair.Zen*. I 59076 and Historical Reconstruction', in *Journal for the Study of Judaism* 45.3 (2014): 305-25.

Lapide, P, and K Rahner, *Heil von den Juden? Ein Gespräch*. Mainz: Matthias-Grünewald-Verlag, 1983.

Lawton, W, *The better time to be: Utopian attitudes to society among Sydney Anglicans, 1885 to 1914*. Kensington, NSW: University of New South Wales Press, 1990.

Llewelyn, J, 'Responsibility with Indecidability', in *Derrida: A Critical Reader*. Edited by D Wood; Oxford: Blackwell, 1992, 72-96.

Lindsay, E and J Scarfe (editors), *Preachers, Prophets & Heretics: Anglican Women's Ministry*. Sydney: UNSW Press, 2012.

Lings, KR, *Love Lost in Translation: Homosexuality and the Bible*. USA: Trafford Publishing, 2013.

Loader, W, *Enoch, Levi, and Jubilees on Sexuality*. Grand Rapids, MI: Eerdmans, 2007.

— *The Dead Sea Scrolls on Sexuality*. Grand Rapids, MI: Eerdmans, 2009.

— *Sexuality in the New Testament*. Louisville, KY: WJKP, 2010.

— *The Pseudepigrapha on Sexuality*. Grand Rapids, MI: Eerdmans, 2011.

— *Philo, Josephus and the Testaments on Sexuality*. Grand Rapids, MI: Eerdmans, 2011.

— *The New Testament on Sexuality*. Grand Rapids, MI: Eerdmans, 2012.
— *Making Sense of Sex: Attitudes towards Sexuality in Early Jewish and Christian Literature*. Grand Rapids: Eerdmans, 2013.
Lorenzen, T, *Resurrection and Discipleship: Interpretive Models, Biblical Reflections, Theological Consequences*. Maryknoll, NY: Orbis Books, 1995.
Maddox, M, *God under Howard: The Rise of the Religious Right in Australian Politics*. Crows Nest: Allen & Unwin, 2005.
Marar, Z, *Intimacy: Understanding the Subtle Power of Human Connection*. Durham: Acumen, 2012.
Marchal, PA, 'The Usefulness of an Onesimus: The Sexual Use of Slaves and Paul's Letter to Philemon', in *Journal of Biblical Literature* 130 (2011): 749–70.
Mascall, EL, *The Secularisation of Christianity: An Analysis and a Critique*. London: Darton, Longman & Todd, 1965.
MacCulloch, D, *Thomas Cranmer: A Life*. New Haven/London: Yale University Press, 1998.
McCarthy, T, *The Great Dock Strike 1889*. London: Weidenfeld and Nicolson, 1988.
McGuire, BP, *Friendship and Community: The Monastic Experience, 350–1250*. Kalamazoo: Cistercian Publications, 1988.
McLean, BH, *Biblical Interpretation and Philosophical Hermeneutics*. Cambridge: Cambridge University Press, 2012.
Morimoto, A, 'Contextualised and Cumulative: Tradition, Orthodoxy and Identity from the Perspective of Asian Theology', in *Studies in World Christianity* 15:1 (2009): 39–55.
Moltmann, J, *The Church in the Power of the Spirit: A Contribution to Messianic Ecclesiology*. London: SCM, 1977.
— *Neuer Lebensstil: Schritte zur Gemeinde*. München: Chr Kaiser, 1977.
Moxnes, H, *Jesus and the Rise of Nationalism: a New Quest for the Nineteenth Century*. London: IB Tauris, 2012.
Musurillo, HA, *The Acts of the Pagan Martyrs: Acta Alexandrinorum*. Oxford, Clarendon, 1954.
Newman, JH, *An Essay on the Development of Christian Doctrine*. Hammondsworth, UK: Pelican, 1974.

Nussbaum, M, *The New Religious Intolerance: Overcoming the Politics of Fear in an Anxious Age*. Cambridge, Mass: Belknap Press, 2012.

Ochs, P, *Peirce, Pragmatism and the Logic of Scripture*, Cambridge: Cambridge University Press, 1998.

Palmer, B, *High and Mitred: Prime Ministers as Bishop Makers 1837-1977*. London: SPCK, 1992.

Parker, JW (editor), *Essays and Reviews*. London: JW Parker, 1860.

Parker-Pope, T, 'Gay marriage: Same, But different', in *International Herald Tribune* 3 July, 2013, 10.

Patrick, G, *The Miner's Bishop: Brooke Foss Westcott*. Peterborough: Epworth, 2nd Ed, 2004.

Perrin, E and B Siegel, 'Promoting The Well-Being of Children Whose Parents Are Gay or Lesbian', in *Pediatrics* 131/4 (2013): 1374-83.

Petzer, JH, 'The History of the New Testament—Its Reconstruction, Significance and Use in New Testament Textual Criticism', in *New Testament Textual Criticism, Exegesis and History*. Edited by B Aland and J Delobel; Kampen: Kok Pharos, 1994, 11-36.

Pew Forum, 'Graphics Slideshow: Changing Attitudes on Gay Marriage' 2012. <http://www.pewforum.org/Gay-Marriage-and-Homosexuality/Graphics-Slideshow--Changing-Attitudes-on-Gay-Marriage.aspx>

—'Gay Marriage and Homosexuality in America' 2012. <http://www.pewforum.org/Topics/Issues/Gay-Marriage-and-Homosexuality/>

— *A Survey of LGBT Americans*, 2013. <http://pewsocialtrends.org/2013/06/13/a-survey-of-lgbt-americans>

Pickard, S, 'Innovation and Undecidability: Some Implications for the Koinonia of the Anglican Church', in *Journal of Anglican Studies*, 2.2 (2004): 87-105.

—*Theological Foundations for Collaborative Ministry*. Farnham: Ashgate, 2009.

Poettcker, G, 'Beyond Nietzsche's War Rhetoric: Ascesis, Sacrifice, and the Recovery of Health'. <www.girard2014.de/_download/3df600a35a8c4cd1acf2b4d81806f8ae>

Pomeroy, SB, *Women in Hellenistic Egypt: from Alexander to Cleopatra*. Detroit, Mich: Wayne State University Press, 1990.

Popovic, M, *Reading the Human Body: Physiognomics and Astrology in the Dead Sea Scrolls*. Leiden: Brill, 2007.

Porter, M, *Sydney Anglicans and the Threat to World Anglicanism*. London: Ashgate, 2011.
—'Backlash: The New Threat to Ordained Women', in *Preachers, Prophets & Heretics*. Edited by E Lindsay and J Scarfe; Sydney: UNSW Press, 2012, 374-91.
Preece, G, 'Accommodation of gay culture not scriptural', in *The Melbourne Anglican* 6/3/2012.
Rahner, K *Foundations of Christian Faith: An Introduction to the Idea of Christianity*. London: Darton, Longman and Todd, 1997.
Rajak, T, *Translation and Survival: The Greek Bible of the Ancient Jewish Diaspora*. Oxford: Oxford University Press, 2009.
Ricoeur, P, 'Biblical Hermeneutics', in *Semeia* 4 (1975): 29-148.
Robertson, G, *The Statute of Liberty: How Australians Can Take Back Their Rights*. North Sydney: Vintage, 2009.
Roscoe, ES, *The Bishop of Lincoln's Case*. London: William Clowes, 1889.
Rothblum, ED, KF Balsam and SE Solomon, 'Narratives of same-sex couples who had civil unions in Vermont: The impact of legalising relationships on couples and social policy', in *Sexuality Research and Social Policy*, 8 (2011): 183-91.
de Rougemont, D, *Passion and Society*. London: Faber & Faber, 1962.
Sakharov, N, *I love therefore I am: The Theological Legacy of Archimandrite Sophrony*. New York: St Vladimir's Seminary Press, 2002.
Schüssler Fiorenza, E, 'Challenging the Rhetorical Half-Turn: Feminist and Rhetorical Biblical Criticism', in *Rhetoric, Scripture and Theology: Essays from the 1994 Pretoria Conference*. Edited by SE Porter and TH Olbricht; Sheffield: Sheffield Academic Press, 1996, 48-60.
Shea, V and W Whitla (editors), *Essays and Reviews: The 1860 Text and its Reading*. USA: University of Virginia Press, 2000.
Sheppard, ARR, 'R.E.C.A.M. Notes and Studies No. 6: Jews, Christians and heretics in Acmonia and Eumeneia', in *Anatolian Studies* 29 (1979): 169-80.
Solomon, A, *Far from the Tree: Parents, Children and the Search for Identity*. London: Chatto & Windus, 2013.
Stead, MR, *The Intertextuality of Zechariah 1-8*. New York: T&T Clark, 2009.

—'Herman Who? The Hermeneutics of the Homosexuality Debate'. <www.stjamesturramurra.org.au/stead/files/HermanWhoThe HermeneuticsoftheHomosexualityDebate.pdf>

Steiner, G, *Real Presences*, Chicago: University of Chicago Press, 1989.

Stern, KB, 'Vandals or Pilgrims? Jews, Travel Culture and Devotional Practice in the Pan Temple of Egyptian El-Kanais', in *'The One who Sows Bountifully': Essays in Honor of Stanley K. Stowers*. Edited by CJ Hodge, SM Olyan, D Ullucci and E Wassermann; Providence, RI: Brown University Press, 2013), 177–88.

Still, J and M Worton, 'Introduction' to *Intertextuality: Theories and Practices*. Edited by M Worton and J Still; Manchester: Manchester University Press, 1990, 1–44.

Taylor, MC, *About Religion: Economies of Faith in Virtual Culture*. Chicago: University of Chicago Press, 1999.

Tcherikover, VA and A Fuks (editors), *Corpus Papyrorum Judaicarum* [*CPJ*]. Cambridge, MA: Harvard University Press, 1957.

Thatcher, A, 'Beginning Marriage: Two Traditions', in *Religion and Sexuality*. Edited by Michael A Hayes, W Porter and D Tombs; Sheffield: Sheffield Academic Press, 1998, 415–26.

Thompson, MD (editor), *Human Sexuality: and the 'Same Sex Marriage' Debate*. Sydney: Anglican Youthworks, 2015.

Thomson, H and S MacNeil (editors), 'Taking Stock: The Joy and challenge of ordained women in the Anglican Church of Australia', in *St Mark's Review* 228.2 (2014): 1–141.

Thorley, P, 'German Romantic Idealism', in *The Cambridge Companion to British Romanticism*. Edited by S Curran; Cambridge: Cambridge University Press, 2nd Ed., 2010, 74–94.

Torrance, T, *Theological Science*, Oxford: Oxford University Press, 1969.

—*The Trinitarian Faith*. Edinburgh: T&T Clark, 1988.

Treloar, G, *Lightfoot the Historian: The Nature and Role of History in the Life and Thought of J.B. Lightfoot (1828–1889) as Churchman and Scholar*. Tübingen: Mohr Siebeck, 1998.

Turner, B, *Religion and Modern Society: Citizenship, Secularisation and the State*, Cambridge: Cambridge University Press, 2011.

Tyack, C, 'Friendship is the Basic Form of Love', in *Changing Attitude Australia Newsletter*, Feb 2014 at <http://www.changingattitude.

org.au/wp/wp-content/uploads/2014/02/CAA-Newsletter-Feb-2014.pdf>.

Vincent, A, *La Religion des Judéo-Araméens d'Éléphantine*. Paris: Geuthner, 1937.

Vernon, M, *The Philosophy of Friendship*. Basingstoke: Palgrave Macmillan, 2005.

VHREOC (Victorian Human Rights and Equal Opportunities Commission) 'Victoria's Charter of Human Rights and Responsibilities', nd . http://www.humanrightscommission.vic.gov.au/index.php/the-charter.

Warner, M, '"Set in Tradition and History": Genesis 2:24 and the Marriage Debate', in *Pieces of Ease and Grace: Biblical Essays on Sexuality and Welcome*. Edited by AH Cadwallader; Adelaide: ATF Press, 2013, 1–15.

Westcott, BF, *Introduction to the Study of the Gospels*. London: Macmillan, 1860.

— 'The Revised Version of the New Testament', in *The Expositor* III.5 (1887): 346–54.

— *Essays in the History of Religious Thought in the West*. London: Macmillan, 1891.

— *Lessons from Work*. London: Macmillan, 1901.

— *Christian Social Union Addresses*. London: Macmillan, 1903.

Westcott, A, *Life and Letters of Brooke Foss Westcott*. London: Macmillan, 2 vols, 1903.

de Wet, C., 'On Method in the Study of Early Christian History: Problems, Limits and Challenges', in *Journal of Early Christian History* 3.2 (2013): 1–3.

White, JL, *Light from Ancient Letters*. Philadelphia: Fortress Press, 1986.

White, P, *Voss: A Novel*. London: Eyre & Spottiswoode, 1957.

Whitehorne, JEG, 'Sex and Society in Greco-Roman Egypt', in *Actes du XVe congrès international de papyrology, Pt 4*. Edited by J Bingen and G Nachtergael; Brussels: Fondation Égyptologique Reine Élisabeth, 1979, 240–46.

Williams, R, *On Christian Theology*. Oxford: Blackwell, 2000.

— *Resurrection: Interpreting the Easter Gospel*. Cleveland, OH: The Pilgrim Press, 2nd Ed, 2002.

— *Writing in the Dust: Reflections on the 11 September and its Aftermath*. London: Hodder & Stoughton, 2002.

— *The Archbishop of Canterbury's Address to the Thirteenth Ordinary General Assembly of the Synod of Bishops on The New Evangelization for the Transmission of the Christian Faith*, 10 October 2012, Rome. <http://rowanwilliams.archbishopofcanterbury.org/articles.php/2645/archbishops-address-to-the-synod-of-bishops-in-rome#sthash.ky9vuE1H.dpuf>

Wink, W, *Manifesto for Biblical Studies*, revised and re-published as *The Bible in Human Transformation*. Philadelphia: Fortress Press, 1973.

Wiseman, N, *The Real Presence of the Body and Blood of Our Lord Jesus Christ in the Blessed Eucharist, Proved from Scripture*. Dublin: James Duffy, 1836.

Wittgenstein, L, *Philosophical Investigations, The German Text, with a Revised English Translation*. Oxford: Blackwell Publishing, 2003.

Wood, D (editor), *Derrida: A Critical Reader*. Edited by D Wood; Oxford: Blackwell, 1992.

Wood, JT, *Discoveries at Ephesus*. London: Longmans, Green & Co, 1877.

Wright, NMcI (editor), *Five Uneasy Pieces*. Adelaide: ATF Press, 2011.

Yeo, R, *Notebooks, English Virtuosi and Early Modern Science*. Chicago: University of Chicago, 2014.

Zeldin, T, *An Intimate History of Humanity*. London: Vintage, 1998.

Zizioulas, J, *Communion and Otherness: Further Studies in Personhood and the Church*. London/New York: T & T Clark, 2006.

Index of Biblical References and Other Ancient Sources

Genesis	
1:26, 27	71, 129
2:16	67
2:24	
3	129
3:5	x
4	158–9
12:1	x

Exodus	
3:5	x
3:8	x
3:14–15	68
3:14	x
33:11	60

Leviticus	
18:7–8	13
20	13

Joshua	
7	177
7:26	177

1 Samuel	
18:1–3, 20	60

2 Samuel	
1:26	60

2 Chronicles	
20:7	60

Psalms	
41:9	60
88:18	60

Isaiah	
1:18	168
41:8	60
66:1–2	163

Jeremiah	
29:7	x

Matthew	
3:7	178
3:11	178
5:6	189
5:27–30	130
7	81
8:5–13	181
8:22	53
10:34	177
10:37	50
11:3	178
12:7	163
15:21–28	181
19:1–12	100
19:12	22
21:26	161
21:27–28	
21:31–32	22
22:23–33	50
22:34–46	72

23:4	50	**Acts of the Apostles**	
25:31–46	46	2:14–42	45
		4:32–5	60
Mark		10:9–16	172
2:27	50	10:19	45
3:28–30	163	10:28	xv, 178
7:13	163	10:28b	33
7:24–30	181	10:34–35	45
8:35	53	15	32
10:2–12	100	15:28	93, 102, 108
10:21	53	16:9	x
10:41–45	27		
11:17	x	**Romans**	
12:18–27	50	1	16
		1:18	129
Luke		5:15–21	148
6:27–28	187	8:17–23	x
7:1–10	181	8:24	ix
9:62	53	14	46, 141
9:32	162		
10:29	72	**1 Corinthians**	
12:51	177	5:1ff	14
14:26	50, 54	5:9	14
16:18	100	6	16
17:33	53	6:9–10	14
20:27–40	50	7:7–8	22
20:34–35	22	7:10–13	100
23:12	60	8	141
		10	141
John		13:12	xi, 63
1:14	162	16:1	14
8	158		
8:11	130	**Galatians**	
8:44	174	3:28–29	163, 171
9	173, 174	5:22	158
10:10b	148		
13:23	60	**Philippians**	
14:27	177	2:5–11	162
15:13–15	60	3:1–17	162
15:15	55		
19:16–23	189	**Colossians**	
19:25–27	190	1:19	148
20:30–31	14	2:9	148
21	45	4:16	14
21:15–17	60		
21:20	60	**1 Thessalonians**	
		5:27	14

2 Thessalonians
2:15   14

1 Timothy
1:14   148

Philemon
2   14

Hebrews
5:5–10   162
11:16   ix

James
2:23   60

2 Peter
3:15–16   14

1 John
3:2   69

Revelation
2:7   14
2:11   14
2:17   14
2:29   14
3:6   14
3:13   14
3:22   14
6:15–17   177
22:18–19   14

Other Ancient Sources
Papyri and Inscriptions

Corpus Inscriptionum Judaicarum (CIJ)
2.1537   18

Corpus Papyrorum Judaicarum (CPJ)
1   18
4   17
5   18
7   18
39   17
126   18
427   17

Corpus Inscriptionum Latinarum (CIL)
4.1375   19
4.1655   19
4.1782   20
4.2402   20
4.2403   20
4.2406   20
4.5244   20

Papiri greci e latini [PSI]
4.340   19

PCairo Zenon
1.59076   16–20

PCowley
14   17
21.2   17

POxyrhynchus
1160   19

Other Ancient Sources Texts

Acts of the Pagan Martyrs 16

Basil of Caesarea
On the Holy Spirit
1.3   6
2.4   ix–x

Damascus Document (CD)
12.10–11   18

Herodotos
2.104.2–3   17

Josephus
Antiquities
12.160   19

Juvenal
Satires
14.104   20

Martial
Epigram

7.30	20
7.82	20
11.94	20

(Ps-) Quintilian
Minor Declamations
298	19
335	14

Seneca
Epistles
122.7	20

Controversies
10.4.17	20

Sibylline Oracles
3.596–600	19

Tertullian
Against the Heretics 142

Index of Modern Authors

A
Aland, K	13
Alison, J	43, 44, 46, 56, 57, 138, 161–82
Angelou, M	1
Armstrong, PW	3
Atherton, J	7
Avis, P	27, 143, 144

B
Bachelard, S	xv, 43–58, 168, 169
Bagnall, RS	16
Baile, D	20
Barclay, JDG	19
Barnett, P	25
Bates, S	31, 78
Bayer, O	21
Berdyaev, N	xiv, 148
Best, G	7
Bieżunka-Malowist, I	17
Bird, M	24, 25, 99
Bita, N	32, 34, 36
Blaskow, N	161–82
Boer, R	24
Bonhoeffer, D	64
Bouma, G	29–42
Bourdieu, P	12, 22, 27
Brittain, CC	126
Burgon, J	5

C
Cadwallader, AH	ix–xi, xv, 1–28, 60, 99, 172, 181
Carr, EH	15
Chamberlain, L	66-7, 72
Charry, ET	136
Colenso, J	5
Collins, JJ	13
Collins, RF	17
Congar, JJ	10
Cooper, A	xiv
Cooper-Clarke, D	14
Cotter, W	23
Crafton, BC	xiv
Critchley, S	147
Croucher, R	33

D
Darwin, C	3
Derrida, J	146–7
Descartes, R	68, 72
Dessaix, R	65
Doe, N	154
Doering, L	18
Donaldson, JW	5
Driver, J	27

E
Edwards, D	61

F
Fuks, A — 17

G
Gaden, J — 172
Gagnon, RJA — 13, 14, 15
Garrett, G — 147
Giddens, A — 159
Giles, KR — 6, 11, 14, 25
Giordano, C — 20
Girard, R — 161, 176, 178, 182
Goldsworthy, K — xiii–xvi, 96
Goldsmith, B — 128
Grabbe, LL — 18
Grayling, AC — 64, 65
Griffin, GM — 27
Gunderson, J — 20
Gwatkin, HM — 3

H
Habel, N — 71
Hanks, TD — 22
Harding, J — 60
Hauerwas, S — 48–51
Hazelton, L — 169
Hearon, HE — 9
Heidegger, M — 101–3, 107
Hellerman, J — 158–9
Hengel, M — 17
Hill, W — 141
Hooker, R — 148
Horbury, W — 17
Hort, FJA — 2, 4, 13, 15

I
Ivarsson, F — 19, 20

J
Jewel, J — 142
Jowett, B — 5–6, 8
Jüngel, E — 70–1

K
Kahn, I — 20
Kaye, B — 25
von Kellenbach, K — 107
King, FJ — 12, 13
Knowles, GB — 3
Krautbauer, A — 18–19
Kristeva, J — 21

L
Lapide, P — 68
Lawton, W — 9
Lightfoot, JB — xv, 1, 2, 3, 4, 5, 6, 10, 11, 12–13, 24
Lindsay, E — 7, 95, 96
Lings, KR — 14
Llewelyn, J — 146
Llewellyn, S — 18–19
Loader, W — 13–17, 19, 20, 21, 22, 24
Lorenzen, T — 44

M
MacNeil, S — 96
McCarthy, T — 7
MacCulloch, D — xiii
McKinnon, A — 126
McLean, BH — 101, 102
Maddox, M — 24
Marar, Z — 62–4, 70, 73
Marchal, JA — 19
Marsh, H — 5
Mascall, EL — 95
Maurice, FD — 5
Moltmann, J — 64–6, 73, 74
Morimoto, A — 103–5, 106, 108
Moxnes, H — 23
Musurillo, HA — 16

N
Nestle, E — 2
Newman, JH — 5, 143
Noy, D — 17
Nussbaum, M — 138

O
Ochs, P — 149

P
Palmer, B — 7
Patrick, G — 7
Peirce, C — 149
Peterson, E — 172
Pickard, S — xv, 26, 65–6, 135–59
Poettcker, G — 182
Pomeroy, SB — 19
Popovic, M — 17
Porter, M — 31, 79, 87, 88, 96
Preece, G — 21, 24, 25, 99

R
Rahner, K — 68, 140
Rajak, T — 17
Reid, D — 59–74
Reynolds, J — 146
Ricoeur, P — 148
Rilke, RM — xiii, xvi
de Rougemont, D — 61

S
Sakharov, N — 72
Sakharov, S — 72
Scarfe, J — 7, 95, 96
Schüssler Fiorenza, E — 21
Sheppard, ARR — 17
Sherlock, P — xv, 26, 75–183–200
Smith, EJ —
Solomon, A — 73
Stead, MR — 21, 24
Steiner, G — 147, 158–9
Stern, KB — 18
Still, J — 21–2
Sullins, P — 125

T
Tcherikover, VA — 17
Temple, F — 6–7

Thomson, C — 111–33
Thomson, H — 96
Thorslev, P — 97
Tolliday, P — 26, 93–109
Torrance, T — 142, 150
Treloar, G — 11
Turner, B — 144
Tyack, C — 59

V
Vernon, M — 59, 61, 66, 72, 74
Vincent, A — 17

W
Warner, M — 11
Wassell, B — 18–19
Westcott, A — 3, 27
Westcott, BF — xv, 1–11, 13–14, 15, 24, 27, 28
Westcott, F — 3
de Wet, C — 11
White, JL — 17
White, P — 64
Whitehorne, JEG — 16
Williams, R — 45, 54, 106–7, 109, 158, 180
Wink, W — 12, 22
Wittgenstein, L — 99
Wood, JT — 4
Wordsworth, J — 1
Worton, M — 21–2

Y
Yeo, R — 13

Z
Zeldin, T — 62, 72
Zizioulas, J — 66–71, 72, 74

Index of Subject

Alison, James 43, 44, 46, 56, 57, 138, 161–82
Anglican Church of Australia 23, 24, 31, 35, 80, 84, 93, 94
  Decision-making x–xi, xv, 75–8, 82, 87, 94–8
  Politics ix, 7, 23–7, 29, 109, 120, 155, 156
  Synod xv, 24, 25–6, 77–8, 79–81, 82–3, 84, 88, 89, 94–5, 152, 185, 192, 198
  Thirty-nine Articles 5, 151, 152, 156
Anglican Communion, The xv, 1, 76, 77, 78, 79, 84, 107, 111–33, 135, 137, 138, 145, 151–6, 158, 170
Archbishops of Canterbury 1, 6, 11, 31, 54, 106–7, 135
Aristotle 73
Authority 6, 65, 119, 137–8, 151–2, 186, 187, 199
Authoritarianism 27
  Levels 25–6, 76, 89, 137–8, 143, 152–5
  Power 5, 8, 31, 62, 65–6, 87, 89, 120, 121, 126, 151, 189
Australia xi, xiii, 24, 39, 78, 188, 189
  Attitudes to same-sex
    Marriage xiii, 29, 30, 32, 35–6, 41–2, 47, 55, 57, 136
  Demographics 32, 34–6, 40, 41

Basil of Caesarea ix–x, 6
Bible
  Authority 4–5, 93–4, 113, 129, 130, 132, 170–1

Hermeneutics 7–8, 11, 15, 22, 28, 94, 97, 101–3, 106, 111–12, 122, 166, 171, 173, 175–7
  History 4, 8, 10–12, 15–21
  Interpretation x, 1–9, 28, 97, 127, 196
  Methodology 11, 15, 21–23
  Understandings, changes of 4, 9, 27–8, 56–7, 85, 94, 100–1, 143, 149
  Usage in debates 8–9, 24–27, 89, 93–5, 99–100, 113, 127, 145, 151, 170–1, 176, 181, 189, 193
Bishops xv, 2, 5, 6, 7, 11, 24, 75, 79, 80, 81–3, 84, 86, 87, 89, 90, 111–33, 142, 197
  Catholic 167
  Protocols 26–7, 96, 105
Bonhoeffer, Dietrich 64
Book of Common Prayer xiii, 60, 83, 84, 88
Buber, Martin 69

Cambridge Triumvirate, The 2, 28
Chamberlain, Lesley 66–7, 72
Chomsky, Noam 103
  Competence and
    Performance 103–4, 106, 108
Christian Socialism 7–8
Christology 108, 141
Church x, xi, 2, 9, 25, 26, 27, 28, 31, 32, 49–51, 59, 60, 77, 79, 85, 89, 120, 121, 125, 127, 139, 152, 155–7, 172, 184, 185, 188–9, 196
  Cultural change and xiv, 23, 25, 30–1, 42, 46–7, 50, 75, 94, 105, 108, 129, 149, 150, 153, 158, 159, 171
  Welfare arm 38–40

Church of England 2, 5, 86, 107, 113, 124–5, 128
Controversy 137–42, 144, 178, 181
  Dispute resolution 137, 139, 142, 145, 152, 155, 157
  Levels 25–6, 76, 89, 152–5
  Theology and
  Covenant, Anglican 119, 124, 126, 137–8, 152
Cranmer, Thomas, Margaret xiii–xiv

Darwin, Charles 3
Derrida, Jacques 146–7
Descartes, René 68, 72
Desire 5, 19, 46, 69–70, 149, 163, 178, 180, 191, 196
Diversity 26, 34, 175, 192
  in Bible 8, 33
  Religious 28, 31, 34–6, 40, 42, 83, 133, 140, 151–7, 195, 199
  Sexual xi, 2, 29, 32, 33, 83, 88, 89, 136, 138, 140, 183–5, 187, 188, 189, 190, 191, 192, 196, 198–200

Ecclesiology
  Anglican polity 25, 27, 151–7
  Catholicity 46, 125, 138, 154–5,
  Centrality of 140, 141
  Conflict 2, 5–6, 10, 42, 83, 135, 136, 137–42, 144, 157, 178, 181
  Courtesy 147, 170, 192
  Decision-making 82, 86–8, 90, 94–5, 137, 145–6, 152, 154–6
  Division and 29, 33, 89, 117, 127, 139, 144, 156, 162–3
  Enclaves 144, 154
  Freedom and unity 5, 7, 9, 53, 54, 65, 67, 123, 144, 151–7, 172, 184
  Koinonia 151, 153, 154, 157, 159
  Patience 106–7, 157–9
  Sexuality and 59, 76–8
  Subsidiarity 152, 156
  Trust 157–9
Episcopal Church of the United States of America 78–9, 113, 116, 135
Essays and Reviews 5–6, 21
  Frederick Temple 6–7

Ethics 40, 41–2
  Future and ix, x, xiv, 28, 64, 77, 96–8, 106–9, 111, 193
  Moral perception and 41, 43, 121, 184
Eunuchs 22

False sacredness 44–7, 178
  Marriage 43–52, 56–7
  Taboos 44, 45, 46, 52, 56, 57, 198
Family xiv, 34, 41, 59, 62, 72, 101, 190, 191, 193
  Church and 31, 48, 49, 120, 131, 132, 158–9, 177, 180, 181, 184, 185, 186, 190, 199
  Fear ix, x, 22, 52–3, 54, 57, 106, 111, 119, 129, 185, 191, 192
  Dishonesty 180–1
  of God 45, 165–7, 172
  of being wrong 161–82
  Prejudice 2, 24, 150
  Solution 3, 147, 173–5, 176–8, 180–1, 183–4, 187, 194, 195
Feminist hermeneutics 21, 23
  Masculinist studies 23
Five Uneasy Pieces xiv, 8, 12, 13–14, 21, 24, 25, 33, 99
Fox, George 61–2
  Quakers 62, 183
Francis, Saint 51
Freedom 5
  Church resistance 28, 38
  from discrimination 5, 6, 37–8, 40, 42
  of religion 36–7, 39
  rights and 39, 41–2
Friendship v, xiii, xiv, 2, 52, 59–74, 93, 183, 185, 187, 190, 193, 199
  David and Jonathon 60
  Difference and 59, 64, 66–72, 73
  Jesus and 55, 60, 64–5, 172, 190, 191, 193
  Private and public 1, 59, 61, 62–6
  Professionalism and 65–6
  Types of 60–2
Fundamentalism 169, 170, 175–6, 177

Gender 31, 35, 38, 41, 42, 62, 73, 85, 121
Identities 2, 29, 31, 34, 41, 59, 136, 183, 190, 198, 199
Genealogical method 2-3
Girard, René 161, 176, 178, 182
God xv, 43, 44, 46, 49, 50, 53, 54-5, 67-8, 73, 77, 89, 121, 129, 130, 141, 159, 163, 199
 Fear of 45, 165-7, 172
 Incomprehensibility of ix-x, 149, 151
 Marriage and 43, 47, 52, 55-8, 83, 120, 125, 130, 132
 Providence of 5, 43, 82, 93, 97-8, 108, 109, 147-8, 162, 181, 187, 193
 Welcoming xi, 28, 31, 42, 45, 46, 50, 51, 52, 53, 76, 81, 91, 121, 168, 169, 181, 187, 197-8
 Wrath of 45, 171, 174-9
 and see Trinity

Hauerwas, Stanley 48-51
Hegel, Georg WF 97-8
Heidegger, Martin 101-3, 107
Herft, Abp Roger 25-6, 82-4, 89
Hermeneutics 7-8, 11, 15, 22, 28, 94, 97, 101-3, 106, 111-12, 122, 166, 171, 173, 175-7
 Interpreter as key 5, 9, 12, 20, 21, 22, 27, 28, 76-7, 80, 100-3, 107, 142, 144, 145, 150, 151, 153, 176
History xiv, 1-28
 Hermeneutics 7-8, 11, 15, 22, 28, 94, 97
 Literature 5, 8, 11, 14, 15-21, 175
 Material artefacts 4, 15
Homosexuality
 Fidelity xiii, 29, 30, 43, 50, 54, 57, 74, 112, 125, 127, 129, 175, 185, 187, 194, 199
 Legal rights and 32, 39, 42
 Science and 8, 10, 112, 115, 131, 138, 140-1, 164, 168, 174
 Theology of 91, 131
 Women's ordination 85
Hort, Fenton JA 2, 4, 13, 15

Human experience 46, 47, 48, 52, 64, 74, 120, 129
Guidance 33, 47, 61, 68, 73, 79, 94-5, 101-2, 108, 113, 120, 169, 181

Identity xi, 2, 8, 9, 29, 31, 34, 36, 41, 44-5, 47, 53, 54, 59, 70-1, 74, 76, 77, 83, 84, 136, 183, 185, 190, 191, 192, 198, 199
 exclusion and inclusion x, xi, xv, 9, 38, 41, 44-8, 55, 57, 59, 77, 81, 88-90, 121, 123, 127, 133, 161, 168, 173-5, 179, 181, 193, 194, 195
 otherness 67-72, 74, 121
 politics 12, 22, 70
Innovation 135-59
 Doctrine and 86, 135, 141-2, 152, 168
 Novelty and 85, 141, 142, 143
 Undecidability and 138, 139, 144-51
Inter Anglican Theological and Doctrinal Commission 12, 135
Interpersonality 112, 116-17, 122-3, 126
Intersectionality 73
Intertextuality 112, 114-16, 117-21, 124-6
Intimacy 62-6, 73
 Characteristics 63
 Particularity 63, 66, 70-1, 72, 74, 109

James, Saint
 Change in the church 32
 Jerusalem Council 32
Jesus xv, 23, 50, 53-4, 56, 76, 91, 100, 130, 166, 171, 177-8
 Friendship 55, 60, 64-5, 72, 172, 190, 191, 193
 Jewishness 15, 22, 23
 redemption and x, 28, 44-5, 53, 64, 82, 89, 148, 184, 188, 189, 192, 193-6, 199
 the revisionist 44, 90, 158, 161-2, 163-4, 172-5, 187, 190-1
Justice 24, 26, 28, 54, 123, 183, 187-92
 Sexuality and 32

Kierkegaard, Søren 66, 146

Laity 167
  Church decisions and 25–6, 30, 76, 153–4
  Church hierarchy and 39, 167
  Lambeth Conference 78–9, 86, 111–33, 170
  1897 1
  Laity 30
  Consensus fidelium 143–4, 145, 153–4
  Reception 125, 140, 143, 145, 159
Legal Rights 30, 32, 34, 37–8
  Church exemption 37, 38–40
  United Nations charters 36–7, 123
Levinas, Emmanuel 69
Lightfoot, Joseph Barber xv, 1, 2, 3, 4, 5, 6, 10, 11, 12–13, 24
Love xi, 30, 32, 33, 54, 106, 121, 128, 165–7, 168, 171, 174, 185, 187, 191, 195, 197, 198
  Friendship 59–74, 93
  Intimacy xiii, 62–6, 73
  Sexual expression xv, 29, 59, 63, 74, 79–80, 85, 130, 187
  Unconditional 9, 31, 45–6, 51, 52, 53, 55, 57, 129, 163, 178, 184, 193, 195, 196, 199
  see also Marriage

Manning, Cardinal 7
Marriage 48, 80
  Australian statistics 32, 34–6, 47
  Civil unions / celebrants xiii, 26, 41, 78, 83, 128, 192
  Divorce and 30, 32, 41, 48, 52, 57, 100–1, 106, 125
  Equality 29
  God and 52–3, 54–5, 58
  Heterosexual 30–1, 43, 53, 55, 83, 90, 98–9, 113, 115, 120, 128, 130, 132, 199
  Remarriage 33, 41, 100, 181
  Same-sex xiii, xiv, 26, 29–30, 36, 41–2, 43, 55–8, 76, 83–4, 89, 93, 96, 99, 104, 105, 107, 109, 125, 129, 130, 135–40, 144, 150, 153, 185, 186–7, 198
  Theology of 43–58, 91, 93–4, 99–101, 113, 120, 124–5, 131, 155
Maximos the Confessor 69–70
McIntyre, Bp John 26, 28, 81–2, 84, 89
McLean, BH 101, 102
Moltmann, Jürgen 64–6, 73, 74
Montaigne, Michel de 73
Morimoto, Anri 103–5, 106, 108

Niemöller, Pastor Martin 107

Ordination 2, 50, 100
  Gay and Lesbian 25, 28, 59, 75–80, 84, 89, 90, 94, 96–8, 104, 106–7, 109, 113–14, 120, 122–3, 124–5, 128, 129, 130, 135–8, 140, 155
  see also Women's ordination
Orthodoxy 38, 101, 103–6, 108, 116, 119, 126, 127
Otherness 67–72, 74, 121
  Difference and x, 59, 63, 66, 69, 70, 71, 73, 77, 157, 162, 167, 171, 175, 179, 190

Papyri 14, 15–16
  Documents 17
  Literature and 14
  Zenon 16–17
Paul, Saint 14, 16, 17, 19, 20, 25, 46, 141, 148, 162–3, 179
  Council of Jerusalem 32
Peter, Saint 32–3, 45, 60
  Cornelius 33, 172
  Council of Jerusalem 32
Pickard, Stephen xv, 26, 65–6, 139
Pieces of Ease and Grace xiv, 8, 9, 21, 99, 181
Pope, Alexander 97
Prayer and Liturgy ix, 26, 45–6, 103, 128, 133, 177, 183–200
Prophets, Preachers and Heretics 95
Providence 4–5, 97–8

Reciprocity 63–4, 72–3
Revelation x, 5, 82

Church doctrine and 168
Reality 167-9
Reason 163
Sources 8, 50-1, 56, 173-5
Truth and 10, 47, 82, 121, 143, 145, 165-7, 167-9, 170-3, 181, 182, 195, 196
Revised Version 1, 5, 8, 13
Richard of St Victor 61, 64, 67, 73
Robinson, Bp Gene 78-9, 135
Roman Catholic church 108, 143, 168

Sacred x, xv, 12, 53-5, 86, 115, 123, 131, 132, 168, 169
False 43-52, 56-7
Murder 77, 158-9, 175, 177
Profane xv, 5, 33, 44-6, 56, 172
Wrath and 45, 162, 171, 178-9
Sexegesis 24, 99
Finance 24, 25
Giles, Kevin and 25-6
Sydney Diocese 24-5
Sexuality xv, xvi, 9, 10, 13, 14, 15, 16, 23, 28, 63, 73, 76, 77-8, 79, 80-1, 89, 93, 94-5, 97-8, 100, 111, 113-15, 120, 121, 129-32, 167, 180, 184
Controversy and 24-7, 75-91, 116-7
Legislation and 36-9, 42, 57, 78-9, 80, 83, 105, 124, 128, 146, 187, 191-2
Sexual identity xi, xiv, 9, 11, 18-20, 22, 76, 83, 84, 112, 174, 185, 191, 192, 193, 194, 195, 198-9, 200
Sexual diversity 2, 8, 29-42, 43, 55, 57, 59, 119, 128, 129, 135-59, 164, 168, 183, 190
Shortt, Rupert 106-7
Sin xiii, 52, 77, 94, 113, 120, 128, 130, 132, 149, 167
Discipleship and 54, 173-5
Slavery 16-18, 19, 20, 105-6
Spirit, Holy ix, x, 6, 26-7, 45, 46, 146, 148, 151, 158, 159, 162, 172, 178, 179, 193, 194, 195, 196, 199
Church councils and xv, 32, 78, 93-4, 102, 108-9

Steiner, George 147, 158-9
Holy Saturday 157-9

Tertullian 142, 159
Cain and Abel 158-9
Textual criticism 2, 3, 13
Torrance, Thomas 142, 150
Toubias 16-17
Trinity ix-x, 61, 67, 106, 142, 186, 187
Creativity and 148,-9, 196
Doctrine of God 6, 54-5, 67-8, 70-1, 141-2, 149

Undecidability 144-51
Innovation and 153-5, 157-9

Virginia Report, The 152
Vision 45, 98, 157, 172, 195
New Creation 161-5
Optics 162, 168

Westcott, Brooke Foss 1-11, 13-14, 15, 24, 27, 28
Bible and history 1-28
White, Patrick 64
Williams, Rowan 45, 54, 106-7, 109, 158, 180
Hopeful waiting 106-7, 158-9
Windsor Report, The 78-9, 119, 124, 125, 137, 152
Wittgenstein, Ludwig 99
Women's ordination xv, 6-7, 25, 26, 85-7, 88, 96, 99, 105, 109, 145, 181
Precedent 84-9, 93-109, 145-6
Words and meaning x, 3, 6, 10, 15, 27, 28, 99, 101-2, 180
Grammar 103-4
Usage ix, 94, 99, 103-4, 116, 119, 120-1, 186, 189

Lightning Source UK Ltd.
Milton Keynes UK
UKOW01f0443070218
317473UK00002B/177/P